INSTRUCTOR'S RESOURCE MANUAL

Operations Management
Strategy and Analysis

Fifth Edition

Lee J. Krajewski
University of Notre Dame

Larry P. Ritzman
Boston College

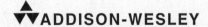ADDISON-WESLEY

An Imprint of Addison Wesley Longman, Inc.

Reading, Massachusetts ◆ Menlo Park, California ◆ New York ◆ Harlow, England
Don Mills, Ontario ◆ Sydney ◆ Mexico City ◆ Madrid ◆ Amsterdam

Instructor's Resource Manual to accompany Krajewski/Ritzman, *Operations Management, Fifth Edition*

Copyright © 1999 Addison Wesley Longman, Inc.

ISBN: 0-201-33119-5

1 2 3 4 5 6 7 8 9 10-CRS-02010099

CONTENTS

PREFACE

This **Instructor's Resource Manual** is one of several ancillaries prepared for instructors using *Operations Management: Strategy and Analysis, Fifth Edition*. The other ancillaries, described in the preface to the text, include the following:

- Solutions Manual
- Test Bank (with *FastFax* testing service)
- Instructor's CD-ROM: PowerPoint Presentations and Computerized Test Bank
- Operations Management in Action Videos
- Operations Management in Action Video Guide
- Operations Management Web Site

CONTENTS OF THE INSTRUCTOR'S RESOURCE MANUAL

COURSE OUTLINES

Introductory courses in operations management are taught in hundreds of ways. Some instructors are on a quarter system while others are on a semester system. Some universities are designing programs where the functional areas of business are taught in modules of anywhere from 5 weeks to 15 weeks at a time. Some professors prefer a functional orientation while others prefer a quantitative orientation. Some teach "megasections" of 250 or more students in a large lecture hall, while others teach smaller sections that foster more interaction with the students. Some prefer to introduce the infrastructure decision areas first, saving the longer term strategic decisions for the end. Finally, some instructors teach at the graduate level while others teach at the undergraduate level. The point of bringing up all of these situations is that the Fifth Edition of *Operations Management: Strategy and Analysis* works equally well in any of them. We have tried to make the text as flexible as possible to accommodate almost any instructor's approach.

In the **Course Outlines** portion of the Instructor's Resource Manual, we suggest six possible plans for using the text over the duration of a "standard" course. The course types represented include undergraduate or graduate, quarter or semester, and functional or quantitative. Suggested cases, readings, and problem assignments are provided. It is very unlikely that you will find one outline that fits your needs exactly. However, the plans introduce various features of the text and the supporting materials. The best parts of each plan can be used to design a course tailored to your specific needs. You may find that we have packaged more material than you need in a given lesson. Simply use the plans as suggestions for how you can use the Fifth Edition in your class.

ANNOTATED CHAPTER OUTLINES

This section contains *detailed* outlines of every chapter and supplement in the text, along with annotated teaching suggestions. The annotated chapter outlines are designed to aid the instructor in preparing for and delivering class sessions, regardless of how closely the instructor is following the organization of the text. They can be used without modification to teach the entire text, or they may be used as a quick review of key points before preparing a lesson or exam. The new in-class application exercises (and their solutions when appropriate) are referenced in these outlines.

IN-CLASS APPLICATION EXERCISES

Many instructors prefer to use problems different than those used as examples or solved problems in the text. To this end, we have prepared a set of new "application" in-class exercises/problems, along with transparency masters of their solutions. The application problems are grouped according to chapter or supplement, 1 per page, at the back of this manual (e.g., AP 3.1 for the first application in Chapter 3). They may be used as transparency masters or student hand-outs as needed. Should you wish to modify the problems, they are also located on the Instructor's CD-ROM in Microsoft Word for Windows 95. As stated above, each application is referenced at an appropriate point in the annotated chapter outlines.

TRANSPARENCY MASTER SOLUTIONS TO IN-CLASS APPLICATION EXERCISES

The solutions to the application exercises are also grouped by chapter or supplement in the back of this manual, and they are highly suitable for use as transparency masters. In many cases, there are several solution masters for a given application problem, so we have numbered the solutions accordingly (e.g., TM A.4a-TM A.4d for the four transparency masters to accompany the fourth application in Supplement A). We have also provided an **Applications & Transparency Masters Table of Contents** (located just before the applications at the back of this manual) to give you an overview of which masters accompany which applications and to share a few notes about various application problems. In some cases, we have left the final solution to an application problem *off* of the master so that the answer can be worked out in class. Whenever this is the case, we have provided the short answer in the annotated chapter outlines. The solutions to the application exercises have been done up in Microsoft PowerPoint and are available on the Instructor's CD-ROM.

CONVERSION TABLE OF CONTENTS FOR THE FIFTH EDITION

For your convenience in switching from the fourth edition of *Operations Management* to the fifth, we have provided the following conversion table, which illustrates how the chapters and supplements have been rearranged.

5ᵗʰ Edition Chapter/Supplement	Status vis-à-vis 4ᵗʰ Edition
Ch 1: Operations as a Competitive Weapon	was Chapter 1
Ch 2: Operations Strategy	was Chapter 2
Supp A: Decision Making	was Supplement A
Ch 3: Process Management	was Chapter 3
Ch 4: Management of Technology	**new chapter**
Supp B: Computer-Integrated Manufacturing	was Supplement B
Ch 5: Work-Force Management	was Chapter 6
Supp C: Learning Curves	was Supplement D
Ch 6: Total Quality Management	was Chapter 4
Ch 7: Statistical Process Control	was Chapter 5
Supp D: Acceptance Sampling	was Supplement C
Ch 8: Capacity	was Chapter 7
Supp E: Waiting Line Models	was Supplement E
Supp F: Simulation Analysis	was Supplement F

Ch 9:	Location	was Chapter 8
Ch 10:	Layout	was Chapter 9
Ch 11:	Supply Chain Management	**new chapter** (previously "Materials Management")
Ch 12:	Forecasting	was Chapter 10
Ch 13:	Inventory Concepts and Systems	was Chapter 12
Supp G:	Special Inventory Models	was Supplement H
Ch 14:	Aggregate Planning	was Chapter 13
Supp H:	Linear Programming	was Supplement I
Ch 15:	Material Requirements Planning	was Chapter 14
Supp I:	Master Production Scheduling	**new supplement**
Ch 16:	Just-in-Time Systems	was Chapter 15
Ch 17:	Scheduling	was Chapter 16
Ch 18:	Managing Projects	was Chapter 17

TEACHING TIPS FOR FIFTH EDITION SUPPORT MATERIALS

The fifth edition of *Operations Management* provides students and instructors with a number of exciting support materials, three of which are new to this edition. These materials include the following:

- new Excel-based OM5 student software on CD-ROM (available for a few dollars over the price of the text alone; text/CD package ISBN 0-201-35728-3)
- new Internet Activities (accessible through the Krajewski/Ritzman OM5 Web site)
- new online "preview library" of operations management software vendors and products
- revised and expanded PowerPoint slides for every chapter and supplement

Below, we present information about each of these items that is intended to help you incorporate them easily into your course.

OM5 STUDENT SOFTWARE

The personal computer and other productivity tools such as spreadsheets have changed the way we approach business problems and manage information. When learning a subject, students must avoid using these tools as a crutch that always provides the right answer. The programming truism GIGO (Garbage In, Garbage Out) is amplified when students are not familiar with the material being taught.

In order to provide students with a truly valuable operations management software tool—one that helps them *learn* the material and experiment with OM concepts on their own—we have made available with the fifth edition of *Operations Management* the "OM5" student software, which consists of a CD-ROM and user guide that may be packaged with each copy of the Krajewski/Ritzman text for only a few dollars over the price of the text alone (use ISBN 0-201-35728-3). The OM5 software consists of nearly 150 Microsoft Excel models that are grouped into three types of learning aides: problem tutorials, problem verifiers, and problem solvers. Together, these three models provide enough structure to guide students through key quantitative concepts, while also allowing them the flexibility to learn through experimentation. Each type of model is explained more fully below.

The models were developed by KMT Software, Inc., a leader since 1991 in creating templates and other software to be used in conjunction with Microsoft Office products. Each model is fully documented and contains programming that automates tasks such as printing and navigation. A custom help system is also included with the models.

Tutorials

As the name implies, the tutorial spreadsheets aim to teach students how to work through an operations management problem by providing them with step-by-step guidance. Referenced throughout the text by an icon in the margin, each tutorial ties into a specific example or solved problem within a chapter. Assigning the tutorials is a great way to reinforce basic concepts or assist students who are having difficulty understanding the material.

The introductory screen of each tutorial spreadsheet provides a brief overview of the technique used to solve a problem:

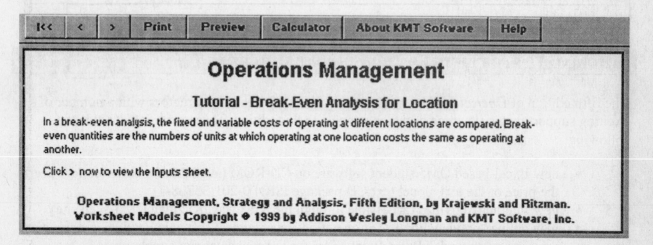

After reading this material, students advance to the tutorial's Inputs sheet (the layout of which varies from model to model):

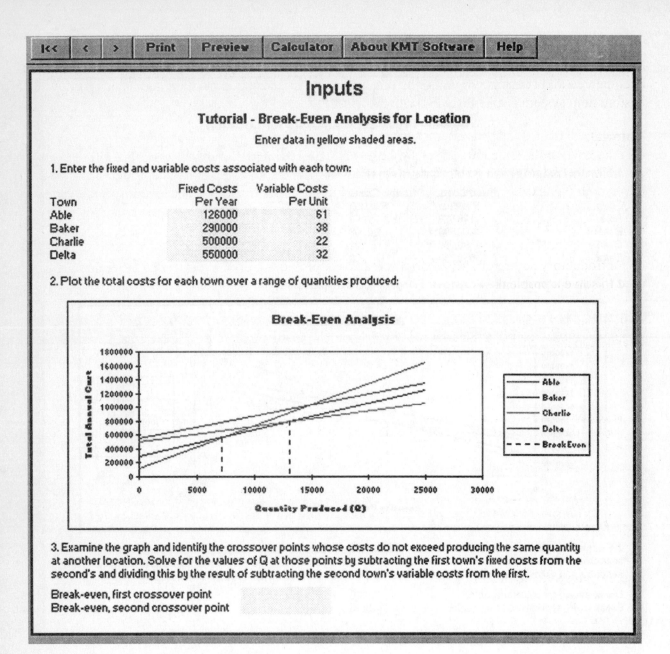

Inputs

Tutorial - Break-Even Analysis for Location

Enter data in yellow shaded areas.

1. Enter the fixed and variable costs associated with each town:

Town	Fixed Costs Per Year	Variable Costs Per Unit
Able	126000	61
Baker	290000	38
Charlie	500000	22
Delta	550000	32

2. Plot the total costs for each town over a range of quantities produced:

3. Examine the graph and identify the crossover points whose costs do not exceed producing the same quantity at another location. Solve for the values of Q at those points by subtracting the first town's fixed costs from the second's and dividing this by the result of subtracting the second town's variable costs from the first.

Break-even, first crossover point
Break-even, second crossover point

The yellow-tinted cells (which appear gray in this manual) are for data input. Some, which are dedicated to the "inputs" or "givens" of a problem, already contain data; others are initially empty. Students may enter data, or change existing data, in any yellow cell. All other cells are locked and cannot be altered. Between major sections of the sheet, students will find verbal descriptions of the mathematical techniques they need to compute one or more performance measures (see step 3 in the example above). Students will need to use paper and pencil or a calculator to do the math as directed. When finished, they enter their results in the yellow cell(s).

When students have finished working through the example as directed, they advance to the Results sheet, which is typically laid out in exactly the same way as the Inputs sheet, but with green-tinted cells replacing the yellow-tinted cells (the green cells also appear gray in this manual):

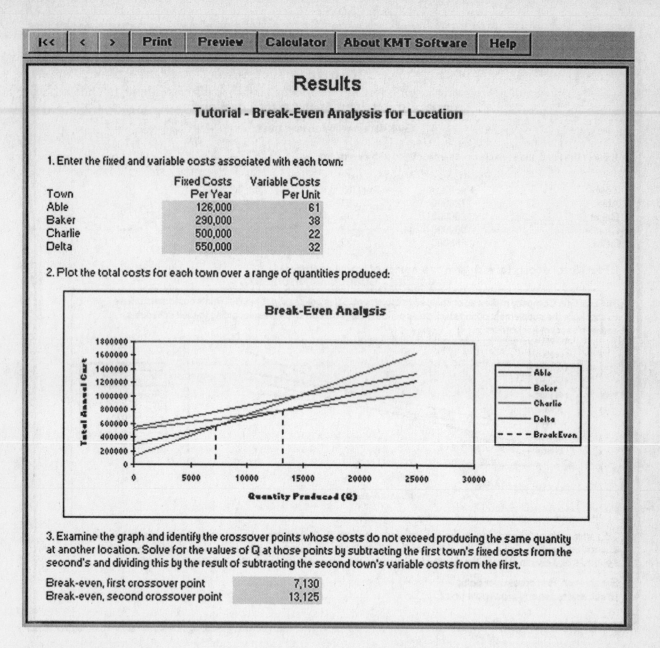

Results

Tutorial - Break-Even Analysis for Location

1. Enter the fixed and variable costs associated with each town:

Town	Fixed Costs Per Year	Variable Costs Per Unit
Able	126,000	61
Baker	290,000	38
Charlie	500,000	22
Delta	550,000	32

2. Plot the total costs for each town over a range of quantities produced:

3. Examine the graph and identify the crossover points whose costs do not exceed producing the same quantity at another location. Solve for the values of Q at those points by subtracting the first town's fixed costs from the second's and dividing this by the result of subtracting the second town's variable costs from the first.

Break-even, first crossover point	7,130
Break-even, second crossover point	13,125

The green cells are for results and contain formulas, which can not be adjusted or overwritten. Some (like the upper four cells in the example above) simply repeat the base values entered in the Inputs sheet. (If these values are adjusted in the Inputs sheet, the changes are reflected in the Results sheet). Other green-tinted cells (such as the final cells in the example above) contain formulas that use Excel's mathematical operators and functions to perform the math requested in the Inputs sheet. Students can use the results in these cells to see whether they came up with the right answer.

If students' answers match those on the Results sheet, they can return to the Inputs sheet, adjust the problem's inputs, work out a new answer, and see whether it still matches the calculated answers found in the Results page. Students who learn best by repetition and who need additional help working through problems independently will gain the most from the tutorials.

Verifiers

The verifiers, again referenced in the text by an icon, are spreadsheet-based solutions to specific problems found in the end-of-chapter material. The models are offered sporadically throughout the end-of-chapter problems to cover certain types of problems, and they allow students to check their work. If you like, you can require students to submit hand-written verification of the problems to ensure that they do not use the verifiers as a crutch.

In a verifier, the introductory page contains a description of the problem found in the text:

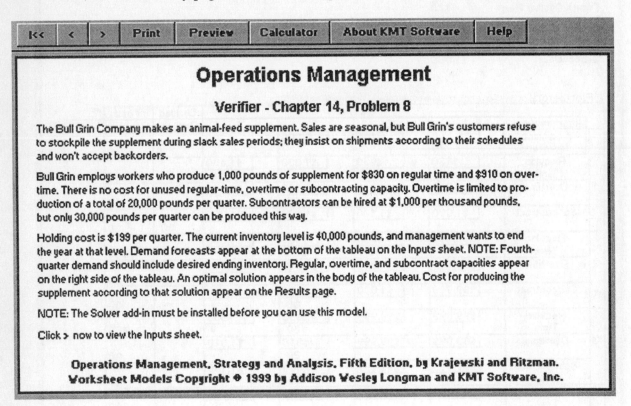

The Inputs sheet has yellow-tinted cells (gray here) that already contain the values called for in the problem:

Inputs

Verifier - Chapter 14, Problem 8

Enter data in yellow shaded areas.

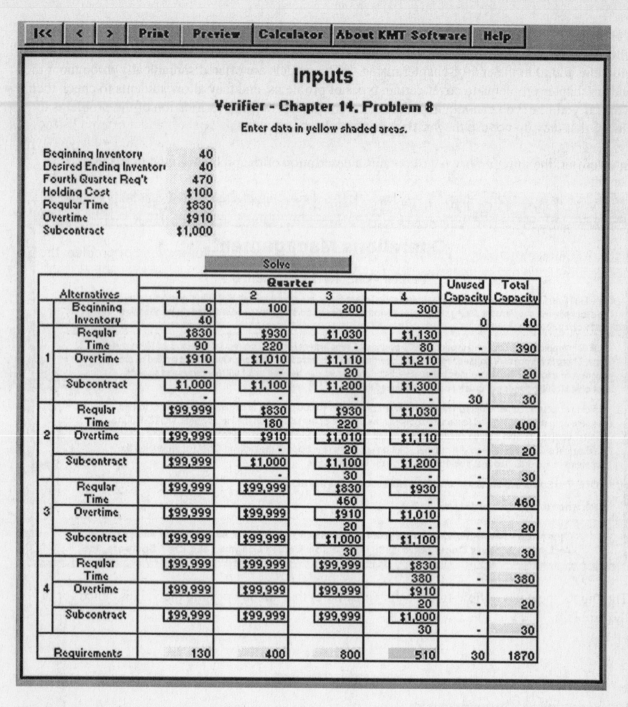

Beginning Inventory	40
Desired Ending Inventory	40
Fourth Quarter Req't	470
Holding Cost	$100
Regular Time	$830
Overtime	$910
Subcontract	$1,000

Solve

Alternatives		Quarter 1	Quarter 2	Quarter 3	Quarter 4	Unused Capacity	Total Capacity
	Beginning Inventory	0 / 40	100	200	300	0	40
1	Regular Time	$830 / 90	$930 / 220	$1,030 / -	$1,130 / 80	-	390
	Overtime	$910 / -	$1,010 / -	$1,110 / 20	$1,210 / -	-	20
	Subcontract	$1,000 / -	$1,100 / -	$1,200 / -	$1,300 / -	30	30
2	Regular Time	$99,999	$830 / 180	$930 / 220	$1,030 / -		400
	Overtime	$99,999	$910 / -	$1,010 / 20	$1,110 / -	-	20
	Subcontract	$99,999	$1,000 / -	$1,100 / 30	$1,200 / -	-	30
3	Regular Time	$99,999	$99,999	$830 / 460	$930 / -	-	460
	Overtime	$99,999	$99,999	$910 / 20	$1,010 / -	-	20
	Subcontract	$99,999	$99,999	$1,000 / 30	$1,100 / -	-	30
4	Regular Time	$99,999	$99,999	$99,999	$830 / 380	-	380
	Overtime	$99,999	$99,999	$99,999	$910 / 20	-	20
	Subcontract	$99,999	$99,999	$99,999	$1,000 / 30	-	30
	Requirements	130	400	800	510	30	1870

The Results sheet contains Excel formulas that provide the correct solution to the problem:

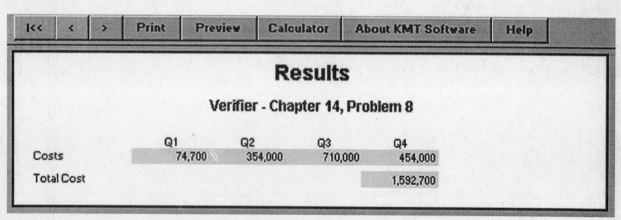

Results

Verifier - Chapter 14, Problem 8

	Q1	Q2	Q3	Q4
Costs	74,700	354,000	710,000	454,000
Total Cost				1,592,700

If you wish, you can have students go back to the Inputs sheet, adjust the values in the yellow-tinted cells, and execute "what if" scenarios to see how the changes in input affect the problem's outcome. Keep in mind, though, that you cannot change the basic parameters of the problem.

Solvers

The solver spreadsheets—perhaps the most innovative and valuable type of model offered by the OM5 software—provide general-purpose computer support for the most popular and widely accepted software applications in operations management. The solvers allow students to apply techniques discussed in the text in a variety of new problem settings. These spreadsheets cover such topics as aggregate planning, financial analysis, process charts, break-even analysis, and many other key OM concepts.

In a solver, the introductory page provides students with a description of the kind of problem the model can solve along with instructions for using the solver:

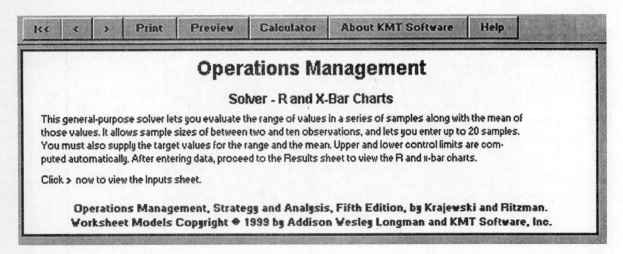

As in tutorials and verifiers, the Inputs sheet contains yellow-tinted cells (gray here) where students provide the input values for the problem they want to solve:

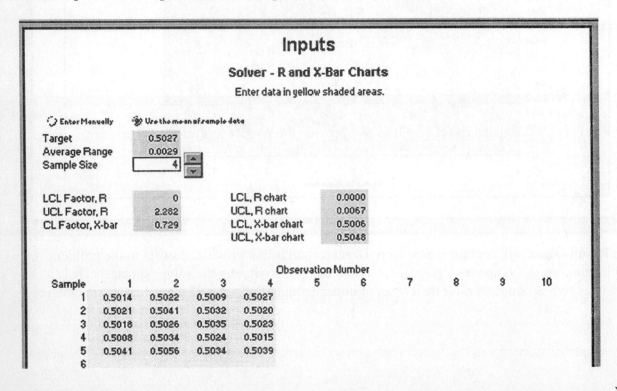

Some solvers provide "controls," such as the two buttons at the top of the example above, that let students select from similar but distinct versions of the type of problem to be solved, or that let them alter the basic parameters of the problem (such as changing the number of periods of data to be entered).

After setting up the problem by entering data and using the control buttons, students can proceed to the Results sheet:

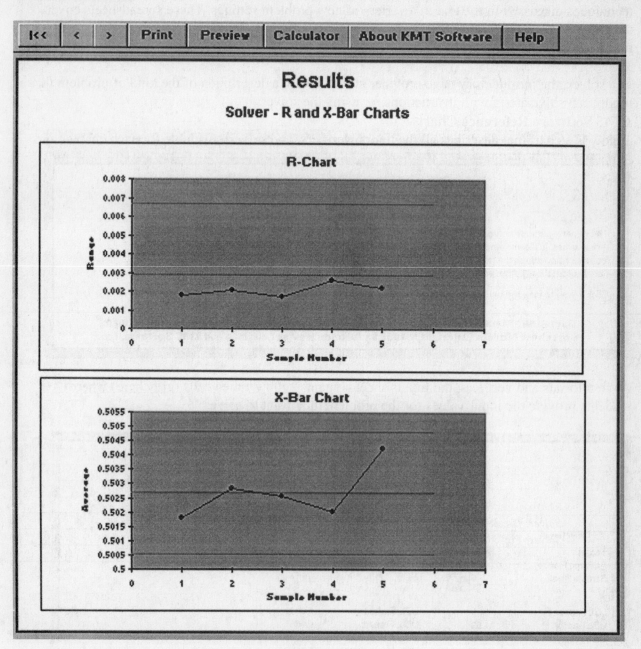

The Results sheet will contain one or more Excel formulas that provide answers to the problem, and in some cases (as above) a graphic for visual insight. Assigning the solver spreadsheets is a great way to help students raise their level of understanding through self-directed experimentation.

The Toolbar

Every model in the OM5 software package features a toolbar at the top of each sheet. which can be seen in the many examples above. All toolbars are identical, which means that navigation, printing, and getting help are consistent no matter which model students are using. Each toolbar contains eight buttons that allow students to navigate among screens, print after previewing the document, link directly to the Windows calculator accessory, get help, and get more information about KMT Software, Inc.

Hardware and Software Requirements

To use the OM5 Software CD-ROM, your students must have access the following:
- An IBM compatible PC
- Microsoft Windows 3.1 or Windows 95
- Microsoft Excel Version 5.0 or higher

OM5 Software Reference Chart

Below is a chart that describes all the tutors, verifiers, and solvers available for each chapter and supplement. For the tutors and verifiers, we have listed the page in the text where the icon for the particular tutor or verifier can be found. Since the solver spreadsheets are general in nature, there are no page references given for them. In addition, we have listed the Windows 95 file name for each spreadsheet.

Chapter/ Supp	Topic of Spreadsheet as Described in Text	Page #	Windows 95 File Name
Chapter 1	*Tutor 1.1:* Productivity Measures (Ex 1.1)	11	Tutor Prod Measures Ch 1 Ex 1.xls
	Verifier: end-of-chapter Problem 1	22	Verifier Chptr 1 Prob 1.xls
Supp A	*Tutor A.1:* Break-Even Quantity (Ex A.1)	69	Tutor Brk Even, Products S-A Ex 1.xls
	Tutor A.2: Break-Even Analysis (Ex A.3)	70	Tutor Brk Even Processes S-A Ex 2.xls
	Tutor A.3: Preference Matrices (Ex A.4)	71	Tutor Pref Matrices S-A Ex 4.xls
	Tutor A.4: Decisions Under Uncertainty (Ex A.6)	74	Tutor Dec Makg under Uncrtnty S-A Ex 4.xls
	Tutor A.5: Decisions Under Risk (Ex A.7)	76	Tutor Dec Makg Under Risk S-A Ex 5.xls
	Tutor A.6: Value of Perfect Information (Ex A.8)	80	Tutor Loc Decns Under Uncrtnty Ch 9.xls
	Verifier: End-of-supplement Problem 2	82	Verifier Supp A Prob 2.xls
	Verifier: End-of-supplement Problem 13	84	Verifier Supp A Prob 13.xls
	Verifier: End-of-supplement Problem 15	85	Verifer Supp A Prob 15.xls
	Verifier: End-of-supplement Problem 16	85	Verifier Supp A Prob 16.xls
	Verifier: End-of-supplement Problem 17	85	Verifier Supp A Prob 17.xls
	Solver: Break-Even Analysis	---	Solver Brk Even Analysis S-A.xls
	Solver: Preference Matrices	---	Solver Pref Matrices S-A.xls
	Solver: Decision Theory	---	Solver Decn Theory S-A. xls
Chapter 3	*Tutor 3.1:* Break-Even Quantity (Fig 3.3)	101	Tutor Brk Even, Processes Ch 3.xls
	Tutor 3.2: Process Charts (annual labor cost)	114-15	Tutor Proc Charts Ch 3 Fig 7.xls
	Verifier: End-of-chapter Problem 5	119	Verifier Chptr 3 Prob 5.xls
	Verifier: End-of-chapter Problem 9	120	Verifier Chptr 3 Prob 9.xls
	Solver: Process Charts	---	Solver Proc Charts Ch 3.xls
Chapter 4	*Verifier:* End-of-chapter Problem 1	152	Verifier Chptr 4 Prob 1.xls
	Verifier: End-of-chapter Problem 2	152	Verifier Chptr 4 Prob 2.xls
	Verifier: End-of-chapter Problem 3	152	Verifier Chptr 4 Prob 3.xls
	Verifier: End-of-chapter Problem 6	153	Verifier Chptr 4 Prob 6.xls
Chapter 5	*Tutor 5.1:* Time Study Sample Size (Ex 5.1)	181	Tutor Time Study Samp Size Ch 5 Ex 1.xls

	Verifier: End-of-supplement Problem 9	666	Verifier Supp H Prob 9.xls
	Solver: Linear Programming	---	Solver Lin Progrmmr S-H.xls
Chapter 15	*Tutor 15.1:* Material Requirements Planning Using the FOQ, POQ, and L4L Rules	686	Tutor Matl Reqt Planning Ch 15.xls
	Verifier: End-of-chapter Problem 7	706	Verifier Chptr 15 Prob 7.xls
	Verifier: End-of-chapter Problem 12	708	Verifier Chptr 15 Prob 12.xls
	Solver: Material Requirements Planning	---	Solver Matl Reqt Planning Ch 15.xls
Supp I	*Tutor I.1:* Master Production Scheduling	726	Tutor Master Prod Sch S-I Ex 6.xls
	Verifier: End-of-supplement Problem 2	728	Verifier Supp I Prob 2.xls
	Verifier: End-of-supplement Problem 5	728	Verifier Supp I Prob 5.xls
	Solver: Master Production Scheduling	---	Solver Mstr Prod Sch S-I.xls
Chapter 16	*Tutor 16.1:* Determining Number of Containers (Ex 16.1)	746	Tutor Num of Containers Ch 16 Ex 1.xls
	Verifier: End-of-chapter Problem 2	757	Verifier Chptr 16 Prob 2.xls
Chapter 17	*Tutor 17.1:* Comparing EDD & SPT Rules (Ex 17.1)	767	Tutor Sgl Dimnsn Rules Ch 17 Ex 1.xls
	Tutor 17.2: Sequencing with CR & S/RO Rules (Ex 17.2)	770-71	Tutor Multi Dimnsn Rules Ch 17 Ex 2.xls
	Tutor 17.3: Scheduling on Two Workstations (Ex 17.3)	773	Tutor Johnson's Rule Ch 17 Ex 3.xls
	Tutor 17.4: Developing a Work-Force Schedule (Ex 17.4)	779	Tutor Work-Force Sch Ch 17 Ex 4.xls
	Verifier: End-of-chapter Problem 1	789	Verifier Chptr 17 Prob 1.xls
	Verifier: End-of-chapter Problem 2	789	Verifier Chptr 17 Prob 2.xls
	Verifier: End-of-chapter Problem 5	790	Verifier Chptr 17 Prob 5.xls
	Verifier: End-of-chapter Problem 8	791	Verifier Chptr 17 Prob 8.xls
	Solver: Workforce Scheduling	---	Solver Work-Force Sch Ch 17.xls
	Solver: Two Machine Scheduler	---	Solver 2 Mach Sch Ch 17.xls
	Solver: Single Machine Scheduler	---	Solver Single Mach Sch Ch 17.xls
Appendix 1	*Tutor A1.1:* Present Value Factors	842	Tutor Pres Value of a Future Amt Ap 1.xls
	Tutor A1.2: Annuities	844	Tutor Pres Value of Annuity Ap 1.xls
	TutorA1.3: Straight-Line Deprecation	846	Tutor Str Line Depr Ap 1.xls
	TutorA1.4: Calculating NPV, IRR, & Payback Period (Ex A1.2)	849	Tutor NPV, IRR, Payback Ap 1 Ex 4.xls
	Solver: Financial Analysis	---	Solver Fin Analysis App 1.xls

INTERNET ACTIVITIES

New to the fifth edition of *Operations Management* are Internet Activities, indicated throughout the text by an icon in the margin. The icons direct students to the Krajewski/Ritzman OM5 Web site, where they then click on the "Internet Activities" button to find the activities grouped by chapter. The activities point them to specific company URLs on the World Wide Web and ask them to answer questions based on their exploration of the company sites. By completing these activities, students learn how real companies use OM to gain competitive advantage. Assigning the Internet Activities to your students is also a great way to help them sharpen their research skills and reinforce their understanding of basic OM concepts. Solutions to selected Internet Activities are posted to a password-protected instructor's page on the OM5 Web site. To access this page, you will need the following ID and password:

ID = operations
password = LK5LR10

SOFTWARE PREVIEW LIBRARY

In addition to Internet Activities, the OM5 Web site also contains a section entitled "Operations Management Software," developed by David Hartvigsen of the University of Notre Dame. This section presents an extensive library of links to OM software vendors and products. The links are organized by chapter or supplement and are broken down into topics, such as decision trees and flow diagrams. Thus, instructors and students have immediate online access to companies whose products perform key OM functions discussed in the text. In essence, the software library bridges the gap between the quantitative techniques used in OM and the enormous software industry that implements and markets these techniques.

In addition to linking to company home pages (many of which allow the viewer to access case studies, client lists, press releases, and other helpful information), the software library also provides links to **downloadable software and demos** and presents students with **Web Activities** related to the vendors and products. The Web activities serve to guide students through the company sites, and they also direct students back to problems and cases in the text that they can solve using downloaded company software. Assigning the Web Activities is a great way to familiarize your students with all kinds of OM software, thus preparing them to use the technical resources they'll encounter in the business world.

POWERPOINT LECTURE PRESENTATION AND OUTLINE SLIDES

The fifth edition Instructor's CD-ROM contains a revised and expanded PowerPoint presentation in PowerPoint 7.0 for Windows 95, prepared by Jeff Heyl of Lincoln University in New Zealand. The CD contains two types of PowerPoint slides: 1) presentation slides, which walk the viewer through all the figures and other key concepts for every chapter and supplement in the text; and 2) lecture outline slides, which provide concise summaries of each chapter and are handy to use as lecture overview transparency masters.

The **presentation slides** illustrate the various tools, techniques, and concepts presented in the figures and other examples in each chapter and supplement of the text. The slides are programmed in PowerPoint to animate models, equations, and analyses, thereby demonstrating the dynamic nature of the operations management field. Graphs are developed step-by-step from basic coordinate systems; the development of equations and variable substitution is clearly shown for many topics; the interrelationship between pieces of a model are shown in ways not possible on the printed page. These presentations work best in a lecture facility with a high-quality video projection system; however, it is possible to print the slides and use them with a standard overhead projector.

Teaching notes accompany many of presentations, explaining the approach to a given sequence of slides and suggesting ways in which the material might be presented. These notes can be accessed slide-by-slide from within PowerPoint. Simply choose "Notes Page" from the View menu at the top of your screen to see the notes prepared for a given slide. PowerPoint allows you to print notes pages with anywhere from one to several slides per page. This is an easy way to generate handouts for students to complement the in-class slide presentations.

Microsoft's **PowerPoint Viewer** is provided on the Instructor CD-ROM for instructors who do not have PowerPoint. The viewer allows you to see and display the slide portions of the presentations in your office or classroom, but it does not enable you to modify the presentations or view the teaching notes.

* * * * *

Preparing an instructor's ancillary package as comprehensive as the one that accompanies the fifth edition of *Operations Management* could not have been accomplished without the help and inspiration of others. We wish to give special thanks to Jeff Heyl for providing the PowerPoint lecture presentation and outline slides and to Dave Hartvigsen for providing much of the Web site content. We also want to thank Ruth Berry for her artful skill in the painless prodding of two old steers who, at times, felt that they had lost their way.

Lee J. Krajewski, Larry P. Ritzman
July 1998

COURSE OUTLINES

Plan A (Case/Quarter)

This plan is an updated version of an outline used at The Ohio State University. The original plan was devised by Professors W. C. Benton, Bill Berry, Dave Collier, Keong Leong, Lee Krajewski, and Peter Ward for the undergraduate program. There were five sections of the course per quarter, with an average class size of 55 students. Typically, three or four teaching assistants taught their own sections. The use of cases and videos greatly enhanced student interaction even though the students did not have to turn in case reports each time. Plan A can also be used as a guide for an MBA course. All cases shown in the plan can be found in the Fifth Edition.

INTRODUCTION TO OPERATIONS MANAGEMENT

Improving Competitiveness in Organizations

TEXTS

Operations Management: Strategy and Analysis, Fifth Edition, Krajewski & Ritzman
Supplementary Packet, The packet contains formula reviews, solutions to the assigned problems, lecture notes, and articles. This packet is an essential aid for the lectures and for preparing for the exams.
OM5 Software, recommended

COURSE OBJECTIVES

Many firms have demonstrated that operations management can be an effective competitive weapon and, in conjunction with well-conceived marketing and financial plans, these firms have made major penetrations into markets worldwide. This course is designed to address the key operations and logistical issues in service and manufacturing organizations that have strategic as well as tactical implications. The specific objectives include:

1. To understand the role of operations management in the overall business strategy of the firm.

2. To understand the interdependence of the operating system with other key functional areas of the firm.

3. To identify and evaluate the key factors and the interdependence of these factors in the design of effective operating systems.

4. To identify and evaluate a range of tools appropriate for analysis of operating systems of the firm.

5. To identify and evaluate comparative approaches to operations management in an international context.

6. To understand the application of operations management policies and techniques to service sector as well as manufacturing firms.

The sessions are designed to promote student participation through the discussion of current events in the business world as they relate to operations management and in-class case analysis.

EVALUATION

Your course grade will be determined in the following way:

Mid Term Exam	30%
Case Reports	30%
Final Exam	30%

As a general policy, no make-up work or exams will be granted unless required for medical reasons, in which case a note from a physician is required.

An important part of the course is the effectiveness of your individual participation in the class discussions. While we expect participation by every member of the class, we will place primary emphasis on the quality of the classroom contributions. In grading class performance, we will give very little emphasis to redundant or extraneous contributions. Contributions that add new insights into the case issues or class discussions, or which build on the work of others in advancing the discussion, will be rewarded.

COURSE OUTLINE

COMPETITIVE ENTERPRISES

1. Course Introduction and Overview   Read: Chapter 1
   - **Case**: Chad's Creative Concepts
   - Video: Au Bon Pain

2. Operations Strategy Framework   Read: Chapter 2, pp. 25-37

PROCESSES

3. Process Choice   Read: Chapter 2, pp. 38-45;
   - **Case:** BSB Inc.: The Pizza Wars Come to Campus   Read: Chapter 3, pp. 87-97
   - Video: King Soopers Bakery

4. Process Design   Read: Chapter 3, pp. 97-116
   - Issues in Process Design
   - **Class Exercise**: Min-Yo Garment Company
   - Problems: 1,2,8

5. Technology Management   Read: Chapter 4
   - Video: Chapparal Steel   Read: Supp B
   - **Case**: Bill's Hardware

TOTAL QUALITY MANAGEMENT

6. A Management Philosophy   Read: Chapter 5, pp. 166-177;
   - Video: TQM at the Christchurch Parkroyal   Chapter 6, pp. 213-223

7. Improving Quality   Read: Chapter 6, pp 223-234
   - **Case**: Jose's Authentic Mexican Restaurant
   - Problems 4,5,9

8. Quality Analysis   Read: Chapter 7
   - Problems: 1,3,4,10,13

STRATEGIC ISSUES IN OPERATIONS

9. Capacity Management   Read Chapter 8

- Problems: 1,2,6,8

10. Capacity Management & Global Operations   Read Chapter 9, pp. 360-372
    - **Case**: Fitness Plus, Part A

11. Location   Read Chapter 9, pp. 373-399
    - **Case**: Imaginative Toys
    - Problems: 1, 3, 9, 11, 24

MATERIALS MANAGEMENT IN OPERATIONS

12. Supply-Chain Management   Read: Chapter 11
    - Video: Inventory and Textbooks
    - Problem: 5

13. Supply-Chain Dynamics
    - **Class Exercise:** Sonic Distributors

14. Inventory Basics & Independent Demand Systems   Read: Chapter 13, pp. 544-564
    - Problems: 1,3,22

15. Independent & Dependent Demand Systems   Read: Chapter 13, pp. 564-569
    - Problem: 23, Chapter 13   Read: Chapter 15, pp. 673-681

16. Dependent Demand Systems   Read: Chapter 15, pp. 681-695
    - Problems: 1,3,7,12

17. Dependent Demand & Just-in-Time Systems   Read: Chapter 15, pp. 695-718
    - **Case:** Flashy Flashers   Read: Chapter 16, pp. 733-749
    - Problems: 1,2,3, Chapter 16

18. JIT Systems   Read: Chapter 16, pp. 749-759
    - **Case**: Copper Kettle Catering

Plan B (Case/ Semester)

This plan features a semester course with a conceptual orientation most likely suited for an introductory course in an MBA program. We have suggested Harvard School cases rather than those found in the Fifth Edition, although many of the cases in the text could be used as "discussion starters" on a cold-call basis. The other feature of this plan is the group project, which has been successfully used at the University of Notre Dame in the MBA program. The students thought it was a unique way to draw together the various functional areas they've studied and still show the importance of operations management. Some lessons of Plan B could be scrapped to make room for group presentations of their projects. The students are always interested in the "new businesses" their fellow students have devised.

GROUP PROJECT

Each student will be assigned to a group of five for the purpose of writing a term paper for the course. The objective of this term project is to tie together the topics of the course and to place the role of operations in perspective relative to other business functions.

1. The paper will discuss the design of a new business of the group's choice. The product or service should be novel and show promise of success in the marketplace. There may be other players in your market, but through your competitive priorities create a niche you can exploit through operations.
2. The paper should focus primarily on the operations management issues, but links to marketing management and financial management should be clear.
3. The operations management decisions to be addressed include, but are not limited to, (a) operations strategy, competitive priorities, and positioning the firm in the marketplace; (b) process choice; (c) capacity determination; (d) location and layout; and (e) inventory, distribution, and total quality management systems. These decisions should be explicitly addressed for the product or service to be provided. Hypothetical data may be used but they should be realistic. Successful attempts to get real data will improve the quality of the paper. Document all contacts you make to get your data as well as literature and Internet sources. The profitability of the product or service should be clearly established.
4. The paper should begin with the business objectives and the market and financial assumptions. The product or service should be described in detail. Each of the decisions in #3 should be addressed in its own section. By the end of the paper it should be obvious that the operations decisions are consistent with the overall business objectives and the distinctive competence of the business.
5. Grading will be based on the following criteria:

   a. Appropriateness of the product or service and the potential for success.
   b. Soundness of the rationale and reasoning presented in the paper.
   c. Comprehensiveness and depth of the paper's content.
   d. Quality of the sources used for references and background information.
   e. Presentational aspects such as organization, format, and grammar.

6. A 100-word (maximum) abstract of the project will be due on Session 20. The company name should be centered on the page in capital letters, and the abstract itself should be single-spaced.
7. The paper is due no later than Session 27. Late papers will suffer a grade decay equivalent to one letter grade per day late.

COURSE OUTLINE

INTRODUCTION AND FLOW STRATEGIES

1. **Case**: Blitz Company   Read Chapters 1 and 2

2.   **Case**: Texas Instruments -- Time Products Division   Read Chapter 10

PROCESS MANAGEMENT AND TECHNOLOGY

3.   **Case**: Max-Able Medical Clinic (A)   Read Chapter 3
4.   **Case**: Siden Motor Products Corporation   Read Chapter 4; Supp B
     [Other options are Mirassou Vineyards (A),
        Chaircraft (B), and Min-Yo Garment (text)]

WORK MEASUREMENT

5.   Prepare assigned problems   Read Chapter 5
6.   **Case**: Knox Electronics
7.   **Case**: Fawcett (Insight) Optical Company

CAPACITY AND LOCATION

8.   Prepare assigned problems   Read Chapter 8 ;
                                                                     Supp E

9.   **Case**: Benihana of Tokyo
10. **Case**: Carborundum, Inc.   Read Chapter 9
     [Other options are Zenith Radio Corporation (AP),
     Mattson Foods, Inc., and New Balance Athletic Shoes USA]

PRODUCTION AND STAFFING PLANS

11. Prepare assigned problems   Read Chapter 14
12. **Case**: Corning Glass Works -- Erwin Automotive
     Plant [Other options are The Swift River Box
     Company, Cross river Products Company, and
     Kool King Division]

SUPPLY-CHAIN MANAGEMENT

13. Prepare assigned problems   Read Chapters 11 and 13
14. **Case**: Heatron, Inc. [An alternative is Walton
         Instruments Manufacturing]
15. **Case**: Blanchard Importing and Distributing Co.
16. **Case**: Sorenson Research Company [Another option is
              Sonic Distributors (text)]

MPS AND DEPENDENT-DEMAND INVENTORY MANAGEMENT SYSTEMS

17. Prepare assigned problems   Read Chapter 15;
18. **Case**: Hot Line, Incorporated   Supp I

JUST-IN-TIME PRODUCTION-INVENTORY SYSTEMS

19. **Case**: Toyo Kogyo Co. LTD. (A)   Read Chapter 16

WORK-FORCE AND PROJECT SCHEDULING

20. Prepare assigned problems   Read Chapters 17 and 18
21. **Case**: Sof-Optics, Inc.
22. **Case**: Space Constructors, Inc.

TOTAL QUALITY MANAGEMENT

23. **Case**: Hank Kolb, Director, Quality Assurance   Read Chapter 6
24. Prepare assigned problems   Read Chapter 7
    Class Exercise: Coin Catapult
25. **Case**: Firestone Tire and Rubber [Another option
    is Steinway & Sons]

CORPORATE AND OPERATIONS STRATEGY

26. **Case**: Litton Microwave Cooking Products (B)
27. **Case**: Steinway & Sons [Other options are Min-Yo Garment Company (text), Hanrahan
    Motors, Mattson Foods, Inc., Sea Pines Racquet Club, and Sensormatic Electronics
    Corporation]

Plan C (Lecture/Functional/Quarter)

This plan might be useful to those instructors who must teach a large undergraduate section or who must rely on teaching assistants without the skills to teach cases. Plan C focuses on the conceptual nature of the problems addressed by operations managers and utilizes selected videos offered with the Fifth Edition. Cases from the Fifth Edition could be added as needed to this plan.

COURSE OUTLINE

1. A Focus on Operations   Read Chapter 1
   - Video: Au Bon Pain

2. Operations Strategy   Read Chapter 2

3. Process Management   Read Chapter 3
   - Video: King Soopers Bakery
   - Problems: 1,2,8

4. Technology Management   Read Chapter 4
   - Video: Chapparal Steel

5. Total Quality Management   Read Chapter 6
   - Video: TQM at the Christchurch Parkroyal
   - Problems: 4,5,9

6. Statistical Process Control   Read Chapter 7
   - Problems: 1,3,4,10,13

7. Capacity   Read Chapter 8
   - Problems: 1,2,6,8

8. Location   Read Chapter 9
   - Problems: 1,3,9,11,24

9. Layout   Read Chapter 10
   - Problems: 1,6,11,12

10. Supply-Chain Management   Read Chapter 11
    - Video: Inventory and Textbooks
    - Problem: 5

11. Independent-Demand Inventory Systems (I)   Read Chapter 13, pp. 544-564
    - Problems: 1,3,22

12. Independent-Demand Inventory Systems (II)   Read Chapter 13, pp. 564-569
    - Problem: 11

13. Master Production Scheduling   Read Chapter 15, pp. 673-681
    - Problems: 1,3,6,8   Read Supp I

14. Material Requirements Planning (I)   Read Chapter 15, pp. 681-695
    - Problem: 7

15. Material Requirements Planning (II)   Read Chapter 15, pp. 695-718
    • Problem: 12

16. Just-in-Time Systems   Read Chapter 16
    • Video: Hewlett-Packard
    • Problems: 1,2,3

17. Managing Projects   Read Chapter 18, pp. 795-818
    • Problems: 1,6,8,11

18. Conclusion and Summary

Plan D (Lecture/Case/Functional/Semester)

This plan expands Plan C to provide a semester course that focuses on the functional aspects of operations management. We have added 15 cases to the plan; many of them can be used, however, as cold-call cases to generate initial discussion about a topic. The cases do not necessarily take much discussion time (as would, say, a Harvard School case), so there is room for lectures on the topics. This outline could also be used as a model for an MBA class.

COURSE OUTLINE

1. A Focus on Operations   Read Chapter 1
   - Video: Au Bon Pain
   - **Case**: Chad's Creative Concepts

2. Operations Strategy (I)   Read Chapter 2, pp. 25-37

3. Operations Strategy (II) and   Read Chapter 2, pp. 38-58
   Process Choice   Read Chapter 3, pp. 87-97
   - **Class Exercise**: Min-Yo Garment Company

4. Process Design   Read Chapter 3, pp. 97-116
   - **Case**: Custom Molds, Inc.
   - Problems: 1,2,8

5. Technology Management   Read Chapter 4
   - Video: Chapparal Steel
   - **Case**: Bill's Hardware

6. Work-Force Management   Read Chapter 5
   - **Case:** The Facilities Maintenance   Read Supplement C
          Problem at Midwest University
   - Problems: 1,2,9,12 in Chapter 5
   - Problems: 1,4 in Supplement C

7. Total Quality Management   Read Chapter 6
   - Video: Quest for Excellence VIII
   - **Case**: Cranston Nissan
   - Problems: 4,5,9

8. Statistical Process Control   Read Chapter 7
   - **Class Exercise**: Coin Catapult
   - Problems: 1,3,4,10,13

9. Capacity (I)   Read Chapter 8
   - Problems: 1,2,6,8

10. Capacity (II) and Waiting Lines   Read Supplement E
    - **Case**: Fitness Plus, Part A
    - Video: Queuing at 1st Bank Villa Italia
    - Problems: 1,4,10 in Supplement E

11. Location and Global Operations   Read Chapter 9
  - **Case**: Imaginative Toys
  - Problems: 1,3,9,11,24

12. Layout (I)   Read Chapter 10, pp. 400-425
  - Problems: 1,6

13. Layout (II) and Forecasting (I)   Read Chapter 10, pp. 425-452
  - **Case**: The Pizza Connection   Read Chapter 12, pp. 491-506
  - Problems : 11, 12 in Chapter 10
  - Problem: 14 in Chapter 12

14. Forecasting (II)   Read Chapter 12, pp. 506-525
  - **Case**: Yankee Fork and Hoe
  - Problems: 1,2,3,4,8,9

15. Supply-Chain Management   Read Chapter 11
  - Video: Inventory and Textbooks
  - Problem: 5

16. Supply-Chain Dynamics
  - **Class Exercise**: Sonic Distributors

17. Independent-Demand Inventory Systems (I)   Read Chapter 13, pp. 544-564
  - Problems: 1,3,22

18. Independent-Demand Inventory Systems (II)   Read Chapter 13, pp. 564-569
  - **Case**: Parts Emporium
  - Problem: 23

19. Master Production Scheduling (I)   Read Chapter 15, pp. 673-681
  - Problems: 1,3,6,8   Read Supp I

20. Material Requirements Planning (I)   Read Chapter 15, pp. 681-695
  - Problem: 7

21. Material Requirements Planning (II)   Read Chapter 15, pp. 695-718
  - **Case**: Flashy Flashers
  - Problem: 12

22. Just-in-Time Systems   Read Chapter 16
  - **Case**: Copper Kettle Catering
  - Problems: 1,2,3

23. Scheduling Operations   Read Chapter 17, pp. 760-777
  - Problems: 3,4,7

24. Scheduling Services   Read Chapter 17, pp. 777-794
  - Video: Scheduling Services for Air new Zealand
  - **Case:** Food King

- Problems: 8,9

25. Managing Projects (I)
   - Problems: 1,6,8,11

Read Chapter 18, pp. 795-818

26. Managing Projects (II)
   - Problems: 12

Read Chapter 18, pp. 818-838

27. Conclusion and Summary
   - **Case:** The PERT Studebaker

Plan E (Lecture/Quantitative/Quarter)

This plan focuses on the tools and techniques for decision making in operations management without losing sight of the big picture. Certain problem areas have to be deleted to make room for the presentation of the tools. The cases that we included are data oriented, with the exception of the first two which are needed to set the stage for the importance of operations management.

COURSE OUTLINE

1. A Focus on Operations
   - **Case**: Chad's Creative Concepts
   - Video: Au Bon Pain
   - Problems: 1,3,12,15,19 in Supplement A

   Read Chapter 1
   Read Supplement A

2. Operations Strategy
   - **Case**: BSB, Inc.: The Pizza Wars Come to Campus

   Read Chapter 2

3. Total Quality Management and Statistical Process Control (I)
   - Problems; 4,5,9 in Chapter 6
   - Problems: 1,3 in Chapter 7

   Read Chapter 6
   Read Chapter 7, pp. 245-261

4. Statistical Process Control (II) and Capacity (I)
   - Problems: 4,10, 13 in Chapter 7
   - Problems: 1,2,6,8 in Chapter 8
   - **Class Exercise**: Coin Catapult

   Read Chapter 7, pp. 261-270
   Read Chapter 8, pp. 299-315

5. Capacity (II) and Waiting Lines
   - Video: Queuing at 1st Bank Villa Italia
   - Problems: 2,4,10 in Supplement E

   Read Chapter 8, pp. 315-326
   Read Supplement E

6. Simulation and Location (I)
   - Problems: 1,2 in Supplement F
   - Problems: 1,3,9,11 in Chapter 9

   Read Supplement F
   Read Chapter 9, pp. 360-381

7. Transportation Method and Location (II)
   - Problem: 24 in Chapter 9

   Read Chapter 9, pp. 381-399

8. Supply-Chain Management
   - Video: Inventory and Textbooks
   - Problem: 5

   Read Chapter 11

9. Forecasting
   - **Case**: Yankee Fork and Hoe
   - Problems: 1,2,3,14

   Read Chapter 12, pp. 491-525

10. Independent-Demand Inventory Systems (I)
    - Problems: 1,3,22 in Chapter 13
    - Problems: 2,4,9 in Supplement G

    Read Chapter 13, pp. 544-564
    Read Supplement G

11. Independent-Demand Inventory Systems (II)   Read Chapter 13, pp. 564-569
    • **Case**: Parts Emporium
    • Problem: 23

12. Aggregate Planning and Linear Programming   Read Chapter 14, pp. 595-628
    • Problems: 2,4 in Chapter 14   Read Supp H, pp. 637-649
    • Problems: 1,2 in Supp H

13. Linear Programming   Read Supp, pp. 649-664
    • Problems: 6,10

14. Material Requirements Planning (I)   Read Chapter 15, pp. 673-681
    • Problems: 1,3,7

15. Material Requirements Planning (II)   Read Chapter 15, pp. 681-695
    • **Case**: Flashy Flashers
    • Problem: 12

16. Just-in-Time Systems   Read Chapter 16
    • Video: Hewlett-Packard
    • Problems: 1,2,3

17. Managing Projects   Read Chapter 18, pp. 795-818
    • Problems: 1,6,8,11

18. Conclusion and Summary
    • **Case:** The PERT Studebaker

Plan F (Lecture/Quantitative/Semester)

This plan extends Plan E and continues to emphasize the problem-solving aspects of operations management. With the exception of the first three cases, the cases have been chosen for their ability to challenge students to apply the techniques presented in the text, either manually or with the computer.

COURSE OUTLINE

1. A Focus on Operations   Read Chapter 1
    - Video: Au Bon Pain   Read Supplement A
    - Problems: 1,3,12,15,19 in Supplement A

2. Operations Strategy   Read Chapter 2

3. Technology Management   Read Chapter 4
    - **Case**: Bill's Hardware   Read Supp B
    - Video: Chapparal Steel

4. Total Quality Management and   Read Chapter 6
    Statistical Process Control (I)   Read Chapter 7, pp. 245-261
    - **Case**: Jose's Authentic Mexican Restaurant
    - Problems: 4,5,9 in Chapter 6
    - Problems: 1,3 in Chapter 7

5. Statistical Process Control (II)   Read Chapter 7, pp. 261-270
    - Problems: 4,10,13 in Chapter 7   Read Supplement D
    - Problems: 1,2,3 in Supplement D

6. Capacity and Financial Analysis   Read Chapter 8
    - **Case:** Fitness Plus, Part A   Read Appendix 1
    - Problems: 1,2,6,8,10 in Chapter 8

7. Waiting Lines   Read Supplement E
    - Video: Queuing at 1st Bank Villa Italia
    - Problems: 2,4,10 in Supplement E

8. Simulation   Read Supplement F
    - Problems: 1,2

9. Location and Global Operations   Read Chapter 9, pp. 360-381
    - Problems: 1,3,9,11

10. Location and the Transportation Method   Read Chapter 9, pp. 381-399
    - Problem: 24 in Chapter 9

11. Layout (I)   Read Chapter 10, pp. 400-425
    - Problems: 1,6

12. Layout (II) and Forecasting (I)   Read Chapter 10, pp. 425-452
    - **Case**: Hightec, Inc.   Read Chapter 12, pp. 491-506

- Problems : 11, 12 in Chapter 10
- Problems: 10, 14 in Chapter 12

13. Forecasting (II)   Read Chapter 12, pp. 506-525
    - **Case**: Yankee Fork and Hoe
    - Problems: 1,2,3,4,8,9

14. Supply-Chain Management   Read chapter 11
    - Video: Inventory and Textbooks
    - Problem: 5

15. Independent-Demand Inventory Systems (I)   Read Chapter 13, pp. 544-564
    - **Case**: Parts Emporium
    - Problems: 1,3,11,22

16. Purchasing and Distribution   Read Supplement G
    - **Case**: Wolf Motors
    - Problems: 2,4,10 in Supplement G

17. Aggregate Planning   Read Chapter 14, pp. 595-628
    - **Case**: Memorial Hospital
    - Problems: 2,4,8,9

18. Linear Programming (I)   Read Supp H, pp. 637-649
    - Problems: 1,2

19. Linear Programming (II)   Read Supp H, pp. 649-664
    - Problems: 6,10

20. Material Requirements Planning (I)   Read Chapter 15, pp. 673-681
    - Problems: 1,3,7

21. Material Requirements Planning (II)   Read Chapter 15, pp. 681-695
    - **Case**: Flashy Flashers
    - Problem: 12

22. Just-in-Time Systems   Read Chapter 16
    - Video: Hewlett-Packard
    - Problems: 1,2,3

23. Scheduling Operations   Read Chapter 17, pp. 760-777
    - Problems: 3,4,5,7

24. Scheduling Services   Read Chapter 17, pp. 777-794
    - Video: Scheduling Services at Air New Zealand
    - **Case**: Food King
    - Problems: 9,10

25. Managing Projects (I)   Read Chapter 18, pp. 795-818
    - Problems: 1,6,8,11

26. Managing Complex Projects (II)
- **Case**: PERT Studebaker
- Problems: 12

Read Chapter 18, pp. 818-838

27. Conclusion and Summary

ANNOTATED CHAPTER OUTLINES

Chapter 1: Operations as a Competitive Weapon

A. Course Introduction

1. Today's objectives:
   - What are the course requirements?
   - **What is OM? [Ask the students to share their ideas on a business they would like to start. Discuss the major OM, Marketing, and Finance decisions.]**
   - Why study OM?

2. Course objectives:
   - Strategy **and** Analysis

3. Syllabus
   - Go over course outline
   - Performance measures
   - Office hours and other administrivia
   - Questions
   - Nature of assignments

B. What is Operations Management?
[Discuss with respect to a hospital versus a local manufacturer.]

1. Inputs
   a. human resources
      - workers
      - managers
   b. capital
      - equipment
      - facilities
   c. purchased materials and services
   d. land
   e. energy

2. Special inputs
   a. customer participation (internal/external)
   b. internal and external information

3. Processes: definition and examples
   a. manufacturing — physical, chemical
   b. airline — locational
   c. school — educational

    d.   store — exchange

    e.   theater — attitudinal

    f.   distribution center — break shipping quantities

    g.   hospital — physiological

    h.   congress — deliberative

4. Outputs

    a.   goods and services

    b.   environmental impact

    c.   political and economic impact

5. Operations

    Places (circles) where input resources utilized and transformation processes occur.

Input examples

Hospital	**[Medical professionals, building, diagnostic equip]**
Manufacturer	**[Workers, managers, drills, metal, energy]**

Output examples

Hospital	**[Healed patients (hopefully)]**
Manufacturer	**[Physical products]**

Transformation examples:

Hospital	**[Physiological, behavioral]**
Manufacturer	**[Physical change of shape, mechanical]**

C. Operations Management as a Set of Decisions

1. Decisions define the scope and content of OM. Five categories:

    a.   Strategic choices affect company's future direction.

- What are the competitive priorities?
- What is flow strategy?
- What are quality objectives?

    b.   Process

- What work done in-house?
- Amount of automation?
- Ways to provide leadership in technological change?
- Degree of job enlargement?
- Time estimates for work requirements.

c. Quality

- How do we improve quality?
- Use of inspection and statistical methods to monitor quality.

d. Capacity, location, and layout

- What system capacity is needed?
- Where should facilities be located?
- How should the facility layouts be organized?

e. Operating decisions

- How so we coordinate internal and external supply chain?
- Which forecasting method is appropriate?
- How will inventory be managed?
- How do we control output and staffing levels over time?
- What, when, and how many items should be purchased or produced?
- Would Just-in-time techniques benefit out organization?
- Which task should revive top priority?
- How should resources be scheduled?

2. Linking decisions

a. Operations decisions compliment corporate strategy.

b. Decisions **within** operations also should be linked.

3. Strategy (big picture) **and** analysis (calculations)

D. Operations Management as a Function

1. Responsibilities of each function

2. OM draws from several disciplines.

E. Manufacturing and Services: Differences and Similarities

1. Differences:

	Manufacturing	Hospital
Nature of product	[physical, durable]	[Intangible]
Nature of inventories	[raw, intermediate, final]	[Raw]
Level of customer contact	[low]	[high]
Response time needs	[often not critical]	[often critical]
Size of market	[far reaching possible]	[typically local]
Size of facilities	[typically large]	[typically small to medium]
Capital intensity	[capital intensive]	[labor intensive]
Ease of quality measurements	[typically easy]	[typically difficult]

2. Similarities

F. Trends in Operations Management

1. Service sector growth

   a. Three components of the service sector

      - local, state, and federal governments

      - wholesale and retail firms

      - transportation, public utilities, communications, health, financial service, and personal service firms

   b. Keeping manufacturing a vital sector

      - You can't control what you can't produce.

      - Output in manufacturing has been increasing.

      - Two sectors are complementary.

   c. We address both manufacturing and service industries in the course. [Emphasize this point.]

2. Productivity changes

   a. The value of outputs produced divided by the value of input resources

   $$\text{Productivity} = \frac{\text{Output}}{\text{Input}}$$

   b. Use **Application 1.1: Productivity Calculations (AP 1.1)** to give students the chance to make their own productivity calculations. This example comes from a prior Annual Report to the Stockholders from Chrysler. The labor productivity increase was 12.6% this year, and 15.8% last year. The multifactor productivity change is 2.6%.

   c. U. S. Productivity
- Compare and contrast productivity in manufacturing and services
- Role of operations managers in determining productivity
- Link productivity with standard of living
- Global comparisons

   d. Some possible explanations
- Unreliable productivity data for services
- Increased regulation (EPA, OSHA)
- Low investment in new equipment and technology
- Changing work-force composition and attitudes
- Strong unions? (baseball)
- Difficulty in improving on already high productivity
- Operations management is the key to productivity improvements

3. Global competition

   a. Viewing operations in global terms
- world trade in materials and services

   b. Productivity comparisons

   c. NUMMI and Honda **[See MP 1.1]**

4. Competition based on quality, time, and technology

   a. Quality, a part of productivity ratio, is a now prerequisite for competition.
[Mention electronics]

   b. Time, another important basis for competing, is also being emphasized.
[Mention Honda vs. Yamaha]

   c. Technological change is also a source of competitive advantage.
[Mention robotics; Internet]

5. Environmental, ethical, and work-force diversity issues

   a. Decisions about the design and operations of production systems consider the environment, ethics, and workplace diversity issues

   b. Examples **[Discuss oil spills, use of Styrofoam packaging, tobacco]**

E. Operations Management and the Organization

    a. Cross-functional coordination

- Interdependent functions require coordination
- Strongest connection with marketing
- Accounting provides operations performance feedback
- Finance influences investments
- Human resources recruits and trains personnel
- Engineering design should match operation's capabilities

    b. Achieving cross-functional coordination

- Unified strategy, department vision
- Redesigned organizational structure
- Reward systems consistent with cross-functional goals
- Decision support information systems
- Informal social systems,
- Employee selection and promotion

2. Operations management as a competitive weapon

    a. Operations can be either a competitive weapon or a millstone.

    b. Meeting the competitive challenge at selected firms

- Examples include IKEA, GTE Corporation, Merlin Metalworks, and Dillard Stores **[See MP 1.2]**
- Other examples

Chapter 2: Operations Strategy

[Students sometimes have difficulty envisioning the linking of operations to competitive priorities. Use the Min-Yo in-class simulation exercise to establish that link.]

A. Strategy Overview

[Mention Hewlett-Packard's customer-driven operations strategy]

1. Market analysis

   - Categorize customers.

   - Identify customer needs.

   - Assess competitors' strengths.

2. Corporate strategy

   - Provides framework of goals for the organization

3. Competitive priorities

   - Operating system capabilities and strengths required to serve customers

4. Functional strategies

   - Goals and long term plans for each of the functional areas (operations, finance, marketing).

B. Corporate Strategy

1. Strategic choices

   - Determine the mission.

   - Monitor and adjust to changes in the environment.

   - Identify and develop distinctive competencies.

   a. Mission

      - What business are we in? Where should we be ten years from now?

      - Who are our customers (or clients)?

      - What are our basic beliefs?

      - How do we measure success? What are the key performance objectives?

   b. Broad or narrow mission?

      - Too broad — the firm enters businesses in which it has no distinctive competencies.

      - Too narrow — may miss promising growth opportunities.

   c. Environment

      - Environmental scanning: Monitor socioeconomic trends for potential opportunities or threats.

        — competition is broadening product lines, improving quality, or lowering costs

        — economic trends

        — technological changes [Mention Rusty Jones rust proofing.]

- political conditions
- social changes
- availability of vital resources collective power of customers or suppliers

    d. Core competencies: examples **[Mention Volvo's anticipation of environmental changes.]**

       Some distinctive competencies:

- Work force, well-trained and flexible
- Facilities, well-located and flexible
- Marketing and financial skill
- Systems and technology, achieve competitive advantage through innovation

2. Global strategies

    a. Forms of Strategic Alliances

- Collaborative effort **[Mention Kodak.]**
- Joint venture **[Mention joint ventures in China.]**
- Licensing of technology **[Mention Cannon copiers.]**

    b. Locating operations in foreign countries: some differences to consider

- Political environment
- Customer needs
- Customs **[Mention McDonald's restaurants.]**
- Economic situation

C. Market Analysis

1. Market segmentation (Step 1)

- Identify customer groups having common characteristics which differentiate them from other market segments.
- Incorporate market segment needs into product or service design and the operations system design.

    a. Dimensions used to determine market segments **[Use examples familiar to students.]**

- Demographic factors **[Mention Greyhound's market segmentation in MP 2.1.]**
- Psychological factors
- Industry factors

2. Needs assessment (Step 2)

    a. Customer benefit package

- Core product or service
- Set of peripheral products or services

b. Four categories of market needs

- Product/service

- Delivery system

- Volume

- Other [Bring out links to other functional areas]

D. Competitive Priorities

1. Cost

    a. Low cost operations [**Mention items such as salt, flour, nails, etc.**]

2. Quality

    a. High Performance Design [**Mention Club-Med and Fincantieri shipbuilding company in MP 2.2.**]

    - Superior features

    - Close tolerances

    - Greater durability

    - Available, courteous, knowledgeable service

    - Convenient location

    - Product safety

    b. Consistent quality

    - Frequency of conformance to specifications

3. Time [**Discuss time-based competition.**]

    a. Fast delivery time [**Mention Fed Ex**].

    - Short lead time

    b. On-time delivery [**Mention suppliers to auto assembly plants.**]

    - Deliver as promised.

    c. Development speed [**Mention The Limited.**]

    - Time-based competition

    - Reducing response time

    - More products in less time

4. Flexibility

    a. Customization — accommodate unique needs of customers [**Mention cafeterias, hairdressers, and MP 2.3.**]

    b. Volume flexibility — ability to quickly change production rate [**Mention Post Office, lawn fertilizer producers such as Scott's & Sons.**]

5. Selecting competitive priorities

    a. Further improvements in one area sometimes requires a trade-off with other areas

    b. Order qualifiers (a prerequisite to entering the market place)

- Quality **[Mention food products, auto parts suppliers.]**
- Reliability **[Mention TV sets, telephone service.]**

E. Flow Strategy

1. Flexible flow strategy

    a. Processes are grouped by the function they perform.

    b. Products or services are routed from one process to another until finished.

    c. Used for low volumes with a high degree of variety **[Mention manufacturing and service examples, discuss the LFKHS tour.]**

2. Line flow strategy

    a. Processes are grouped by the product or service to be produced.

    b. Products or services flow directly from one process to the next.

    c. Used for high volumes and standardized products or services **[Mention automobile assembly operations, car washes, discuss the Chaparral tour.]**

3. A continuum of strategies

- Positioning strategy can vary by facility, depending on the products and services.
- A continuum of choices exists between extremes of process focus and product focus.

    a. Process-focused strategy

- Equipment and work force are organized around processes.
- Equipment is general purpose.
- Workers have multiple skills.
- Volume is low.
- Routings vary from one order to the next.
- Flow pattern is jumbled.
- The facility (a job shop) can produce a wide range of products.

    b. Product-focused strategy

- The equipment and work force are organized around a small number of products, or a single product line that offers the customer a choice from a defined list of options.
- Equipment is special purpose.
- Workers have few skills.
- Volume is high.

Anno2-4

- Single routing, material may be moved by conveyors.
- The facility (a flow shop) can produce a high volume of just a few products, or a single product line with a nearly infinite number of combinations of options.

  c. Intermediate strategy

- Product volumes are higher than found in job shops.
- Some standardized products are made to stock.
- Some customized products are made to order.
- Flow pattern is jumbled, with some frequently used paths.
- Some equipment may be dedicated to small flow lines to produce popular products made to stock.
- Remainder of equipment is arranged as a job shop.

4. Strategies based on flows

   a. Make-to-stock strategy

- Finished goods items held in stock for immediate delivery
- High volumes, standard products, line flow strategy
- Production based on forecasted demand
- Supports low cost, consistent quality competitive priority

   b. Standardized services strategy

- Services with little variety and high volumes
- Use line flow strategy, but services cannot be stocked in advance
- Supports low cost, on-time delivery, and consistent quality priorities **[Mention U.S. Postal Service, FedEx, UPS.]**

   c. Assemble-to-order strategy

- Assemblies and components held in stock, intermediate flow strategy used
- Final assembly is completed after the customer selects options.
- A very large number of final configurations are possible.
- Forecasting the final configuration is impractical because of the many combinations. **[Mention furniture manufacturer, paint retailer.]**
- Used for services in situations where many standardized services can be packaged for individual customers **[Mention long distance telephone service providers.]**

   d. Make-to-order strategy

- Most required materials are ordered after the customer places the order.
- Produce to customer specifications.
- Flexible processes, flexible flow strategy used
- Supports customization as a competitive priority **[Mention specialized medical equipment, expensive homes.]**

e. Customized services strategy

- Highly individualized services, often in low volumes **[Mention beauty salons, appliance repair shops, interior decorators.]**

- Use a flexible flow strategy.

- Sometimes this strategy is used in high volumes, such as a product repair facility associated with a large retailer.

F. Mass Customization
[Mention Hewlett-Packard in Chapter 2 opener as an example of a mass customizer.]

- Use an assemble-to-order strategy, but typically focus on large volumes.

- Postpone the task of differentiating the product or service until the latest possible moment.

1. Product or service implications

- Design the product or service in modular forms that can be easily and quickly assembled for a specific customer. **[Mention America Online, Ritz-Carlton.]**

2. Process implications

- Design processes as independent modules that can be easily arranged to meet a variety of needs at the latest possible moment. **[Mention retail paint stores, Benetton.]**

[Use the experiential case Min-Yo Garment Company to actively involve students in aligning their market segments with their processes and competitive priorities. You will need at least a complete class period to execute the simulation, but the students like the competitive orientation and the interaction between the functional areas.]

Supplement A: Decision Making

Decision-Making Steps

1. Recognize and clearly define the decision

2. Collect information, analyze alternative courses of action

3. Choose and implement the most feasible alternative

A. Break-even Analysis

1. Evaluating products or services

   - We assume total costs equals fixed costs; which do not vary with volume, plus variable costs; which vary linearly with volume.

   - Use **Application A.1: Break-Even Analysis for Evaluating Products or Services (AP A.1)** for an in-class exercise of graphical solution, algebraic solution, and sensitivity analysis. The expected demand increase is not quite enough to break even.

2. Evaluating processes

   - We assume that the make versus buy or process 1 versus process 2 decision does not affect revenues.

   - The decision alternative is indicated on the basis of the lowest total costs at the expected volume.

   - Use **Application A.2: Break-Even Analysis for Evaluating Processes (AP A.2)** for a make or buy example.

B. Preference Matrix

The preference matrix is used where multiple criteria cannot be merged into a single measure such as dollars.

1. Preference matrix steps

   a. Decision statement—define the decision and the factors that are relevant to that decision. For example in answering the question: "Who shall I marry?", relevant factors may include money, hair, and the desire to upset ones parents.

   b. Assign weights to the relevant factors that reflect how important each is to your decision. It is nice if the weights add to 100%. Later, we could then say that 40% of the decision to marry Skip was because of money, and 30% was because of the desire to upset parents.

   c. Objectives/assumptions—establish the decision criteria, perhaps a scale from 1 (worst) to 5 (best). State your assumptions!

   d. Generate alternatives—techniques such as "brainstorming" or research methods may be employed

   e. Formulate a matrix—relating the relevant factors (rows) to the alternatives (columns) generated in step 3.

   f. Evaluate the alternatives

- Compare each alternative to each relevant factor, then assign a score that describes how well that alternative satisfies that factor.

- Multiply the score times the weight for that factor.

- Add the weighted scores in each column to obtain total points.

   g. Tentative decision—the alternative that best satisfies the objectives is the one that gets the most points.

   h. Assess adverse consequences/qualitative factors—this is where non quantitative values come in. We don't want to make decisions based solely on numbers.

   i. Implement the decision and monitor the results—manage change, look for early warning signals of trouble, mitigate damages, have alternative plans.

2. Criticism of preference matrix

   a. Requires the manager to state criterion weights before examining alternatives, but they may not know in advance what is important and what is not.

   b. Allows one very low score to be overridden by high scores on other factors.

   c. This approach does take time to analyze, so it would not be useful for trivial situations such as deciding which movie to attend.

3. Use **Application A.3: Preference Matrix (AP A.3)** for a quick example of evaluating new service.

C. Decision Theory

1. Decision Process

   a. List a reasonable number of feasible *alternatives*.
   b. List the *events*.
   c. Calculate the *payoff* table showing the payoff for each alternative in each event.
   d. Estimate the *probability* of occurrence for each event.
   e. Select a *decision rule* to evaluate the alternatives

2. Decision making under certainty. The manager knows which event will occur.

3. Decision making under uncertainty. The manager can list the possible events but cannot estimate probabilities.

   a. Four decision rules

- Maximin—For those pessimists who tend to believe that the worst possible event will certainly occur, this decision rule chooses the alternative that has the best result, given the worst event will occur.

- Maximax—For those optimists who tend to believe that the best possible event will certainly occur, this decision rule chooses the alternative that has the best result, given the best event will occur.

- Laplace—For realists who tend to believe that events tend to even out in the long run, this decision rule places equal weight, or assumes equal probability, for each of the possible events.

- Minimax Regret—For Monday morning quarterbacks, and those who focus on past mistakes, this decision rule looks to minimize the worst possible negative effect (regrets) associated with making a wrong decision (and ignoring the positive effects of a good decision).

b. Use **Application A.4: Decision Making Under Uncertainty (AP A.4)** here. The short answers are: arrows for Laplace (Fletcher), barrels for Maximin (Cooper), Wagons for Maximax (Wainwright), and arrows for Minimax Regret.

4. Decision Making Under Risk

a. The manager can list the possible events and estimate their probabilities.

b. The expected value rule is widely used.

5. Value of Perfect Information

a. Identify the best payoff for each event.

b. Calculate the expected value of these best payoffs.

c. Find the difference between expected payoff values with and without perfect information. This is the maximum one would pay for the information.

d. Use **Application A.5: Decision Making Under Risk (AP A.5)** for using expected value and calculating the value of perfect information.

D. Decision Trees

1. The approach

A schematic model of available alternatives and possible consequences

- Useful with probabilistic events and sequential decisions

- Square nodes represent decisions.

- Circular nodes represent events.

- Events leaving a chance node are collectively exhaustive (probabilities sum to one).

- Conditional payoffs for each possible alternative-event combination shown at the end of each combination.

- Draw the decision tree from left to right.

- Calculate expected payoff to solve the decision tree from right to left.

2. Use **Application A.6: Decision Trees (AP A.6)** for an in-class exercise in drawing and analyzing a decision tree.

Chapter 3: Process Management

A. What is Process Management?

1. A process involves the use of an organization's resources to provide something of value.

   - They underlie all work activity throughout the organization.
   - They are nested within other processes along an organization's supply chain.

2. Process management is the selection of the inputs, operations, work flows, and methods that transform inputs into outputs.

   - Begins with deciding what to do in-house and what to outsource.
   - Also deals with the best mix of human skills and equipment, and what done by each.
   - Decisions must be consistent with the process's flow strategy and corporate strategy.

3. When Process Decisions Are Required
   - New or modified product is offered
   - Quality improvement is needed
   - Competitive priorities change
   - Demand volume changes
   - Inadequate current performance
   - Competitors use new technology or a different process
   - Cost of inputs change

B. Major Process Decisions

Five common process decisions [**Note that MP 3.1 ties in ethics and the environment.**]

- Process choice
- Vertical integration
- Resource flexibility
- Customer involvement
- Capital intensity

1. Process choice

   a. Five Basic Choices for Implementing Flow Strategy

      - Project process, high customization, large scope of project
      - Job process, high variety of products or service
      - Batch process, higher volumes, batching of customer orders
      - Line process, high volumes, standardized products or services, dedicated resources, repetitive manufacturing

- Continuous process, high volumes, rigid line flows **[The King Soopers video could be used here, or later at point #6. Be careful about terminology in the video.]**

2. Vertical integration

   a. Attractive when

- High input volume

- Firm has the required skills

- Process integration is important to the future of the firm

   b. Not attractive when

- A supplier can do the work more efficiently **[Mention Atlantic Foods.]**

   c. Backward integration — a type of vertical integration that acquires more of the supply chain toward raw materials.

   d. Forward integration — a type of vertical integration that acquires more of the distribution chain toward the customer. **[Mention Wendy's and IBM.]**

   e. Outsourcing and network companies

- Rely on other firms for most of their production
  - Little backward integration, low capital intensity
  - Quickly move in and out of markets
  - Effective when life cycles are short

- Vulnerable to vertical integration when volume is high or life cycles are long
  - Hollow corporations add little value, investment barriers to competition are low
  - High volume customers can integrate backward to the actual producer, cutting out the hollow corporation
  - Manufacturers can integrate forward toward the customer, again cutting out the hollow corporation

   f. Make or buy **[Relate to Supplement A for problems.]**

- Commonly outsourced services, which are not provided by employees of the firm that needs the service, include:
  - Payroll
  - Security
  - Cleaning
  - Accounting
  - Training
  - Legal
  - Public relations
  - Advertising

- Globalization creates more supplier options.

- Information technology allows competitors to come together as a **virtual corporation** in order to respond to market opportunities.

   b. Own or lease

- Leased equipment is favored when
  - Changes in technology are rapid
  - Frequent servicing is required

— Need for equipment is short term

3. Resource flexibility

   a. Workforce

      - Implications of a flexible work force
        — Requires more education and training
        — Capable of many tasks
        — Alleviates capacity bottlenecks, volume flexibility
        — Reliable customer service
        — Increased job satisfaction

      - Volume flexibility and needed skills determine the type of work force.
        — Steady volume, high skills—permanent work force
        — Variable volume, low skills—part-time or temporary employees to supplement permanent work force
        — Variable volume, high skills—trained flexible force that can be moved to produce whatever the market demands

   b. Equipment

      - General purpose

      - Resource flexibility is crucial to the success of a process-focused flexible flow strategy.

      - Use **Application 3.1: Break-Even Analysis in Process Choice (AP 3.1)** for an in-class exercise. The short answer is **13,000 frames**.

4. Customer involvement

   - Self-service

     — Customers do part of the process formerly done by the manufacturer.

   - Product selection [Mention custom homes]

     — Product specification and design

   - Time and location

     — By appointment or on demand? **[Mention emergency services.]**

     — At supplier's location, customer's location, or third-party location? **[Mention chimney sweeps; tax preparation.]**

   - There is an inverse relationship between customer involvement and capital intensity.

5. Capital intensity

   a. Which tasks will be performed by humans and which by machines?

      - More machines means more capital intensity, and less resource flexibility and less customer involvement.

   b. Automated (capital intensive) operations must have high utilization.

   c. Automation may not fit with competitive priorities being emphasized.

      - More capital intensity is not always best.

    d. Fixed automation favored when **[Mention chemicals and oil.]**

- High demand volume

- Stable product design

- Long life cycle

    e. Flexible automation. **[Mention Cummins Engine.]**

- Useful in both flexible flow and line flow operations

- Can be quickly set up to make a variety of products in small batches

- Flexible manufacturing systems
  — Capital intensive
  — Allow more flexibility in the product produced
  — Shorter design and manufacturing lead time
  — Efficient while producing low-volume, customized products

6. Relationships between decisions **[Emphasize this point. Use King Soopers as a base of discussion.]**

- An underlying variable creating the relationships is volume. **[Discuss *why* this is so.]**

7. Service operation relationships, relative to customized customer involvement and capital intensity

- Professional service

- Service shop

- Mass service

- Service factory

8. Economies of Scope

- Requires a family of products having enough collective volume to utilize equipment fully

9. Gaining focus

- Focused factories

- Focus by process segments, and PWPs

C. Designing Processes

1. Process reengineering

    a. Critical processes **[Mention Bell Atlantic.]**

- Emphasis is placed on core business processes.

- Processes are broadly defined in terms of costs and customer value.

    b. Strong leadership

- Top management makes a compelling case for change.

    c. Cross-functional teams

- Reengineering works best at high-involvement workplaces.

d. Information technology

- Restructuring around information flows can reduce management and work activity.

e. Clean slate philosophy

- Start with the way the customer wants to deal with the company.

f. Process analysis

- Understanding current processes can reveal areas where new thinking will provide the biggest payoff.

2. Process improvement

Two basic techniques for analyzing activities and flows within processes:

- Process charts
- Flow diagrams

a. Characteristics of operations having greatest payoff potential

- Slow in responding to the customer
- Poor quality
- Time consuming, costly
- Bottleneck process, limiting throughput of entire facility
- Disagreeable or dangerous work, pollution
- Little value added, waste of materials or effort

b. Break process into detailed components, asking six questions & why

- *What* is being done? … *Why* is it being done?
- *When* it is being done? … *Why* at that particular time?
- *Who* is doing it? … *Why* have that person or group do it?
- *Where* is it being done? … *Why*? Is that the right place?
- *How long* does it take? … *Why* does it take that long?
- *How* is it being done? … *Why* is it being done that way?
  - a. Flow diagrams
    - Plot the path followed by the person, material, or equipment.
  - b. Process charts

c. Five categories of activities

- Operation   productive work
- Transportation   movement of the study's subject
- Inspection   check or verify, but do not change
- Delay   awaiting operation, transportation, or inspection
- Storage   put away until later, not a delay

d.   Completing a process chart

- Identify each step performed.

- Categorize each step relative to the subject: person, material, or machine. For example, the person may be waiting for a machine to complete an operation.

- Record distances traveled and the time required.

- Calculate summary data: steps, times, and distance.

- Ask the what, when, who, where, how long, and how questions, challenging each of the charted process steps (asking why).

- Plan and implement improvements.

e.   Perhaps do an in-class exercise, such as doing a flow diagram for the Custom Molds case, doing the Advanced Problem on shaving, and possibly creating a process chart with the OM5 Software package.

Chapter 4: Management of Technology

This chapter and the CIM supplement that follows it may not lend themselves very well to an in-class lecture. Perhaps the best strategy is to have the students read the material before class. Then spend class time on the new Bill's Hardware case, the discussion question, the experiences of the class with new technology, or the new video that is being prepared for this chapter.

A. Meaning and Role of Technology

1. The know-how, physical things, and procedures used to produce products and services; also support network

2. Product and process technology

3. Three primary areas

   a. Product technology: translates ideas into new products and services for firm's customers **[PixelVision's flat-panel monitor]**

   b. Process technology: determines methods by which an organization does things **[NYSE's trading process]**

      ▪ technologies along the supply chain

      ▪ technologies by functional area

   c. Information technology used to acquire, process, and transmit information; particularly revolutionary in offices

4. Management of technology

   a. Links R&D, engineering, and management to plan, develop, and implement new technological capabilities

   b. How much to know about technologies in one's own operations

5. Technology's role in business performance

   a. Link of R&D with profitability and new product introductions

   b. High tech not always best

B. Information Technology

1. Four components

   a. Hardware: computer and devices connected to it

   b. Software: computer programs written to make hardware work

   c. Databases: collection of interrelated data or information stored on a data storage device

d. Telecommunications: equipment that makes electronic networks possible; Internet and intranet

2. Impact of internet

   a. World Wide Web

   b. A new distribution channel

C. Creating and Applying Technology

1. R&D Stages

   a. Basic research

   b. Applied research

   c. Development: concept development, technical feasibility, detailed product or service design, and process design

2. Technology fusion: combining several existing technologies and scientific disciplines to create a hybrid technology

D. Technology Strategy

1. Technology as a competitive advantage

2. Fit with competitive priorities

3. Core competencies and strategic fit

4. First-mover considerations

   a. Possible advantages

   b. Risks

5. Economic justification

   a. Traditional techniques

   b. Factoring in uncertainties and intangibles

6. Disruptive technologies

   a. Two properties are:

   • Performance attributes not yet valued by existing customers or products, and

   • Performs worse on some performance attributes that existing or future customers value, but will quickly surpass existing technologies when refined

   b. Dealing with the paradox

E. Implementation Guidelines

1. Technology acquisition

    a. How far back in R&D stream should we get involved?

       - Internal sources
       - Interfirm relationships: outsource to universities or labs with grants, license from another organization, joint venture or alliance, or buy out another firm.
       - Suppliers

2. Technology integration

    - Fragmentation
    - Cross-functional teams and concurrent engineering

3. The human side

    a. Impact of new technology on jobs and people

    b. Education and employee involvement

4. Leadership: good steward, realists, visionaries, advocates, gatekeepers, and project champion

Supplement B: Computer-Integrated Manufacturing

A. Computer-Aided Design and Manufacturing

1. Computer-aided design (CAD); electronic system used to design products and parts

   - Replaces drafting by hand
   - Computer shows several views as designer creates the drawing
   - Stress analysis shows reaction to force, indicating where the design is weak or likely to fail
   - Successful designs are stored, building a library of designs which can be retrieved and reused

2. Computer-aided manufacturing

   a. computers used to:
      - Design production processes
      - Schedule manufacturing operations
      - Track labor costs
      - Send instructions to control machine tools
      - Direct materials flow

3. CAD/CAM system

   - Integrates the design and manufacturing function
   - Translates the computer drawing or image into code which directs and controls a machine to produce parts

B. Numerically Controlled (NC) Machines

   - Most commonly used form of flexible automation
     — One machine has many tools and performs many operations, perhaps machining a detailed part from a block of metal
     — Receives instructions from external source (tape or computer) **[Mention CNC machines.]**
   - Computerized numerically controlled (CNC) machines

C. Industrial Robots

   - Computer-controlled machines programmed to perform various functions
   - Limited reach
     — Increased travel or axes of movement rapidly increases price.
     — Robot must always know where it is relative to the work, precision depends on maintaining a reference point.
   - Usually sightless
     — Tools must be stored in predetermined locations
     — Material must always be presented in the same orientation

  — Some second generation robots have sensors to simulate touch and sight

 • Relatively slow speed (when compared to fixed automation)

  — Usually not suitable for high volume standardized production

D. Automated Materials Handling

1. Materials handling processes cost time and money and add no value to the product

 • Always look for ways to reduce materials handling

 • Materials handling automation justification depends on flow strategy

  — With a flexible flow, materials handling automation is rarely justified

  — With line flow, materials handling automation may be justifiable

 a. Automated Guided Vehicle (AGV)

  • Follow cable or optical (paint stripe) path

  • On board or centralized computer control

  • Route around transportation bottlenecks

  • Just-in-time delivery of parts

 b. AS/RS

E. Flexible Manufacturing Systems

Characteristics of FMS:

• Large initial investment [$5MM to $20MM]

• Little direct labor

• Routing of operations determined by central computer

• Short setup times

• Different machines can perform the same operation

1. Three Key Components of an FMS

 • Several computer-controlled work stations, CNC machines, or robots that perform a series of operations

 • A computer-controlled transport system

 • Loading and unloading stations

2. Strategic Uses of FMS **[Use video: Lessons from Japan]**

 • Intermediate flow strategy

 • Line flow processes where product life cycles are short

3. Flexible manufacturing cells

Chapter 5: Work-Force Management

A. Organizational Restructuring

1. Teamwork

   - Worker participation is key to improving quality.

   - **Employee empowerment** moves decision-making responsibility down to those who have the best information — those who are actually doing the job.

   - **Organizational restructuring**, eliminates some supervisors and middle managers.

   a. Characteristics of teams

   - Common commitment to an overarching purpose

   - Shared leadership roles

   - Performance measures reflect collective "work products"

   - Open-ended discussion rather than managerially defined agendas

   - Do the work together rather than delegation to subordinates

   b. Problem-solving teams, or quality circles **[Mention Wilson Sporting Goods.]**

   - Small groups of supervisors and employees

   - Employees shape their work, more pride, involvement

   - Quality circles die if management fails to implement suggestions.

   c. Special-purpose teams [Mention Victory Memorial Hospital]

   - Address a specific issue of management concern (Ad hoc team).

   - Gives workers a voice in high-level decisions

   - Members represent several departments or functions.

   d. Self-Managing Teams **[Mention Huffy Bicycles.]**

   - Highest level of worker participation

   - Employees design the processes, control their jobs

   e. Some concerns. **[Mention GE Salisbury plant.]**

   - Not everyone wants decision making responsibility or control over their work.

   - Supervisors and middle managers are resistant to change.

     — Different skill sets are required.

     — Organizational restructuring may cost them their jobs.

2. Horizontal organizations **[Mention AT&T, DuPont.]**

   - Hierarchy and functional boundaries are eliminated.

   - Organization is managed across functional areas by multidisciplinary teams.

   a. Key elements

     — Organized around processes

- — Flat organizational hierarchy
- — Management teams
- — Customer-driven performance measures
- — Team-oriented rewards
- — Teams (rather than an individual purchasing agent or account manager) maintain supplier and customer relationships.
- — Training programs for all employees

    b. Links to operations strategy

- Requires major (painful) cultural transformation
- Decide what it takes to be successful in the marketplace.
- Decision should be linked to operations strategy.

        1. Traditional (vertical) organization may suit some mass production industries

- — Repetitive activities
- — Competitive priority is low cost

        2. Flexibility of horizontal organizations is useful when competitive priorities include

- — Product development speed
- — High-performance design
- — Customization and product variety

3. Incentive plans

- Incentives tend to encourage productivity improvements.
- Traditional incentive schemes reward individual behavior rather than team behavior.

    a. Individual-based plans

Piece rate

- Does not promote team efforts
- Does not encourage high-quality work

Pay-for-skills plans

- Reward for skills acquired to make workers more valued as team members **[Mention Mettler-Toledo.]**
- Supports team efforts

Bonus-point plan **[Mention Honda.]**

- Points for employee involvement (such as participation in quality circles)
- Rewards based on points earned

    b. Team-based plans

- Incentives tied to production/quality goals
- *Financial* rewards for teams rather than individuals
- *Public recognition* rewards intrinsic desire for excellence

c. Group-based plans

- Result in higher productivity, value added exceeds costs of plans

Profit sharing

- Paid on profitability levels of the company as a whole

Gain sharing

- Rewards collective performance of a group
- Promotes group efforts to improve productivity

3. Training programs

- Emphasis on efficient process and high quality requires employees having a broad base of skills.

General training

- Leadership, communication, project management, problem solving, mathematics, statistical process control methods, critical thinking, remedial English

Administrative training for team leaders

- Employment practices, performance appraisals, and management skills

Technical training

- Increases skills in aspects of a person's job or a related job

B. Job Design

- Improves efficiency through analysis of the job's work elements
- Improves productivity through consideration of technical and human factors
- Increases the quality of the product or service
- Increases worker satisfaction

Frederick Taylor, Scientific Management

- Traditional job design
- Any operation can be improved by
  — Breaking operation into components
  — Studying each component to improve work methods
- Sought the most efficient and effective way to perform tasks
- Dealt primarily with the technical aspects of job design
  — Best way to reach, grasp, and move objects
  — Number of repetitions before rest
  — Best physical position for worker
- Management trains workers in new work methods
- Management is responsible for coordinating work
- Stressed the need for teamwork between management and workers
- Method works only if economic benefits are shared

1. Job specialization

   - Specialization narrows the range of task

   a. Arguments in favor of job specialization

      - Less training time for limited procedures

      - Repetition leads to faster work pace

      - Lower wages paid to unskilled workers

   b. Arguments against job specialization

      - Low morale, high absenteeism, high turnover, low quality

      - More need for managers to coordinate numerous narrow tasks

      - Specialists have little knowledge about the duties of others; the work force has less flexibility, making it difficult to replace workers (see low morale, high turnover)

   c. Strategic implications **[Provide examples of local companies using various degrees of specialization]**

      - Link the degree of specialization to competitive priorities

      - Specialization tends to support product-focused firms

2. Alternatives to specialization

   a. Reasons people work

      - Economic needs

      - Social needs

      - Individual needs

   b. In narrowly defined jobs there are fewer opportunities to

      - Control the pace of work

      - Receive gratification from the work

      - Advance to a better position

      - Show initiative

      - Communicate with fellow workers

   c. Highly repetitive jobs lead to

      - Boredom

      - Poor job performance

        — High turnover rates

        — Absenteeism

        — Grievances

        — Intentional disruption of production

        — Incomplete work assignments

d. Alternatives to specialization

- Job enlargement — horizontal expansion of responsibility
- Job rotation — workers exchange jobs, no expansion of responsibility
- Job enrichment — vertical expansion of responsibility

C. Work Standards

- Skill, effort, and stamina vary from one employee to another.

1. Work standards as a management tool

Ways managers use work standards: **[Mention NUMMI use of work standards]**

- Establishing prices and costs
- Motivating workers
- Comparing alternative process designs
- Scheduling
- Capacity planning
- Performance appraisal

2. Areas of controversy

a. Standards set "too high" or "too low"

b. Use of work standards for piecework incentives

- May defeat their purpose of increased productivity because workers become secretive about work methods devised to increase output
- Workers may increase quantity at the expense of quality

D. Methods of Work Measurement

Methods of work measurement:

- Time study method
- Elemental standard data
- Predetermined data approach
- Work sampling method

1. Time study method

- Time study is the method used most often for setting time standards.

a. Steps in a time study:

Step 1. Selecting work elements—each should have definite starting and stopping points. Separate incidental operations from the repetitive work.

Step 2. Timing the elements—Use either the continuous or snap-back method. Irregular occurrences should not be included in calculating the average time.

Step 3. Determining sample size—varies with confidence, precision, and variability of the work element times.

Step 4. Setting the standard—Apply subjective performance rating factor, calculate normal times, normal time for the cycle, and adjust for allowances.

Use **Application 5.1: Time Study Method (AP5.1)** to give the students an opportunity to go through the four steps in a time study on their own.

    b. Judgment in time study

- Where should we set the starting and stopping points to define the work elements without making them too long or too short?

- Should we include time for infrequent events?

- Should we eliminate data for unusual events? In other words, is it really unusual for Lucy to have difficulty?

- What is the appropriate amount for allowances?

- Requiring the greatest amount of judgment is the performance rating. Was Lucy really slacking off, working at 90% of her normal speed while packing? How could you prove it was 90%, and not 95%?

    c. Overall assessment of time study

+ Most frequently used method for setting time standards

+ Qualified analysts can typically set reasonable standards

− Not appropriate for "thinking" jobs

− Not appropriate for nonrepetitive jobs

− Inexperienced persons should not conduct time studies because errors in recording information or in selecting work elements can result in unreasonable standards

− Workers may object to judgment and subjectivity involved

2. Elemental standard data approach

- Useful when a high degree of similarity exists

- Time standards are developed for common work elements.

- Study results are stored in a database for later use in establishing standards for jobs requiring those elements.

- Allowances must still be added.

- An equation may be used to account for the effect on time required by certain variable characteristics of the jobs.

- Specifying job variables for use in the equation is difficult and may not produce good estimates.

- This approach reduces the number of time studies needed, but does not eliminate time studies.

3. Predetermined data approach

    a. Break each work element into micromotions: reach, move, disengage, apply pressure, grasp, position, release, and turn.

    b. Find tabular value of time for each micromotion, accounting for mitigating factors: weight, distance, size, degree of difficulty.

    c. Normal times of micromotions are added for the task.

    d. Adjust for allowances to arrive at the standard time.

Advantages of predetermined data approach:

- Standards can be set for new jobs.

- Work methods can be compared without a time study.

- Greater consistency of results, variation due to recording errors and difference between workers is removed.

- Defuses objections to biased judgment in performance rating

Disadvantages of predetermined data approach:

- Impractical for jobs with low repeatability

- Data may not reflect the actual situation in a specific plant.

- Performance time variations can result from many factors.

- Actual time may depend on the specific sequence of motions.

- Considerable skill is required to achieve good standards.

4. Work sampling method

- Results in a proportion of time spent doing an activity, rather than a standard time for the work

- Requires a *large* number of random observations spread over the length of the study

- Proportion of observations in which the activity occurs is assumed to be the proportion of time spent on the activity in general

Work sampling procedure

Step 1.   Define the activities.

Step 2.   Design the observation form.

Step 3.   Determine the length of the study.

Step 4.   Determine the initial sample size.

Step 5.   Select random observation times.

Step 6.   Determine observer schedule.

Step 7.   Make observations.

Step 8.   Decide whether further sampling is required.

Use **Application 5.2: Work Sampling Method (AP5.2)** to see whether the students understand the work sampling approach. The short answers are as follows:

STEP 4.   The answer is 385 observations, using 20% as an initial estimate.

STEPS 5 & 6.   You need 12 per hour to get 385 observations in 32 hours.

STEP 7. Suppose you find 96 unacceptable delays for pitchers, and 46 unacceptable delays for batters. The proportions are 0.25 and 0.18 respectively.

STEP 8. You need 65 more observations.

    a. Overall assessment of work sampling

       + No special training required of observers

       + Several studies can be conducted simultaneously

       + More economical for jobs having long cycle times, since the observer need not be present for the entire duration

       + Workers prefer this method to time studies

       − A large number of observations are required

       − Usually not used for repetitive, well-defined jobs

5. Managerial considerations in work measurement

    a. Total quality management

       • These techniques *can* be used in the spirit of continuous improvement (provided management earns cooperation of labor)

    b. Increased automation

       • There is less need to observe and rate worker performance, because work is machine paced

       • Work sampling may be electronically monitored

Supplement C: Learning Curves

Two types of learning

- *Individual* — with instruction and repetition, workers learn to perform their jobs more efficiently
- *Organizational*
    - experience in product and process design
    - automation, capital investment
    - methods changes

[Mention Samsung from MPC.1]

A. The Learning Effect
[Discuss the general learning curve concept]

1. Background

    a. First developed in aircraft industry

    b. Each doubling of quantity reduced per-unit production time by 20%

    c. Rate of learning may be different for different products and different companies

2. Learning curves and competitive strategy

    a. Learning curves enable managers to project the manufacturing cost per unit for a given cumulative production quantity.

    b. Product design changes disrupt the learning effect.

    c. Firms making standardized products compete on low cost, and use high volume to quickly move costs down the learning curve. Low costs discourage competitors from entering the market

B. Developing Learning Curves

1. The direct labor required for the nth unit k_n, is

    $$k_n = k_1 n^b$$
    where
    $$b = \frac{\log r}{\log 2}$$

    r = learning rate

2. Assumptions

    a. The direct labor required to produce the $n+1$st unit will always be less than the direct labor required for the nth unit.

    b. Direct labor requirements will decrease at a declining rate as cumulative production increases.

    c. The reduction in time will follow an exponential distribution.

Use **Application C.1: Estimating Direct Labor Requirements (AP C.1)** for an exercise using the learning model.

C. Using Learning Curves

1. Bid preparation

   - Use learning curves to estimate labor cost.

   - Add material costs and profit to obtain bid amount.

2. Financial planning

   - Use learning curves to estimate cash needed to finance operations.

3. Labor requirement estimation

   - Estimate training requirements.

   - Develop hiring plans.

Use **Application C.2: Estimating Cumulative Labor Hours (AP C.2)** for an example of using the learning model to test budget constraints.

D. Managerial Considerations in the Use of Learning Curves

1. It may be difficult to obtain a good estimate of the learning rate for an organization.

2. The simpler the product, the less the learning rate.

3. The entire learning curve is based on the time required for the first unit, which may itself be the result of an estimation process.

4. Learning curves are used to greatest advantage in the early stages of new product or service production.

5. Implementing team approaches change organizational learning rates.

6. Learning curves are only approximations.

Chapter 6: Total Quality Management

A. Quality: A Management Philosophy

- Quality was not always a top priority.

- 1980s — manufacturers realized need to listen to the customer or lose market share

1. Customer-driven definitions of quality

    - Quality has multiple dimensions.

    - One or more definitions of quality may apply.

    [Ask the students for examples of "good" and "poor" quality.]

    - Conformance to Specifications — Does the product or service meet or exceed advertised levels of performance? **[Mention Seagate disk drives.]**

    - Value — Does the product serve the customers' purposes considering this price?

    - Fitness for Use — Appearance, style, durability, reliability, craftsmanship, serviceability … How well does the product perform its intended purpose?

    - Support — Even when the product performs as expected, if service after the sale is poor, the customers' view of quality diminishes.

    - Psychological Impressions — Atmosphere, image, or aesthetics

2. Quality as a competitive weapon **[Mention companies that have used quality as a competitive weapon.]**

    - Perception plays as important a role as does performance.

    - Producers that can match their operating capabilities with consumer preferences have a competitive advantage.

    - Good quality can also pay off in higher profits **[Mention *Industry Week* survey.**
        - Increased volume
        - Increased price
        - Reduced production cost

    It is important to note that when one considers all of the costs of poor quality, it actually can be less costly to produce a good product than to produce an inferior one.

B. Employee Involvement

1. Cultural change **[Mention Kawasaki.]**

    - Cultural change must be motivated by top management.

    - Everyone is expected to contribute.

    - External customers buy the product or service.

    - Internal customers are employees in the firm who rely on output of other employees.

    An assembly line is a chain of internal customer-supplier relationships, with an external customer purchasing the finished goods.

2. Individual development **[Mention Honda.]**

   - On-the-job training programs can improve quality.

   - Cross-train on related jobs so people understand how their work affects internal customers' work.

   - Managers need to develop teaching skills.

3. Awards and incentives **[Mention Honda.]**

   - Tie monetary incentives directly to quality improvements.

   - Recognition is also an improvement of quality

C. Continuous Improvement

1. Getting started with continuous improvement **[Mention CIGNA Property and Casualty and Timken.]**

   - SPC training

   - Make SPC a normal aspect of daily operations.

   - Build work teams and employee involvement.

   - Utilize problem-solving techniques within the work teams.

   - Develop operator process ownership.

2. Problem-solving process Deming Wheel

   - Plan — Select a process needing improvement, document process, analyze data, set improvement goals, discuss alternatives, assess benefits and costs, develop a plan and improvement measures.

   - Do — Implement plan, monitor improvements.

   - Check — Analyze data to evaluate effectiveness of the plan.

   - Act — Document and disseminate improved process as a standard procedure.

D. The Costs of Poor Quality

1. Prevention

   Costs in this category include time, effort, and money to:

   - Redesign the processes to remove causes of defects

   - Redesign the product to make it simpler, easier to produce

   - Train employees

   - Train suppliers

2. Appraisal

   - Costs incurred to identify and assess quality problems

   - Inspection

   - Quality audits

   - Statistical quality control programs

3. Internal failure

   Costs from defects discovered before the product or service is sold

   - Yield Losses — The material costs associated with scrap losses

   - Rework — Time, space, and capacity to store, reroute to correct defects

4. External failure [Mention Hubble space telescope and Jack-in-the-Box.]

   Costs when a defect is discovered after the customer has received the product or service

   - Loss of market share

   - Warranty service

   - Litigation

   - Increased regulation

   What are the "hidden" costs of internal and external failures?

   - More labor

   - More machine capacity

   - Increased work-in-process inventory

   - Extended lead times

   - Increased chance of defects reaching the customer

   - Increased pressure to produce more to make up for defects

   - Reduced employee morale

   - More defects

E. Improving Quality Through TQM

1. Benchmarking

   Four basic steps of benchmarking [Mention competitive, functional, internal types.]

   - Planning—Identify process, leader, performance measures.

   - Analysis—Measure gap, identify causes.

   - Integration—Establish goals and resource commitments.

   - Action—Develop teams, implement plan, monitor progress, return to Step 1.

2. Product and service design [Mention dbase IV.]

   - Design changes can increase defect rates. [See MP 6.2 for international considerations.]

   - Stable designs reduce quality problems.

   - Stable designs may become obsolete in the marketplace.

Use **Application 6.1: Reliability Analysis (AP 6.1)** for a reliability example. The short answers are 74.48% for the old car and 68.52% for the new car.

3. Process design [Mention First National Bank of Chicago.]

   - New equipment can overcome quality problems.

- Concurrent engineering ensures that production requirements and process capabilities are synchronized.

4. Quality function deployment (QFD)

   Six questions for using QFD:

   a. Voice of the customer—What do customers need and want?

   b. Competitive analysis—Relative to competitors, how well are we serving customers?

   c. Voice of the engineer—What technical measures relate to our customers' needs?

   d. Correlations—What are the relationships between the voice of the customer and the voice of the engineer?

   e. Technical comparison—How does our product or service performance compare to that of our competition?

   f. Trade-offs—What are the potential technical trade-offs?

5. Purchasing considerations

   - Buyer must emphasize quality, delivery, and price.

   - Work with the supplier to obtain defect-free parts.

   - Specifications must be clear and realistic.

   - Allow time to identify qualified suppliers.

   - Improve communication between purchasing, engineering, quality control, and other departments.

6. Tools for improving quality

   Seven tools for organizing and presenting data [**Carefully go through the cause-and-effect diagram.**]

   - Checklists—record the frequency of occurrence

   - Histograms—summarizes data measured on a continuous scale

   - Bar charts—bar height represents the frequency of occurrence

   - Pareto charts—a bar chart organized in decreasing order of frequency

   - Scatter diagrams—a plot of two variables showing whether they are related

   - Cause-and-effect, fishbone, or Ishakawa diagram

   - Graphs—a variety of pictorial formats, such as line graphs and pie charts

F. Malcolm Baldrige National Quality Award
[Mention well-known companies who have received the award.]

- Established in 1987

- Named for Secretary of Commerce Malcolm Baldrige

- Improved quality as a means of reducing the trade deficit

- Learn strengths and weaknesses and find ways to improve operations

- Seven Criteria

G. International Quality Standards

1. What is ISO 9000?

   - Certified companies are listed in a directory.

   - Compliance with ISO 9000 standards indicates quality claims can be documented

2. ISO 14000 – An Environmental Management System

    - Standards require that companies keep track of their raw materials use and the generation, treatment, and disposal of hazardous wastes.

    - Companies must prepare a plan for ongoing improvement in environmental performance.

    - Standards cover the following areas:

        — Environmental management system

        — Environmental performance evaluation

        — Environmental labeling

        — Life-cycle assessments

3. Benefits of ISO Certification **[Mention ABB Process Automation, DuPont.]**

    - External—potential sales advantage

    - Internal—provides guidance in starting the TQM journey

Chapter 7: Statistical Process Control

Examples of Problems Detected by SPC

[Define SPC and relate to other tools in Chapter 6.]

- An increase in the proportion of defective components
- An increase in the average number of service complaints
- A process frequently fails to conform to design specifications

A. Sources of Variation

- All sources of variation can be attributed to one of two source categories: common causes and assignable causes.

1. Common causes

   - Random, or unavoidable sources of variation within a process

   a. Characteristics of distributions

      1. Mean—the average observation
      2. Spread—the dispersion of observations around the mean
      3. Shape—whether the observations are symmetrical or skewed

   b. Common cause variation is normally distributed (symmetrical) and *stable* (the mean and spread do not change over time).

2. Assignable causes

   - Any cause of variation that can be identified and eliminated.
   - *Change* in the mean, spread, or shape of a process distribution is a symptom that an assignable cause of variation has developed.
   - *After* a process is in statistical control, SPC is used to detect *significant change*, indicating the need for corrective action. **[Emphasize this point.]**

B. The Inspection Process

- Use of inspection to simply remove defectives is improper. It does nothing to prevent defects. We cannot "inspect" quality into a part.

1. Quality measurements **[See MP 7.1 for attribute measures in healthcare.]**

   a. Variables — a characteristic measured on a continuous scale

      - Advantage: if defective, we know by how much — the direction and magnitude of corrections are indicated.
      - Disadvantage: precise measurements are required.

b.	Attributes — a characteristic counted in discrete units, (yes-no, integer number)

- Used to determine conformance to complex specifications, or when measuring variables is too costly

- Advantages:

	— Quickly reveals when quality has changed, provides an integer number of *how many* are defective

	— Requires less effort, and fewer resources than measuring variables

- Disadvantages:

	— Doesn't show by *how much* they were defective, the direction and magnitude of corrections are not indicated

	— Requires more observations, since each observation provides little information

2.	Sampling

a.	Complete inspection

- Used when

	— Costs of failure are high relative to costs of inspection

	— Inspection is automated

- Some defects are not detected because of

	— Inspector fatigue

	— Imperfect testing methods

b.	Sampling plans

- Used when

	— Inspection costs are high

	— Inspection destroys the product

- Some defectives lots may be purchased and some good lots may be rejected when

	— The sample does not perfectly represent the population

	— Testing methods are imperfect

- Sampling plans include

	— Sample size, *n* random observations

	— Time between successive samples

	— Decision rules that determine when action should be taken

c.	Sampling distributions

- Sample means are usually dispersed about the population mean according to the normal probability distribution (reference the central limit theorem described in statistics texts). **[It is important to distinguish between the distribution of sample means and the process distribution itself.]**

d. Control charts

- Used to judge whether action is required

- A sample characteristic measured above the upper control limit (*UCL*) or below the lower control limit (*LCL*) indicates that an assignable cause probably exists. **[Be sure that the student understands that the *UCL* and *LCL* are not product or service specifications.]**

e. Steps for using a control chart:

- Take a random sample, measure the quality characteristic, and calculate a variable of attribute measure.

- Plot the statistic; if it falls outside the control limits, look for assignable causes.

- Eliminate the cause if it degrades quality. Incorporate the cause if it improves quality. Recalculate the control chart.

- Periodically repeat the procedure.

f. Indicators of out of control conditions

- A trend in the observations (the process is drifting)

- A sudden or step change in the observations

- A run of five or more observations on the same side of the mean (If we flip a coin and get "heads" five times in a row, we become suspicious of the coin or of the coin flipping process.)

- Several observations near the control limits (Normally only 1 in 20 observations are more than 2 standard deviations from the mean.)

g. Two types of error can result from sampling

- Type I error—Process declared out of control when in fact it really is in control

- Type II error—Process considered in control when in fact it is not

[Discuss the relationship of control limit spread to Type I and Type II errors.]

3. Inspection station location

a. Purchased input materials

— Could use acceptance sampling **[Refer to Supplement D or use this opportunity to do a lecturette on acceptance sampling.]**

b. Work in process

— Not after every process

— Before it is covered up

— Before costly, irreversible, or bottleneck operations so that resources are used efficiently

c. Final product or service

— Before stocking or shipping to the customer

— Customers often play a major role in final inspection of services

C. Statistical Process Control Methods

- Measure current quality.

- Detect whether the process has changed.

1. Control charts for variables

   • Quality characteristics include variables, which are measured over a continuum.

   a. Range charts

      • Monitor process variability

        — First remove assignable causes of variation.

        — While process is in control, collect data to estimate the average range of output that occurs.

      To establish the upper and lower control limits for the R-chart, we use Table 7.1, which provides two factors; D_3 and D_4. These factors establish the UCL_R and LCL_R at three standard deviations above and below $\overline{R}$.

      $$UCL_R = D_4\overline{R}$$
      $$LCL_R = D_3\overline{R}$$

   b. $\overline{x}$- charts

      • The process average is plotted on the $\overline{x}$- chart after the process variability is in control.

      • The upper and lower control limits can be established in two ways.

        — If the standard deviation of the process distribution is known, we could place UCL and LCL at "z" standard deviations away from the mean, depending on the desired confidence interval.

        $$UCL_{\overline{x}} = \overline{\overline{x}} + z\sigma_{\overline{x}}$$
        $$LCL_{\overline{x}} = \overline{\overline{x}} - z\sigma_{\overline{x}}$$

        where

        $$\sigma_{\overline{x}} = \frac{\sigma}{\sqrt{n}}$$

        — Or we could use Table 7.1 to find A_2, which when multiplied by the previously determined $\overline{R}$, places UCL and LCL three standard deviations above and below the mean.

        $$UCL_{\overline{x}} = \overline{\overline{x}} + A_2\overline{R}$$
        $$LCL_{\overline{x}} = \overline{\overline{x}} - A_2\overline{R}$$

   c. Using $\overline{x}$- and R-charts to monitor a process

      • Construct the R-chart.

      • Compute the range for each sample.

      • Plot the ranges on the R-chart.

      • Construct $\overline{x}$-chart.

      • Compute the mean for each sample.

      • Plot the sample means on the $\overline{x}$-chart.

      • Use **Application 7.1: Control Charts for Variables (AP 7.1)** to demonstrate the construction of R- and x-bar charts. Since the range is out of control, the x-bar calculation is moot. Consider dropping sample 6 because of an inoperative scale. The resulting control charts indicate that the process is actually in control.

2. Control charts for attributes **[Mention examples from banking and manufacturing. Emphasize that defects can be counted.]**

   a. *p*-chart — population proportion defective

      - Take a random sample of n units.

      - Count the number of defectives.

      - Proportion defective = number of defectives ÷ sample size

      - Plot sample proportion defective on a chart. If it is outside the range between the upper and lower control limits, search for an assignable cause. If cause is found do not use these data to determine the control limits.

        $$UCL_p = \bar{p} + z\sigma_p$$

        $$LCL_p = \bar{p} - z\sigma_p$$

        where

        $$\sigma_p = \sqrt{\frac{\bar{p}(1-\bar{p})}{n}}$$

      - Two things to note:

        — The lower control limit cannot be negative

        — When the number of defects is less than the *LCL*, then the system is out of control in a good way. We want to find the assignable cause. Find what was unique about this event that caused things to work out so well.

      - Use **Application 7.2: *p*-Chart for Attributes (AP 7.2)** for an example of a *p*-chart problem. The short answers are: $\bar{p} = 0.025; UCL_p = 0.064; LCL_p = 0;$ *IN CONTROL*

   b. *c*-chart — more than one defect per unit

      - Take a random sample of one.

      - Inspect the quality attribute.

      - Count the number of defects.

        $$UCL_c = \bar{c} + z\sigma_c$$

        $$LCL_c = \bar{c} - z\sigma_c$$

        where

        $$\sigma_c = \sqrt{\bar{c}}$$

      - Plot the number of defectives on a chart. If it is outside the range between the upper and lower control limits, search for the assignable cause. If cause is found do not use these data to determine the control limits.

   c. The Poisson distribution mean and standard deviation are both described using the same number, $\bar{c}$. The mean equals $\bar{c}$, and the standard deviation equals $\sqrt{\bar{c}}$.

   d. We set upper and lower control limits in a manner similar to *p*-charts.

   e. Use **Application 7.3: *c*-Chart for Attributes (AP 7.3)** for an example of a *c*-chart.

D Process Capability

   - Control limits are based on the mean and variability of the *sampling distribution*, not the design specifications. **[This is an important point that is difficult for the students.]**

1. Defining process capability

   A process is capable when

   - The specified tolerance width is greater than range of actual process outputs

     and

   - The process is centered near the nominal or target value

   a. Process capability ratio

      - Compares the tolerance width (upper spec – lower spec) to the range of actual process outputs. The portion of a distribution within ± 3 σ of the mean will include the vast majority (99.74%) of the actual process outputs.

      - The process is capable when the ratio

      $$C_p = \frac{\text{Upper specification} - \text{Lower specification}}{6\sigma} \geq 1.00$$

      - Process capability ratios greater than one (say 1.33) allow for some shift in the process distribution before bad output is generated.

   b. Process capability index
      - Indicates whether the process is sufficiently centered by measuring the distance between the process center and the specification limits and then comparing that to 3σ.

      - The process capability index is

      $$C_{pk} = \text{Minimum of} \left[\frac{\overline{\overline{x}} - \text{Lower specification}}{3\sigma}, \frac{\text{Upper specification} - \overline{\overline{x}}}{3\sigma} \right]$$

      - If the process capability index is less than one, the process center is too close to one of the specification limits, and will generate too many defects.

2. Determining the capability of a process using continuous improvement.
   [Mention Ross Products in MP 7.2.]

   Step 1. Collect data, calculate mean and standard deviation for the process.

   Step 2. Construct the process control charts.

   Step 3. Compare the random samples to the control limits. Eliminate the assignable causes and recalculate the control limits as appropriate until 20 consecutive random samples fall within the control limits. This indicates that the process is in statistical control.

   Step 4. Calculate the process capability ratio and the process capability index. If the process is capable, document changes to the process and monitor the output using control charts. If it is not capable, eliminate the causes of variation and recalculate the control limits. Return to step 3.

Use **Application 7.4: Process Capability Analysis (AP 7.4)** to bring together the concepts of statistical control and process control.

3. Quality engineering

   - An approach combining engineering and statistical methods to *optimize* product design and manufacturing processes

   - Before Taguchi, managers assumed the goal was to produce products falling anywhere between their design tolerances.

   - Quality loss function is optimum (zero) when the product's quality measure is exactly on the target value.

Continually search for places ways to reduce all variability **[There are two excellent experiential exercises at the end of chapter 7. The first gets the students to construct their own variables control chart and then plot real data generated from a coin catapult. The second uses the coin catapult to generate the data for an attributes control chart. Both exercises could be used as a capstone for this chapter, or as a reinforcement of the material as it is discussed during the lesson.]**

Supplement D: Acceptance Sampling

A. Acceptance Plan Decisions

- The consumer, sometimes in cooperation with the producer, specifies the parameters of the acceptance sampling plan.

- The two parameters which completely specify a sampling plan are

  — n, the sample size

  — c, the acceptance number

Definitions:

- Producer, origin of the material

- Consumer, destination of the material

- Sampling plan, a decision guide to control the risks of the producer and consumer

- Acceptable quality level (AQL), a percentage of defects stated by the consumer in the contract, and the aim of the producer

- Lot tolerance proportion defective ($LTPD$), the worst level the customer can tolerate. The customer would not be happy, but probably wouldn't sue

- α, the producer's risk: the probability of making a type I error, which is rejecting a good lot

- β, the consumer's risk: the probability of making a type II error, which is accepting a bad lot

1. Quality and risk decisions

   a. Acceptable quality level (AQL)

      - Quality level *desired* by the consumer (emphasis added)

        — Producer's risk (α) is the probability that a shipment having exactly this level of quality (the AQL) will be rejected when the lot is sampled using the specified sampling plan (n, c).

        — Rejecting a good (AQL) lot is a Type I error.

      - Consumers also desire low producer's risk because sending good materials back to the supplier disrupts the consumer's production processes due to material shortages, increases lead time, and creates poor supplier relations.

   b. Lot tolerance proportion defective

      - The worst level of quality that the consumer can tolerate

        — Consumer's risk, (β) is the probability a shipment having exactly this level of quality (the $LTPD$) will be accepted when the lot is sampled using the specified sampling plan (n, c).

        — Accepting a bad ($LTPD$) lot is a Type II error.

2. Sampling plans

   a. Single-sampling plans (for attributes)

      - The plan states the sample size, n, and the *acceptable* number of defectives found in that sample, c.

      - The accept-reject decision is based on the results of one sample.

Single-sampling procedure for determining whether to accept a lot:

- Take a random sample, n, from a *large* lot.

- Measure the quality characteristic.

- If the sample passes the test (defects $\leq c$), accept the lot.

- If the sample fails (defects $> c$).

  — There may be complete inspection of the lot, or

  — The *entire lot* is rejected.

- A good lot could be rejected if the sample happens to include an unusually large number of defects.

- A bad lot could be accepted if the quality in the sample is better than in the lot.

b. Double-sampling plan

- The double-sampling plan states two sample sizes, (n_1 and n_2), and two acceptance numbers (c_1 and c_2).

- Double-sampling plans reduce costs of inspection for lots with very low or very high proportion defective.

Double-sampling procedure for determining whether to accept a lot:

- Take a random sample of relatively small size n_1, from a *large* lot.

- Measure the quality characteristic to find the number of defectives in the original sample.

  — If the sample passes the test (defects $\leq c_1$), accept the lot.

  — If the sample fails (defects $> c_2$), the *entire lot* is rejected.

  — If $c_1 <$ defects $\leq c_2$, then

  — Take a larger second random sample, n_2; compare the total number of defects found in both samples to c_2.

  — If the sample passes the test (defects $\leq c_2$), accept the lot.

  — If the sample fails (defects $> c_2$), the *entire lot* is rejected.

c. Sequential-sampling plan

- A refinement of the double-sampling plan

- Results of random samples, tested one-by-one, are compared to sequential-sampling chart.

- Chart guides decision to reject, accept, or continue sampling.

- Average number of items inspected (ANI) is generally lower with sequential sampling.

B. Operating Characteristic (OC) Curves

- Perfect discrimination between good and bad lots requires 100% inspection.

- Select sample size n and acceptance number c to achieve the level of performance specified by the AQL, α, LTPD, and β.

1. Drawing the OC curve

- Each item inspected is either defective or not defective (binomial).

- When $n \geq 20$ and $p \leq 0.05$, the Poisson distribution approximates the binomial distribution.

- The Poisson distribution is used to prepare (OC) curves.
- The OC curve shows the probability of *accepting* a lot P_a, as a dependent function of p, the true proportion of defectives in the lot.
- For every possible combination of n and c, there exists a unique operating characteristics curve.

2. Steps for drawing an operating characteristics curve, given n and c:

- Select a value for p, the true proportion of defectives in the lot; calculate np, which is the average number of defectives we would expect to find in samples of size n taken from a lot with p proportion of defectives.
- Find np in the left column of the Poisson distribution.
- Read across that row to the column identifying the c value specified by the sampling plan.
- The probability of exactly c or fewer defects occurring in a sample of size n is found at the intersection of the np row and the c column. We have found P_a, the probability of *accepting* the lot for the selected value of p. Plot this point on a graph with P_a on the vertical axis, and p on the horizontal axis. Return to step 1, selecting a different value for p, and continue this process for a range of p values.

Use **Application D.1: Drawing the OC Curve (AP D.1)** to demonstrate the construction and use of the OC curve. The short answers are:

- Finding α (probability of rejecting *AQL* quality)

  $p = 0.03$

  $np = 5.79$

  $P_a = 0.965$ Therefore $\alpha = 0.035$

- Finding β (probability of accepting *LTPD* quality)

  $p = 0.08$

  $np = 15.44$

  $P_a = 0.10$ Therefore $\beta = 0.10$

2. Explaining changes in the OC curve

   a. Sample size effect

   b. Acceptance level effect

C. Average Outgoing Quality

- AOQ is the expected (or **A**verage) proportion of defects that a particular sampling plan would allow to pass through (**Q**uality **O**utgoing from) inspection.
- Rectified inspection — defects found during the sampling process are removed and reworked or replaced with conforming material.
- Rejected lots are subjected to 100% inspection.
- Different sampling plans have different *AOQ*'s and *AOQL*'s.
- The *AOQL* is found by calculating *AOQ* at several values for p, then setting *AOQL* equal to the highest occurring *AOQ*.

Use **Application D.2: Average Outgoing Quality (AP D.2)** to demonstrate the model for computing AOQ.

Chapter 8: Capacity

[Introduce with Chase Bank and the financial services industry.]

A. Capacity Planning

- This activity is central to the long-term success of an organization.

- Capacity planning considers questions such as:

    - How much of a cushion is needed?

    - Should we expand capacity before the demand is there or wait until demand is more certain?

1. Measuring capacity

- No single capacity measure is universally applicable.

- Capacity can be expressed in terms of outputs or inputs.

    - Output measures—the usual choice for line flow processes
        — Low amount of customization
        — Product mix becomes an issue when the output is not uniform in work content.

    - Input measures—used for flexible flow processes
        — High amount of customization
        — Output varies in work content; a measure of total units produced is meaningless.
        — Output is converted to some critical homogeneous input, such as labor hours or machine hours.

    - Average utilization rate, expressed as a percentage:

    $$\text{Utilization} = \frac{\text{Average output rate}}{\text{Maximum capacity}} \times 100\%$$

    - The average output rate and the capacity must be measured in the same terms.

    a. Peak capacity

    - Peak capacity
        — Calling for extraordinary effort under ideal conditions which are not sustainable
        — Nameplate-rated capacity, engineering design

    b. Effective capacity

    - Economically sustainable under normal conditions

    c. Increasing maximum capacity

    - The effective capacities of multiple operations within the same facility are different.

    "A **bottleneck** is an operation that has the lowest effective capacity of any operation in the facility and thus limits the system's output."

    - Expansion of a facility's capacity occurs only when bottleneck capacity is increased.

    - Flexible flow processes may have floating bottlenecks due to widely varying work loads on different operations at different times.

    - Job shops have low equipment utilization rates.

2. Economies of scale

   - **Economies of scale:** Increasing a facility's size decreases the average unit cost

   a. Spreading fixed costs

      - As the facility utilization rate increases, the average unit cost drops because fixed costs are spread over more units.

      - Increments of capacity are often rather large.

   b. Reducing construction costs

      - Costs for permits, environmental studies, utility hookup fees and the like are often independent of facility size.

      - Doubling facility size usually does not double costs.

   c. Cutting costs of purchased materials

      - Higher volumes give the purchaser more bargaining power and the opportunity for quantity discounts.

   d. Finding process advantages

      - As volume increases, processes shift toward a line flows.

      - High volume may justify investment in more efficient technology.

      - Benefits of dedicated resources include reduced inventory, reduced setups, enhanced learning effects, and process improvements.

3. Diseconomies of scale

   - Excessive size can bring complexity, loss of focus, and inefficiencies which raise the average unit cost.

   - Characterized by loss of agility, less innovation, risk avoidance, and excessive analysis and planning at the expense of action.

   - Nonlinear growth of overhead leads to employee ceilings.

   - Loss of focus **[See Focused Facilities in Chapter 3.]**

4. Capacity strategy

   a. Sizing capacity cushions

      - Average utilization rates near 100% indicate
        — Need to increase capacity
        — Poor customer service or declining productivity

      - Utilization rates tend to be higher in capital-intensive industries.

   Factors Leading to Large Capacity Cushions

   - When demand is variable, uncertain, or product mix changes

   - When finished goods inventory cannot be stored

   - When customer service is important

   - When capacity comes in large increments

   - When supply of material or human resources is uncertain

Factors leading to small capacity cushions

- Unused capacity costs money.

- Large cushions hide inefficiencies, absenteeism, unreliable material supply.

- When subcontractors are available to handle demand peaks

b. Timing and sizing of expansion

- Expansionist strategy
  — Keeps ahead of demand, maintains a capacity cushion
  — Large, infrequent jumps in capacity
  — Higher financial risk
  — Lower risk of losing market share
  — Economies of scale may reduce fixed cost per unit
  — May increase learning and help compete on price
  — Preemptive marketing

- Wait-and-see strategy
  — Lags behind demand, relying on short-term peak capacity options (overtime, subcontractors) to meet demand
  — Lower financial risk associated with overly optimistic demand forecast
  — Lower risk of a technological advancement making a new facility obsolete
  — Higher risk of losing market share

- Follow-the-leader strategy
  — An intermediate strategy of copying competitors' actions
  — Tends to prevent anyone from gaining a competitive advantage

c. Linking capacity and other decisions

- Capacity cushions, resource flexibility, inventory, and longer lead times all serve as buffers against uncertainty.

- A change in one area may affect decisions in the other areas.
  — Competitive priorities—fast delivery requires large capacity cushions
  — Quality management—higher quality reduces uncertainty
  — Capital intensity—pressure for high utilization and lower capacity cushion
  — Resource flexibility—a buffer to be balanced with capacity cushion
  — Inventory—an alternative form of buffer
  — Scheduling—stability reduces uncertainty, allowing smaller cushions
  — Location—new facilities require suitable locations
  — Other functional are as—Marketing provides demand forecasts; finance provides capital; human resources recruits and trains the work-force.

B. A Systematic Approach to Capacity Decisions

Step 1: Estimate capacity requirements

- Begin with a long-range forecast of demand, productivity, competition, and technological change.

- Long-range forecast errors will be large.

- Convert demand into comparable units of capacity.

- Use **Application 8.1: Estimating Capacity Requirements (AP 8.1)** for an in-class exercise. The short answer is **3.83 or 4 machines**.

Step 2: Identify gaps

- This is the difference between projected demand and current capacity.

- Use the correct capacity measure. The correct measure is determined by what is critical to the bottleneck operation.

- Capacity can be expanded only if the bottleneck is one of the expanded operations. Otherwise, expansion just increases idle time.

- Multiple operations and inputs add complexity because floating bottlenecks could change the dimensions of the capacity measure.

- Use **Application 8.2: Identifying Capacity Gaps (AP 8.2)** for an in-class exercise.

Step 3: Develop alternatives

- Base case ... do nothing

- Alternative timing and size of capacity additions/closings
  — Expansionist strategy
  — Wait-and-see strategy
  — Expand at a different location
  — Use short-term options ... overtime, temporary workers, subcontracting

Step 4: Evaluate the Alternatives

- Qualitative concerns

  - Fit with overall capacity strategy

  - Uncertainties in demand, competitive reaction, technological change, and cost

- Quantitative concerns

  - Net present value of after-tax cash flows

- Use **Application 8.3: Developing Capacity Alternatives (AP 8.3)** for an in-class exercise.

C. Tools for Capacity Planning

1. Waiting line models **[Relate to Supplement E for problems.]**

   Reasons waiting lines (or queues) form

   - Variable times between successive jobs or customer arrivals

   - Variable processing or service times

2. Decision trees **[Relate to Supplement A for problems.]**

   - Can be applied to a wide range of decisions

   - Valuable for capacity decisions when demand is uncertain and when sequential decisions are involved

Supplement E: Waiting Line Models

A. Introduction

1. Why waiting lines form

   - When current demand temporarily exceeds current service rates

   - If both demand and service rates are constant, no waiting line forms

2. Use of waiting line theory

   - Applies to many service or manufacturing situations. Decisions can be on process, capacity, layout, inventory, and scheduling.

   - Service is the act of processing a customer (or manufacturing job).

B. Structure of Waiting Line Problems

1. Customer population

   - The source of input to the service system

   - Whether the input source is *finite* or *infinite* will have an affect on the waiting line characteristics.

     - When several customers from a finite source are already in the waiting line, the chances of new customer arrivals is reduced.

     - When the input source is infinite, customers already in the waiting line do not affect probability of another arrival.

   - Whether the customers are *patient* or *impatient* also affects waiting line characteristics.

     - Patient customers wait until served.

     - Impatient customer arrivals either *balk* at long lines (leave immediately), or join the line and *renege* (leave after becoming discouraged with slow progress).

2. The service system

   a. Number of lines

   - A single-line arrangement is favored when servers are capable of general service.
     — Keeps servers uniformly busy
     — Levels waiting times among customers, gives sense of fairness

   - A multiple-line arrangement is favored when servers provide a limited set of services.
     — Customers wait in the appropriate line for a particular service.

   b. Arrangement of service facilities

   - Single-channel, single-phase—customers form one line, all services performed by a single-server facility

- Single-channel, multiple-phase—servers specialize in one part of service

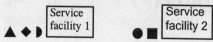

- Multiple-channel, single-phase—

First available server   Customers stay in the line first joined

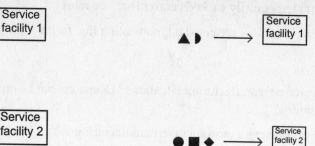

- Multiple-channel, multiple-phase

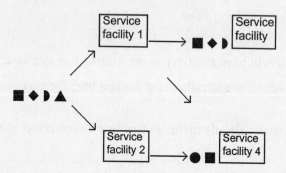

- Mixed arranged, unique services, services can't be described neatly in phases

3. Priority rule

- First-come, first-served (FCFS)—priority discipline is assumed

- Other rules, [earliest due date (EDD), shortest processing time (SPT)] are discussed in Chapter 17.

- Preemptive discipline—Allows a high priority customer to be served ahead of another who would have been served first according to the normal priority discipline (such as FCFS).

C. Probability Distributions

1. Arrival distribution

- Customer arrivals can often be described by the Poisson distribution.

$$P(n) = \frac{(\lambda T)^n}{n!} e^{-\lambda T}$$

- Arrival rate: the probability of n arrivals in T time periods

- Interarrival times, the average time between arrivals: the probability that the next customer will arrive in the next T time periods

2. Service time distribution

- Service time: The probability that the service time will be no more than T time periods can be described by the exponential distribution.

$$P(t \leq T) = 1 - e^{-\mu T}$$

- The exponential distribution assumes that each service time is independent of those that preceded it.

  - Does not account for learning effect

  - Very short and very long service times exhibited in the exponential distribution might not ever actually occur.

D. Using Waiting Line Models to Analyze Operations

1. Balance costs against benefits of improving service system.

2. Also consider the costs of *not* making improvements.

   Waiting line operating characteristics

   a. Line length—Long lines indicate poor customer service, inefficient service, or inadequate capacity.

   b. Number of customers in system—A large number causes congestion and dissatisfaction.

   c. Waiting time in line—Long waits are associated with poor service.

   d. Total time in system—May indicate problems with customers, server efficiency, or capacity.

   e. Service facility utilization—Control costs without unacceptable reduction in service.

E. Decision Areas for Management

   a. Arrival rates—Adjust through advertising, promotions, pricing, appointments.

   b. Number of service facilities—Adjust service system capacity.

   c. Number of phases—Consider splitting service tasks.

   d. Number of servers per facility—work force size

   e. Server efficiency—training, incentives, work methods, capital investment

   f. Priority rule—Decide whether to allow preemption.

   g. Line arrangement—single or multiple lines

      - Models for some other waiting line situations have been developed.

      - Formula complexity increases rapidly.

      - All models assume steady state conditions.

      - Simulation can be used to model the characteristics of waiting lines with a variety of distributions and non steady-state conditions.

3. Single-server model

    a. Assumptions and formulas

Assumptions		Formulas
Number of servers:	1	$\rho = \dfrac{\lambda}{\mu}$
Number of phases:	1	$P_n = (1-\rho)\rho^n$
Input source:	infinite; no balking or reneging	$L = \dfrac{\lambda}{\mu - \lambda}$
Arrival distribution:	Poisson; mean arrival rate = λ	$L_q = \rho L$
Service distribution:	exponential; mean service time = $1/\mu$	$W = \dfrac{1}{\mu - \lambda}$
Waiting line:	single line; unlimited length	$W_q = \rho W$
Priority rule:	first-come, first served	

   b. Use **Application E.1: Single Server Model (AP E.1)** to demonstrate the single server model. The short answers are $\rho = 0.8$; $L = 4$; $L_q = 3.2$; $W = 0.2$ **hr**; and $W_q = .16$.

   c. Use **Application E.2: Analyzing the Service Rate (AP E.2)** to show how the single server model can be used to analyze capacity issues. The short answer is **25.88**, or about **26 customers per hr**.

4. Multiple-server model

    a. Assumptions and formulas

Assumptions		Formulas
Number of servers:	s	$\rho = \dfrac{\lambda}{s\mu}$
Number of phases:	1	$P_0 = \left[\displaystyle\sum_{n=0}^{s-1} \dfrac{(\lambda/\mu)^n}{n!} + \dfrac{(\lambda/\mu)^s}{s!}\left(\dfrac{1}{1-\rho}\right) \right]^{-1}$
Input source: Arrival distribution:	infinite; patient, no balking or reneging Poisson; mean arrival rate = λ	$P_n = \begin{cases} \dfrac{(\lambda/\mu)^n}{n!}P_0, & 0 < n < s \\[2ex] \dfrac{(\lambda/\mu)^n}{s!\,s^{n-s}}P_0, & n \geq s \end{cases}$
Service distribution:	exponential; mean service time = $1/\mu$	$L_q = \dfrac{P_0(\lambda/\mu)^s \rho}{s!(1-\rho)^2}$
Waiting line:	single line unlimited length	$W_q = \dfrac{L_q}{\lambda}$
Priority rule:	first-come, first served	$W = W_q + \dfrac{1}{\mu}$
		$L = \lambda W$

b. Use **Application E.3: Multiple-Server Model (AP E.3)** to demonstrate the multiple-server model for a situation with two servers. The short answers are $\rho = 0.8$; $P_0 = 0.11$; $L_q = 2.84$; and $W_q = 0.14$ hr.

5. Finite-source model

a. Assumptions and formulas

Assumptions		**Formulas**
Input source:	finite; equal to N customers	$$P_0 = \left[\sum_{n=0}^{N} \frac{N!}{(N-n)!} \left(\frac{\lambda}{\mu} \right)^n \right]^{-1}$$
		$\rho = 1 - P_0$
Number of servers:	1	
Number of phases:	1	$L_q = N - \frac{\lambda + \mu}{\lambda}(1 - P_0)$
Arrival distribution:	exponential interarrival times; mean $= 1/\lambda$	$L = N - \frac{\mu}{\lambda}(1 - P_0)$
Service distribution:	exponential; mean service time $= 1/\mu$	$W_q = L_q\left[(N-L)\lambda\right]^{-1}$
Waiting line:	single line; limited to no more than $N - 1$	$W = L\left[(N-L)\lambda\right]^{-1}$
Priority rule:	first-come, first served	

b. Use **Application E.4: Finite Source Model (AP E.4)** to demonstrate the finite source model.

c. Use **Application E.5: Hilltop Produce (AP E.5)** to demonstrate the single-server model in an elaborate example. **[It is effective to use the video on queuing to lead off this session. Another option is to show the OM5 software solving the applications, either real time or with samples of output.]**

Supplement F: Simulation Analysis

A. Definition

1. Reproduces system behavior
   - Study alternative solutions

2. Model that describes operations
   - Once developed, can manipulate variables to measure effects

3. Examples of use
   - Differs from waiting line models because equations on operating characteristics are not known
   - Other uses: inventory policies, maintenance policies, location, and so forth

B. Reasons for Using Simulation

1. Problem complexity
   - Nonlinear relationships
   - Too many variables or constraints
   - Empirical probability distributions

2. Experimentation without system disruption
   - Less costly
   - No impact on production schedules

3. Time compression
   - Gather years of experience in minutes on computer

4. Gaming
   - Sharpen managerial decision-making skills

5. Option of "Last Resort," but used extensively in practice
   - Doesn't necessarily find optimal solution
   - Evaluates only the alternatives proposed

C. Simulation Process

Monte Carlo Simulation: Random numbers are used to generate the simulation events.

1. Data Collection

   a. Data intensive

2. Random-number assignment

   a. What is a random number?

3. Model formulation

   a. Decision variables

      - Controlled by decision maker
      - Change from one simulation run to the next
      - Examples are number of service channels or priority rule

   b. Uncontrollable variables

      - Random events that decision maker cannot control
      - Examples are arrival rate or supply uncertainties

   c. Dependent variables

      - Reflect the values of the decision variables and uncontrollable variables
      - Operating characteristics or performance measures such as idle time or overtime costs

   d. Use **Application F.1: Monte Carlo Simulation (AP F.1)** to demonstrate the construction and execution of a simulation model.

4. Analysis

   a. Comparisons

      - Compare results for different sets of decision variables
      - Run length must be long enough
      - Statistical tests

   b. Significance

      - Can be statistically significant, but not managerially significant

Chapter 9: Location

[Ask students to give an example where a facility's location makes a difference, or introduce with examples, such as Au Bon Pain and White Castle.]

A. Globalization and Geographic Dispersion of Operations

- Tendency to concentrate similar operations in one geographic area is lessening
- Exception is JIT manufacturing, which relies on supplier proximity
- Trend toward foreign businesses building facilities in this country

1. Globalization of services

   - Services represent 20% of total world trade.
   - Airlines, education, consulting, and restaurants are globally active services.

2. Reasons for globalization

   Four developments spurring globalization:

   1. Improved transportation and communication technologies
   2. Reduced regulations on financial systems
   3. Increased demand for imported goods
   4. Lowered international trade barriers

   Disadvantages of overseas manufacturing:

   - Giving away proprietary technology
   - Threat of nationalization
   - Alienation of U.S. customers
   - Increased response times
   - Increased training requirements

3. Hot spots of global activity

   a. East Asia

      - Increasingly important role in the world economy, despite its recent slump
      - Rapidly industrializing nations

   b. Mexico

      - Maquiladoras build facilities to client specifications and help foreign firms recruit, train, and pay Mexican employees.

        + Save about $15,000 per employee per year

        − Lower productivity

        − Less work-force stability

        − Problematic transportation and utility infrastructure

        − Considerable training requirements

c. European Union (EU)

- EU corporations trade freely and avoid quotas and duties.

- EU corporations manufacture core parts within the EU.

- Japanese multinationals are investing in EU to manufacture autos and other durable goods.

d. East Europe and the former Soviet Union

- Uncertain pace of growth

- Population about double that of the U.S.

4. Managing global operations
[Describe some challenges in global operations, such as the examples in Managerial Practice 9.1.]

a. International operations require a global view of market opportunities.

b. New standards of quality and fast delivery

Challenges of managing multinational operations:

- Other languages—competitors fluent in several languages

- Different norms and customs—shape business values

- Work-force management—different management styles

- Unfamiliar laws and regulations—affect policies and practices

- Unexpected cost mix—the most efficient mix of labor, capital, and material costs depends on their relative costs, which change with location .

c. To what degree should corporate production methods be transplanted overseas, and how much control should be centralized at the home office?

- At one extreme, a firm relies on its home offices for strategic direction and is more centralized.

- At the other extreme, a firm has a worldwide vision, but allows for local differences. These are highly decentralized organizations with a wide mix of product strategies, cultures, and consumer needs.

B. Factors Affecting Location Decisions

- Use comprehensive checklist of factors for which the degree of achievement is sensitive to location, or is significant to the decision.

- Divide location factors into dominant factors derived from competitive priorities and secondary factors.

1. Dominant factors in manufacturing (in decreasing order of importance):

a. Favorable labor climate

- Wage rates

- Training requirements

- Attitudes toward work

- Worker productivity

- Union strength

b. Proximity to markets

- Particularly important when outbound transportation rates are high

c. Quality of life

- High quality of life is required to attract technically skilled workers.
  — Good schools: Educated workers are interested in educating their children
  — Low crime: Skilled workers desire to retain their possessions.
  — Recreation: Local recreational opportunities are important to professionals who have discretionary income, but scarce time.

d. Proximity to suppliers and resources

- Important to industries dependent on bulky or heavy raw materials
  — Breweries near sources of water
  — Electric utilities near water and coal
  — Saw mills near trees
  — Food processors near produce farms

e. Proximity to the parent company's facilities

- Important to plants that supply parts to other facilities or frequently rely on other facilities for coordination and communication

f. Utilities, taxes and real estate costs

- Costs and availability of utilities vary by location. Electricity is costly in California and the Northeast, water is precious in the Southwest, and telephone service may be inadequate in rural areas.
- Local governments may provide tax relief, training subsidy, debt financing, and other incentives.
- A square mile of farm land can be purchased for the same price as an acre of land in some major cities.

g. Other factors

- Room for expansion
- Accessibility to alternative modes of transportation
- Relocation costs
- Community attitudes toward growth, education, regulations
- Work force education and skills
- Condition of local infrastructure
- Avoiding import quotas, tariffs

2. Dominant factors in services

a. Proximity to customers

- Location is a key factor in determining customer convenience.

b. Transportation costs and proximity to markets

- Important to warehousing and distribution operations
- Delivery time can be a competitive advantage.

c. Location of competitors

- Estimating the impact of competitors is complicated.
  - Anticipate competitors reaction.
  - Avoiding established competition often pays.
  - Exception is **critical mass**.

d. Site-specific factors

- Level of retail activity
- Residential density, discretionary income level
- Traffic flow and visibility

e. Example: location factors at a fast-food restaurant

C. Locating a Single Facility
(assuming no interdependence with other existing facilities)

1. Selecting on-site expansion, new location, or relocation

- On-site expansion
  + Keeps management together.
  + Reduces construction time and costs.
  + Avoids splitting up operations.
  − Diseconomies of scale
  − Poor materials handling
  − Increasingly complex production control
  − Lack of space at the present site

- Building a new plant
  + In the event of strike, fire, or natural disaster, does not have to rely on production from a single plant.
  + Escape unproductive labor.
  + Modernize with all new technology.
  + Reduce transportation costs.

- Relocate (move out of existing facility)
  — Relocating firms tend to be small.
  — They don't move very far.
  — They often are single-plant companies needing space and needing to redesign their production processes and layouts.

2. Comparing several sites

   a. Systematic Site Selection Process

- Identify important location factors and categorize them into dominant and secondary categories.

- Consider alternatives; narrow the choices.

- Collect data.

- Analyze data quantitatively, transportation costs, taxes

- Evaluate qualitative factors.

   b. Use **Application 9.1: Preference Matrix (AP 9.1)** for an in-class exercise.

3. Applying the load-distance method

- Proximity to markets, suppliers, resources and other company facilities is related directly to distance.

- Objective: minimize the total weighted loads moving into and out of the facility.

   a. Distance measures

- **Euclidean distance** is the straight-line, shortest distance between two points ... as the crow flies, so to speak.

- **Rectilinear distance** assumes that the trip between two points is made with a series of 90° turns.

- Use **Application 9.2: Distance Measures (AP 9.2)** for in-class exercise. Perhaps also do Internet Activity 9.2 to find the distance between any two locations chosen by the class.

   b. Calculating a load-distance score

- Multiply each load (weight or trips per time period) between facilities times the distance (Euclidean or rectilinear) the load travels. The load-distance score is the sum of the products.

- Compare load-distance scores for alternative locations. Locations that generate big loads going short distances reduce *ld*. Of the points investigated, the location minimizing *ld* is the tentative best location.

- Other factors, price of land, zoning, suitability of land for building, etc. may require consideration of other sites.

- Use **Application 9.3: Load-Distance Method (AP 9.3)** for an in-class exercise. This method is often difficult for students without an example.

   c. Center of gravity

- Finding the *x,y* coordinates of center of gravity

    — This solution is not usually the optimal location, so investigate locations in the neighborhood.

- Use **Application 9.4: Center of Gravity (AP 9.4)** for an in-class example.

4. Using break-even analysis

- Break-even is discussed in Supplement A.

Basic Steps

1. Estimate fixed and variable costs for each alternative location.

2. Plot total cost lines.

3. Approximate the ranges for which each location has lowest cost.

4. Solve algebraically for break-even points.

- Use **Application 9.5: Break-Even Analysis (AP 9.5)** to draw graphs and then solve algebraically. The short answer is: Baltic Avenue if 6 months or less, St. Charles Place if longer.

D. Locating Within a Network of Facilities
(assuming interdependence with other existing facilities)

1. Three Dimensions of Multiple-Facility Location Problems

   a. Location—What is the best location for new facilities?

   b. Allocation—How much work should be assigned to each facility?

   c. Capacity—What is the best capacity for each facility?

2. The transportation method

   - Determines the allocation pattern that minimizes transportation costs from multiple sources to multiple destinations

   - The method does not consider other facets of the multiple-facility location problem, such as community attitudes or work force skills.

   a. Setting up the initial tableau

      - Create a matrix with one row for each source (origin or plant) and one column for each sink (destination or warehouse).

      - Make an additional column at the right for plant capacities and an additional row at the bottom for warehouse demands.

      - Add dummy plant or warehouse if needed.

      - Insert the transportation cost per unit from each plant to each warehouse in the upper right-hand corner of each cell.

      - Use **Application 9.6: The Transportation Method (AP 9.6)** for an in-class example of setting up. If classroom is equipped, obtain the solution with the OM5 Software.

   b. Finding a solution

      - The least-cost allocation pattern that satisfies all demands and exhausts all capacities is found by using the transportation method.

   c. The larger solution process. Other costs and various qualitative factors also must be considered as additional parts of a complete evaluation.

3. Other methods of location analysis

   - Many location analysis problems are complex.

   - Analysis of complex location situations involves extensive calculations.

   - Three basic computer models have been developed for this purpose.

a. Heuristics

"Solution guidelines, or rules of thumb, that find feasible — but not necessarily the best solutions to problems are called **heuristics**."

- Heuristics efficiently handle general views of a problem.

b. Simulation

- Simulation models evaluate location alternatives by trial and error.

c. Optimization

- These procedures find the "best" answer, but it is the best answer to a simplified and less realistic view of the problem.

Chapter 10: Layout

A. What Is Layout Planning?

1. A definition:

   The physical arrangement of economic activity centers within a facility. A center can be anything that consumes space.

2. Four choices

   a. What centers should we include?

      - Reflect process decisions

      - Maximize productivity

   b. How much space and capacity for each center?

      - Inadequate space can reduce productivity and privacy and create hazards.

      - Excess space is costly and can isolate employees. Often use space standards to guide designers.

   c. How to configure the space?

      - The amount of space, its shape, and elements in it

      - Atmosphere

   d. Where should each be located?

      - Two aspects of location: relative and absolute

      - Relative location can affect travel time, material handling cost, and communication.

      - Absolute location can affect cost to change layout and customer reactions.

B. Strategic Issues

1. Fit with competitive priorities

   a. J.C. Penney **[Discuss Managerial Practice 10.1 or some other example.]**

   b. Other examples

2. Layout types

   a. Process layout

      - Organizes resources around the process and groups work stations or departments according to function

      - Intermittent, low volume, high-variety

      - Flow strategy of King Soopers cake line

      - Advantages
        + General purpose, flexible resources are less capital intensive
        + Less vulnerable to changes in product mix or new market strategies
        + Equipment utilization can be higher, because not dedicated to one product line
        + Employee supervision can be more specialized

- Disadvantages
  - Slower processing rates
  - Lost production time during setups
  - More capital and more floor space tied up with inventory
  - Longer manufacturing lead times
  - Costly materials handling, requiring variable path devices
  - Production planning and control more difficult
- A major challenge in designing process layouts is to identify dominant flow patterns among the jumbled traffic and to locate centers so that materials handling is minimized.

b. Product layout

- Dedicates resources to a product or closely related product family

- Repetitive, high-volume, continuous production

- Workstations or departments are arranged in a linear path, which is consistent with the routing sequence of the product.

- Positioning strategy of King Soopers bread line: product focus

- Advantages
  + Faster processing rates
  + Lower inventories
  + Infrequent setups

- Disadvantages
  - More risk of layout redesign
  - Less flexible
  - For low volume, dedicated resources have low utilization

- Challenge in designing product layouts
  - Minimize resources used to achieve desired output rate
  - Balance tasks, equalize the workload assigned to resources

c. Hybrid layout

- Combines elements of both a flexible flow and line flow

- Facility with both fabrication and assembly operations

- Cells and flexible automation

  — Group technology (GT)

  — One worker-multiple machine (OWMM) stations

- Flexible manufacturing systems (FMS)

- Retail

d. Fixed-position layout

- Product is fixed in place. Resources come to the product, minimizing number of times product must be moved.

- Used for:

  — Very large products, ships, roads, power plants, airplanes

  — Service of fragile or bulky items

3. Performance criteria

   a. Capital investment: cost per square foot

   b. Materials handling

- Large flows should go short distances
- Includes stockpicking in warehouse, customer convenience in store, and communication in office

   c. Flexibility

- Facility remains desirable after significant changes
- Can be easily and inexpensively adapted in response to them

   d. Other criteria

- Labor productivity
- Equipment maintenance
- Work environment
- Organizational structure

C. Creating Hybrid Layouts

If volumes not high enough for dedicating line to single product, may achieve benefits with OWMM or GT.

1. One worker, multiple machines (OWMM) cell

   a. Is there enough volume to have a one-person line? One worker operates several *different* machines simultaneously to achieve line flow. The machines operate on their own for much of the cycle. The worker interacts with the machines as required, performing loading, unloading, or other operations that have not been automated.

   b. Benefits are similar to those of flow lines: lower WIP inventory, reduced frequency of setup, labor savings through low cost automation, simplified materials handling, and reduced cycle time through overlapped operations.

2. Group Technology (GT)

- Group parts into families that have identical processing steps.
- Changeover from producing one part to another requires only minor setup adjustments.
- Product family volume justifies dedication of machines, which are arranged into flow lines called *cells*.

   a. **Step 1:** Group parts or products into *families*. Similar characteristics on:
- Manufacturing requirements
- Size and shape
- Routings
- Demand

   b. **Step 2:** Create a GT *cell* for each family to achieve improvements in:
- Setup time
- WIP inventory
- Materials handling
- Cycle time
- Opportunities to automate

c. Example
- Process flows before and after change
- Three product families that account for majority of production
- Discuss Cummins Engine

D. Designing Process Layouts

1. Gather Information (Step 1)

   a. Space requirements by center and available space and current block plan

   - Tie space requirements to capacity plans.

   - Add "circulation" space—that is, aisles wide enough to move materials to and from the center—and space to access the machines for maintenance or disassembly.

     — Recall that process layouts have higher WIP. Provide space for that inventory at each center.

     — Also recall that rework requires space.

   b. Closeness ratings

   - Which items need to be close to each other, and which should not be close to each other?

   - Trip matrix and REL chart

   c. Other considerations

   - Absolute location criteria—departments fixed in place: relocation costs, foundations, noise levels, impulse buys in store near exit, and so forth

2. Develop a block plan (Step 2)

   - Most elementary way is trial and error, looking for patterns. Can supplement effort with computer help, such as the Process Layout Solver from the OM5 software.

   - Use **Application 10.1: Process Layout (AP 10.1)** to demonstrate the use of a trip matrix when evaluating a block plan and spotting possible improvements in it.

3. Design a detailed layout (Step 3)

   a. More exact sizes, shapes, and detail; show aisles, stairs, machines, desks, and the like

   b. Examples of visual representation

E. Aids for Process Layout Decisions

1. Combinatorial problem

2. Automated Layout DEsign Program (ALDEP): sequence of entering departments

   a. First, randomly choose one.

   b. Each successive department should have a strong REL rating with one just entered. If no such relationship, choose randomly.

3. Computerized **R**elative **A**llocation of **F**acilities **T**echnique (CRAFT)

    a. Origins in space program and backboard wiring problem

    b. Successive pair exchanges

    c. Improvement heuristics, some of most effective to this day

F. Warehouse Layouts

1. Out-and-back selection pattern
   - Simplest situation
   - One item picked at a time; go from dock to storage area and back

    a. Decision rule to minimize ld-score
   - Equal areas: Place departments with most trips closest to the dock.
   - Unequal areas: Place departments with highest trip-to-area ratio closest to the dock.

    b. Use **Application 10.2: Warehouse Layout (AP 10.2)** for an in-class example of developing layout for a plant warehouse.

2. Other Options

    a. Shifting demand

    b. High density designs **[shown in the video about the Addison-Wesley warehouse]**

    c. Different layout patterns

   - Out-and-back pattern
   - Route collection system
   - Batch picking system
   - Zone system

3. Addison-Wesley Distribution Center

G. Office Layouts

1. Recent Harris Poll: A 1400-worker poll revealed that 75 percent felt a better layout would improve their productivity.

2. Hawthorne study: Management indirectly used layout as a "spatial language" to say:

    a. You are special

    b. Out of supervisor's watchful eyes

    c. Satisfied social needs

3. Proximity

    a. The usual approach is to design office layouts around work flows and communication patterns.

    b. The assumption is that proximity helps with understanding, mutual interests, and even friendship.

4. Privacy

   a. Crowding and noise can hurt performance and attitudes.

   b. Example: A Chicago newspaper company went from a traditional to an open-office plan: plush carpets, baffled ceilings, and more eye appeal, but no doors and no partitions over three feet high. A survey of attitudes was taken before and after the change. Attitudes were worse on all counts.

5. Options in office layout

   • Privacy is expensive. The capital investment in open-plan layouts is about 40 percent less. An open plan maximizes flexibility.

   • A trade-off between privacy and proximity is possible.

   a. Traditional layouts

     • Closed offices for some

     • Open areas for others

   b. Office landscaping

     • Everyone in the open: plants, screens, and portable partitions for semiprivate space

     • Examples: Quickborner office landscape from Germany, Johnson Wax headquarters

   c. Activity settings

     • Home base: a personal nook; position no longer means place

     • Multiple work places

   d. Telecommuting or electronic cottages

H. Designing Product Layouts

1. Common characteristics

   a. Arranges work stations in sequence

   b. Line flow from station to station, with each performing a set of work elements

   c. Small or nonexistent inventory buffers

   d. Production line or assembly line

2. Line Balancing

   a. Two basic questions

     • How many stations are needed?

     • What work elements are assigned to each?

   b. Immediate predecessors

   c. Precedence diagram

     • AON network

     • Cannot add a work element until all of its immediate predecessors are shown. Have students finish the partially completed diagram.

   d. Desired output rate

     • Matching demand to the production plan

- Job specialization and number of shifts worked: A typical automobile assembly plant is 60 cars per hour.

e. Cycle time

- Inverse of desired hourly output rate; convert to same time units as given for work elements

- In general,

$$c = \frac{1}{r}$$

f. Theoretical minimum number of stations

- Productivity is maximized by minimizing the number of stations.

- The ultimate in balance is when the sum of work-element times at each station equals c.

- The theoretical minimum assumes perfect balance, which may not be possible.

- In general,

$$TM = \frac{\Sigma t}{c} \qquad \text{(round up)}$$

g. Visualizing the solution: Big Broadcaster at Green Grass **[If classroom facilities permit, use the OM5 software to run the problem.]**

h. The computer output shows the efficiency of the solution. This measure is one of three related goals.

$$\text{Idle time} = nc - \Sigma t$$

where

n = number of stations

c = cycle time

Σt = total time per unit assembled

$$\text{Efficiency (\%)} = (\_t/nc)(100)$$

$$\text{Balance delay (\%)} = 100 - \text{Efficiency}$$

i. Theoretical maximum efficiency. The efficiency of a solution is found with TM stations. In our example, it is 90.6%.

j. Use **Application 10.3: Product Layout (AP 10.3)** for an in-class example of drawing a precedence diagram, and then calculate the cycle time, the theoretical number of stations, and the various performance measures.

k. Finding a solution

- Do not dwell on this procedure at the outset, as it makes more sense to the students after the following application is finished.

Step 1. Begin with station $k = 1$. Make a list of candidate work elements to assign to station k. Each candidate must satisfy three conditions:

   a. It has not yet been assigned to this or any previous station.

      b.   All its predecessors have been assigned to this or a previous station.

      c.   Its time cannot exceed the station's idle time, which accounts for all work elements already assigned. If none has been assigned, the station's idle time equals the cycle time.

      If no such candidates can be found, go to step 4.

Step 2.   Pick a candidate. Two decision rules are commonly used for selecting from the candidate list.

      a.   Pick the candidate with the *longest work-element time*.
- Works in the most difficult ones first, saving the smaller ones for rounding out each station.

      b.   Pick the candidate having the *largest number of followers*.
- C has three followers.
- Keeps options open for rest of solution.

      Assign the candidate chosen to station k. If there are ties, break them randomly.

Step 3.   Calculate the cumulative time of all tasks assigned so far to station k. Subtract this total from the cycle time to find the station's idle time. Go to step 1, and generate a new list of candidates.

Step 4.   If some work elements are unassigned, but none are candidates for station k, start a new station $k + 1$ and go to step 1. Otherwise, you have a complete solution.

- Use **Application 10.4: Product Layout (AP 10.4)** here. Continue with this application to develop a line balancing solution.

3.   Other Considerations

   a.   Pacing

   b.   Behavioral factors
- Job enlargement and rotation
- Craft lines
- Involving worker groups in decisions
- Arranging stations to facilitate interaction
- Personnel selection

   c.   Number of models produced
- Mixed-model line
- Advantages
- Disadvantages

   d.   Modify cycle times
- May increase efficiency
- Rebalancing frequency

Chapter 11: Supply-Chain Management

[The concepts of this chapter can be reinforced by allocating class time for the Sonics Distributors in-class simulation. See the section on supply-chain dynamics below.]

- Definition: supply-chain management seeks to synchronize a firm's functions and those of its suppliers to match the flow of materials, services, and information with customer demand. **[Mention Dell Computer's supply chain design.]**

- SCM is a strategic weapon.

A. Overview of Supply-Chain Management

- An analogy for inventory flows is the water flows from a tank.

- A basic purpose of SCM is the manage the flow of materials.

- The three categories of inventories are raw materials (RM), work-in-process (WIP), and finished goods (FG).

- Manufacturers spend 60 percent of sales on purchased materials and services, and service providers spend as much as 40 percent. The management of materials flows is therefore important from a cost perspective alone.

1. Materials management

    a. Encompasses materials and services purchasing, inventory management, production planning, staffing, scheduling, and distribution.

    b. The segmented structure is "traditional" and creates three departments: purchasing, production control, and distribution.

    c. The integrated structure combines the three traditional departments into one that is called materials management or logistics management. **[Reinforce the notion of the domains of responsibility for each of the three areas by reviewing the simple example of a bakery in the text.]**

2. Supply chains

    a. Definition: an interconnected set of linkages between suppliers of materials and services that spans the transformation of raw materials into products and services and delivers them to a firm's customers. **[Ask students to provide some of the suppliers for a local business. Discuss the aspect of tiers.]**

    b. Control over suppliers can be gained through backward vertical integration or, more typically, through contractual agreements.

3. Supply chains for service providers

    a. Service providers must purchase materials from manufacturers and services from other service providers.

    b. Examples **[Discuss Arizona Public service in MP 11.1]**

4. Integrated Supply Chains—the phases

    a. Phase 1– independent supply-chain entities

    b. Phase 2–internal integration

    c. Phase 3– supply-chain integration: This form integrates the internal and external supply-chain entities.

B. Purchasing

- Purchasing is the management of the acquisition process, which includes deciding which suppliers to use, negotiating contracts, and deciding whether to buy locally. It is a crucial activity for any organization.

1. The acquisition process

    a. Recognize a need. **[MP 11.1 has the purchasing needs of a public utility.]**

    b. Select suppliers. This step is important to designing a supply chain that responds to the firm's competitive priorities.

    c. Place the order.

    d. Track the order.

    e. Receive the order.

2. Electronic purchasing

    a. EDI has changed the traditional image of purchasing by reducing the paper shuffling that used to take place.

    b. Electronic commerce **[Mention Wal-Mart, Kodak, GE.]**

    c. Implications for SCM are reduced ordering costs, less time to place an order, and the potential to include more suppliers in the supply chain.

3. Supplier selection and certification

    a. Supplier selection—Three criteria often used are price, quality, and delivery. **[Mention Maimonides Medical Center which selected a supplier that enabled drastic reductions in inventory per bed.]**

    b. Supplier certification—Typically involves visits by cross-functional teams to do an in-depth evaluation of the supplier's processes.

4. Supplier relations

    a. Competitive orientation—a zero sum game. The purpose is to drive costs down to the minimum level. Power in the supply chain relates to the purchasing clout a firm has. **[Use Premier, Inc. as an example in the health care industry.]**

b. Cooperative orientation—a partnership between buyers and sellers. This orientation implies long-term commitments, joint work on quality, and buyer support of infrastructure. Typically, fewer suppliers are needed in this arrangement. **[Use the VW factory in Brazil as an example of an extreme case of a cooperative orientation. Also discuss MP 11.2 for the headaches that can occur with sole sourcing.]**

5. Outsourcing

   a. Degree of sourcing control. Managers must choose the appropriate contract relationship with suppliers. Long-term options include ownership and strategic alliances, and short-term options include contracts for a given shipment of materials or services.

   b. The degree of sourcing control is inversely related to the flexibility to change the supply chain when needed.

6. Centralized versus localized buying

   a. Centralized—increases purchasing clout

   b. Localized—often reduces lead times and enables closer coordination with local production schedules

7. Value analysis

   a. Value analysis is an intensive examination of the materials, processes, information systems, and material flows in the production of a good or service.

   b. Benefits include reduced costs, better profits, increased customer satisfaction, and often improved employee morale.

   c. Value analysis can improve the internal supply chain, but its greatest potential lies in applying it to the external supply chain. **[MP 11.3 discusses Chrysler's SCORE program for suppliers.]**

C. Distribution

- Distribution is the management of the flow of materials from manufacturers and service providers to customers and from warehouses to retailers, involving the storage and transportation of products.

1. Placement of finished goods inventory

   a. Forward placement puts the inventory close to the customer and enhances fast delivery times and reduced transportation costs, but may require duplicated stocking of the same item in several locations.

   b. Backward placement means keeping the inventory at the manufacturer and supports customization of the finished goods. This is often referred to as pooling the inventory. **[See MP 11.4 for an example of backward placement by IBM.]**

2. Selection of transportation mode

   a. Highway—supports flexibility of routings

   b. Rail or water—support low cost operations

c. Pipelines—support high volume, low cost operations.

d. Air transportation—supports fast delivery

3. Scheduling, routing, and carrier selection **[Discuss the implications of these decisions on the operations of a supply chain.]**

D. Measures of Supply-Chain Performance

1. Inventory measures

a. Average aggregate inventory value—the total value of all items held in inventory for a firm. The value is expressed at *cost* (as opposed to price) to avoid the differences that occur in prices over time. This measure is used in two other important measures.

b. Weeks of supply—Average aggregate inventory value divided by weekly sales (at cost). From an inventory cost perspective, the lower the weeks of supply, the better.

c. Inventory turns—Annual sales (at cost) divided by the average aggregate inventory value. The greater the turns, the lower the average inventory levels. **[Note that inventory turns or weeks of supply can be calculated for an individual item as opposed to an entire inventory. In such a case you can perform the calculations in 'units' rather than costs.]**

Use **APPLICATION 11.1 : Inventory turnover** (AP11.1) to demonstrate the calculations for weeks of supply and inventory turns.

2. Links to financial measures

[Students do not have a difficult time with the weeks of supply or the inventory turns calculations, but the have a lot of difficulty understanding how these measure relate to typical financial measures they discuss in accounting or finance classes. Reserve some time to discuss the following measures and how they relate to the inventory measures.]

a. current assets

b. working capital

c. contribution margin

E. Links to Operations Strategy

[It is important to discuss the expansion of the theory of an individual firm with its competitive priorities to the theory of a network of firms linked in a supply chain for the support of the firm's competitive priorities. Supply chains can be designed to achieve certain competitive priorities.]

1. Efficient versus responsive supply chains

a. Efficient supply chains—main purpose is to minimize inventories and maximize efficiency of the members of the supply chain. Demands are highly predictable, new product introductions infrequent, and variety is minimal. This design supports low cost operations, consistent quality, and on-time delivery.

b. Responsive supply chains—The main purpose is to react quickly to marketing demands. Demand predictability is low and the firm offers a high degree of product variety. The focus is on reaction time, and the primary competitive priorities are development speed, fast delivery times, customization, volume flexibility, and high performance design.

2. Design of efficient and responsive supply chains.

a. Efficient supply chains—Features include line flows; low capacity cushions; low inventory investments; and short lead times (but not so as to increase costs). **[Discuss Campbell Soup Company in MP 11.5 as an example.]**

b. Responsive supply chains – Features include flexible or intermediate flows; high capacity cushions; inventories as needed to enable fast delivery; and lead times that are aggressively shortened (even if costs increase). **[Discuss Dell Computer Company as an example—see Chapter 11 opener.]**

F. Supply-Chain Dynamics

[Dynamics in supply chains are an interesting phenomenon and can be demonstrated in class. See the experiential learning exercise, Sonic Distributors, at the end of chapter 11. This in-class simulation exists at two levels. Students can be given a highly defined scenario and asked to simulate the operation of the supply chain so defined. Alternatively, you can allow the students to test their own supply-chain designs and see how well they do "under fire." Either way, this section and the one on efficient versus responsive supply chains set up the use of the simulation.]

- A recent survey by AIAG found that it takes four to six weeks for materials release information to reach the last tier in an automotive supply chain.

1. External supply-chain causes

   a. volume changes

   b. product/service mix changes

   c. late deliveries

   d. underfilled shipments

2. Internal supply-chain causes

   a. internally generated shortages

   b. engineering changes

   c. New product/service introductions

   d. Product/service promotions

   e. information errors

Chapter 12: Forecasting

A. Demand Characteristics

[Define the term *"forecast"* and give examples]

1. Patterns of demand

   a. Horizontal—the average level of demand

   b. Trend—an upward or downward slope

   c. Seasonal—usually an annually repeating pattern, but could be based on time of day, week, or month

   d. Cyclical—Business cycles often span 4 to 8 years, while life cycles vary widely in duration. It is difficult to quantitatively address this component, because a sufficient data history is rarely available.

   e. Random—By definition, this component can never be forecast using statistical processes. If an identifiable pattern in the errors exists, they are not random.

2. Factors affecting demands

   a. External factors

      - Management cannot directly control external factors.

      - An external factor may positively affect one product while reducing the demand for another.

      - Leading, coincident, and lagging indicators **[Give examples.]**

   b. Internal factors: demand management

      - The timing of demand is important to efficient utilization of resources and production capacity.

      - Advertising and promotions encourage customers to make purchases during off-peak demand periods.

      - Developing products that have different seasonal peak demands tends to level production resource requirements.

      - Appointments match demand for services to schedules of available capacity. When demand exceeds capacity, the appointment lead time lengthens until customers balk.

B. Designing Forecasting Systems

1. What should we forecast?

   a. Level of aggregation

   b. Units of measurement

      - Prices fluctuate, masking changes in demand for units of output.

      - Forecasting units of *output* may not be possible in custom manufacturing or services. Instead, forecast in terms of critical *input* resources such as labor hours.

2. What type of forecasting technique is appropriate?

    a. Short term

- Time series methods are the most often used in the short term.

    + Inexpensive to generate large numbers of forecasts

    + Good quality (small errors) for short-term forecasts

- Causal models not used as extensively for short term forecasts.

    + Usually more accurate than time series forecasts

    − More time to develop

    − More time consuming to compute

    − Less likely to be understood and used

    − More training required

- Judgment methods are used only on a rare exception basis. They are too costly to apply to thousands of routine short-term forecasts.

    b. Medium term

- Time series should not be used. Time series are useful in quickly generating a large number of forecasts. However a relatively small number of forecasts are required to make projections by product family.

    − Unlikely that existing patterns will continue very far into future

    − Poor results

- Causal models are most often used in the medium term.

    + Better at identifying turning points in trends

- Judgment methods

    + Also can identify turning points

    + Used when historical data not available

    - Still very costly

    c. Long term

- Aggregate demand for a product family expressed in homogeneous units, such as dollars of sales, tons of steel

- Causal models adjusted for judgment

- Judgment methods

3. Forecasting with computers

- Forecasting software packages are widely available. **[Mention Wal-Mart's CFAR in MP 12.1.]**

- Three categories

    — Manual systems

    — Semiautomatic systems

    — Automatic systems

- Package selection depends on (1) fit with musts and wants, (2) cost of the package, (3) level of clerical support required, (4) amount of programmer maintenance required.

C. Judgment Methods

1. Sales force estimates

   - Sales force provides personal estimates of future demands.

   - Advantages

     + Sales force should have good information about customer's purchasing plans.

     + Forecasts are separated by district or region.

     + Forecasts are easily aggregated to any level of detail.

   - Disadvantages

     – Forecasts may be biased.

     – The sales force may not be able to tell the true intentions of their customers.

     – Potential for sales personnel to underestimate sales so that they look good when reviewed.

2. Executive opinion

   - Opinions of a group of executives are summarized.

   - May be used to modify an existing forecast to account for unusual circumstances

   - Disadvantages

     — Consumes expensive executive time

     — Executives may independently modify forecasts based on individual opinion

3. Market research

   - A systematic approach to creating and testing hypotheses about the market

   - Data are usually gathered by survey.

   - Pitfalls

     — Accuracy decreases as projections increase into the long term.

     — Numerous hedges and qualifications in the findings

     — Low response rate to surveys

     — Respondents may not be representative of the market.

   Activities for designing and conducting a market research study:

   a. Design a questionnaire.

      — Requests economic and demographic information

      — Asks interest in product

   b. Decide method of administering survey.

      — Telephone

      — Mail

      — Personal interview

   c. Select a representative population to survey.

d. Collect, then analyze data.

— Interpreting responses

— Poor response rate may skew the data.

4. Delphi method

- A process of gaining consensus from a group of experts while maintaining anonymity

- Anonymity is important so that a respected guru doesn't dominate the results.

- Used for technological forecasting

- Pitfalls

    — The process can take a long time.

    — Anonymity might also produce irresponsible opinions.

    — All forecasts (regardless of method) are wrong.

    — Results are sensitive to questionnaire design.

Steps in the Delphi Method:

a. Questions about progress in a technological field are sent to a group of experts who are developing that technology.

b. Experts respond, arguing in support of their responses.

c. A report that summarizes the responses is prepared.

d. The report is returned to the experts for another round.

e. Experts modify or reassert their responses.

f. Process repeats two to four times to achieve some form of consensus.

5. Guidelines for using judgment forecasts

a. Adjust quantitative forecasts when their track record is poor and the decision maker has important contextual knowledge.

b. Make adjustments to quantitative forecasts to compensate for specific events.

D. Linear Regression

1. Causal approach

a. Relates a dependent variable to one or more independent variables by linear equation.

b. Independent variables could be the external or internal factors that are assumed to affect demand.

2. Linear regression equation for one independent variable

a. $Y = a + bX$ (the theoretical relationship)

where: Y = dependent variable

X = independent variable

a = intercept of the line

b = slope of the line

[Show simple regression line relative to data; give examples.]

b. The objective is to find values of <u>a</u> and <u>b</u> that minimize the sum of the squared deviations of the actual data points from the graphed line.

c. Use the data below, and the OM5 software, to demonstrate a simple linear regression analysis.

Forecast the number of appetizers that could be sold at a price of $3.00 each.

	X (Price)	Y (Appetizers)
1.	$2.70	760
2.	3.50	510
3.	2.00	980
4.	4.20	250
5.	3.10	320
6.	4.05	480

- What is the regression line?
  [ANS: $Y = 1450.12 - 276.28X$]

- If the price is set at $3.00, how many appetizers will be sold?
  [ANS: 621.28]

  How good is the forecasting equation? **[ANS: $r = 0.84$; $r^2 = 0.71$. The coefficient of determination of only 0.71 indicates other variables have an appreciable effect on sales.]**

E. Time Series Methods

1. Naive forecast method **[Use the data in Application 12.1: Estimating the Average (AP 12.1) to motivate the naïve approach.]**

    - What is the forecast for month 5? **[ANS: 790]**

2. Simple moving average method

    a. The procedure:

    $$F_{t+1} = \frac{D_t + D_{t-1} + \ldots + D_{t-n-1}}{n}$$

    where: D_t = actual demand in period t

    n = total number of periods in the average

Use **Application 12.1: Estimating the Average, Part a. (Simple Moving Average) (AP 12.1)** to demonstrate the moving average method. The short answers are:

Forecast for month 5 = **780**

Forecast for month 6 = **802**

b. Implications of increasing n **[Discuss the differences in responsiveness.]**

3. Weighted moving average method

    a. The procedure:

$$F_{t+1} = W_1 D_t + W_2 D_{t-1} + \cdots + W_n D_{t-n+1}$$

    where

$$\sum_1^n W_i = 1$$

Use **Application 12.1: Estimating the Average, Part b. (Weighted Moving Average)** **(AP 12.1)** to demonstrate the weighted moving average method. The short answers are:

        Forecast for month 5 = **786**

        Forecast for month 6 = **802**

4. Exponential smoothing method

    a. The procedure:

$$F_{t+1} = D_t + (1 - \alpha)A_{t-1}$$

    Where α = smoothing parameter with a value between 0 and 1.

Use **Application 12.1: Estimating the Average, Part c. (Exponential Smoothing Average)** **(AP 12.1)** to demonstrate the exponential smoothing method. The short answers are:

        Forecast for month 5 = **784**

        Forecast for month 6 = **789**

    b. Advantages

- Simplicity
- Minimal data requirements compared to moving average
- Inexpensive

    c. Disadvantages

- Lags behind changes in underlying average.
- Does not account for any factors other than the series past performance.

5. Trend-adjusted exponential smoothing

    a. Smooth (average) estimates for the series average as well as the trend.

    b. Procedure:

    Average: $A_t = \alpha D_t + (1 - \alpha)(A_{t-1} + T_{t-1})$

    Average trend: $T_t = \beta(A_t - A_{t-1}) + (1 - \beta)T_{t-1}$

    Forecast for p periods in the future: $= A_t + pT_t$

        where: A_t = exponentially smoothed average of the series in period t

            T_t = exponentially smoothed average of the trend in period t

          α, β = smoothing parameters

Use **Application 12.2: Forecasting Using Trend-Adjusted Exponential Smoothing (AP 12.2)** to demonstrate the trend-adjusted method.

6. Seasonal Patterns

    a. Procedure:

        Step 1: Calculate the average demand per period for each year of past data.

        Step 2: Divide the actual demand for each period by the average demand per period to get a seasonal factor for each period. Repeat for each year of data.

        Step 3: Calculate the average seasonal factor for each period.

        Step 4: To get a forecast for a given period in a future year, multiply the seasonal factor by the average demand per period in that year.

Use **Application 12.3: Forecasting Using the Multiplicative Seasonal Method (AP 12.3)** to demonstrate the multiplicative seasonal method.

F. Choosing a Time Series Method

1. Forecast errors

    a. Forecast error is the difference between the forecast and actual demand.

    b. Cumulative sum of forecast errors (CFE)

      - Useful for bias measurement

      - Used in tracking signals

    c. Average forecast error equals CFE divided by the number of data points.

    d. Mean squared error (MSE)

      - Measures dispersion of forecast errors

      - Places greater weight than MAD on large errors

    e. Standard deviation (σ)

      - Measures dispersion of forecast errors

      - Want to have small values of σ

    f. Mean absolute deviation (MAD)

      - Measures dispersion of forecast errors

      - Easier for managers to understand than standard deviation

      - $MAD = 0.8\,\sigma$

      - $\sigma = 1.25 MAD$

    g. Mean absolute percent error (MAPE)

      - Relates forecast error to level of demand

      - Puts the size of a forecast error in proper perspective

Use **Application 12.4: Calculating Measures of Forecast Error (AP 12.4)** to show how the measures of forecast errors differ what they tell the forecaster about the performance of the forecasts.

2. Tracking signals

   a. Indicates whether a method of forecasting has any built-in biases

   b. Tracking signal $= \dfrac{\text{CFE}}{\text{MAD}}$

   c. Using the tracking signal in practice.

3. Criteria for selecting time series methods

   a. Statistical criteria

      - Minimize bias

      - Minimize MAD

   b. Managerial expectations

      - Projected stable demands suggest low values of α and higher values of n.

      - Projected changing patterns suggest high values of α and lower values of n.

   c. Forecast error last period

Chapter 13: Inventory Management

A. Inventory Concepts

1. A definition

    Inventory is a stock of anything held to meet some future demand. It is created when the rate of receipts exceeds the rate of disbursements. **[Use the water tank analogy in Chapter 11.]**

2. Pressures for small inventories

    a. Collectively called "inventory holding cost." The cost to keep an item on hand for a year typically ranges from 25 percent to 40 percent of the item's value.

    b. Cost components

    - Interest or opportunity cost—time value of money

    - Storage and handling—warehouse facilities and labor

    - Taxes and insurance—usually proportional to inventory value

    - Shrinkage

        — Pilferage

        — Obsolescence

        — Deterioration

3. Pressures for high inventories

    a. Customer service: For customers that have immediate or seasonal demands, finished goods inventory can speed up delivery and reduce:

    - Stockouts—when standard item not on hand when demand occurs, and sale lost

    - Backorders—customer order not filled when promised or demanded but is filled later

    b. Ordering costs: Costs associated with purchasing, follow-up, receiving, and paperwork are incurred each time an order is placed. By ordering in larger quantities, the resulting inventory provides a means of obtaining and handling materials in economic lot sizes. **[Mention MP 13.1 here.]**

    c. Setup costs: Work orders have similar costs associated with each setup, and machines may be unproductive for several hours each time the product is switched.

    - Labor and time to make changeover

    - May include scrap and rework

    d. Labor and equipment utilization

    - Setup time reduction: Throughput at bottleneck resources can be increased by placing larger production orders, reducing total setup time.

    - Fewer missing components: Inventories protect against supply errors, shortages, stockouts, and delivery uncertainties.

    - Stabilizing output rates: Inventories can be used to cover peaks in demand, level production activities, stabilize employment, and improve labor relations.

    e. Transportation cost

    - Outbound: Transportation costs can be reduced by building inventories and shipping full carloads.

- Inbound: per unit inbound material transportation costs can be reduced by ordering large lot sizes.

   f. Quantity discounts. Ordering large quantities can provide a hedge against future price increases and provide a means to obtain quantity discounts.

4. Types of Inventory

   Here we break inventory into four types, classifying inventory by how it is created. Separate inventories cannot be identified physically, but helps understand how it is created and controlled.

   a. Cycle inventory

   - Created by ordering in larger quantities so as to place orders less frequently. The longer the cycle, the bigger the **lot size** (Q).

   - A larger Q can help with customer service, ordering cost, setups, transportation rates, and purchasing cost.

     Two lot-sizing principles:

     — Q varies directly with the elapsed time (cycle) between orders. A one-month cycle means an average Q of one month's supply.

     — Cycle inventory varies from Q to 0, or an average of:

     $$\text{Average cycle inventory} = \frac{Q + 0}{2} = \frac{Q}{2}$$

   b. Safety stock inventory

   - Helps with customer service and hidden costs of missing parts

   - Created by placing an order sooner than typically needed

   - The replenishment order most likely will arrive ahead of time, protecting against three uncertainties:
     — Demand
     — Lead time
     — Supply

   c. Anticipation inventory

   - Used to absorb uneven rates in
     — Demand
     — Supply

   - Created by smoothing output rates, stockpiling during the slack season or overbuying before a price increase or capacity shortage

   - Examples: manufacturers of air conditioners or greeting cards

   d. Pipeline (transit) inventory

   - Created by the time spent to move and produce inventory

   - All orders that have been placed but not yet received

   - Can be found in any one of three stages:
     — **Inbound:** scheduled receipts of purchased materials paid for but not ready to use

- **Within the plant:** WIP inventory, including all scheduled receipts for orders sent to the shop

- **Outbound:** finished goods that have been shipped but not yet received and paid for by the customer

- Pipeline inventory: Sometimes it is 0 (nothing on order) and sometimes Q (one open order). But on the average, it is

Average pipeline inventory $= \overline{D}_L = dL$

Use **Application 13.1: Estimating Inventory Levels (AP 13.1)** to demonstrate the approaches for estimating inventory levels.

5. Inventory reduction

Managers want cost-effective ways to reduce inventories.

a. There are basic tactics, which we call **levers**.

- The **primary lever** must be activated to really cut inventory.

- A **secondary lever** reduces the penalty cost of applying the primary lever and reduces the need to have inventory in the first place.

b. Cycle

- Primary: Reduce lot size, Q.
  However, making such reductions in Q without making any other changes can be devastating.

- Secondary levers

  - Streamline methods for placing orders and making setups.

  - Increase repeatability, eliminate the need for changeovers.

c. Safety stock

- Primary: Place orders closer to the time when they must be received. **[Mention Sport Obermeyer in MP 13.2 here.]**

  However, this approach can lead to unacceptable customer service—unless demand, supply, and delivery uncertainties can be minimized.

- Secondary levers

  - Improve demand forecasts

  - Reduce lead time

  - Reduce supply uncertainties, communicate with suppliers, use preventive maintenance

  - Capacity cushions and cross-trained workers

d. Anticipation inventory

- Primary: Match demand rate with production rate.

- Secondary levers

  - Add new products with different demand cycles

  - Provide off-season promotional campaigns

  - Offer seasonal pricing plans

e. Pipeline inventory

- Primary: Reduce lead time.

- Secondary levers

  — Find more responsive suppliers, improve materials handling.

  — In cases where lead time varies with lot size, decrease Q.

6. Inventory placement

Managers make in part these decisions by designating an item either as special or standard.

a. **Special:** made (or purchased) to order; just enough to cover a customer request

b. **Standard:** made (or purchased) to stock and normally available when needed

c. Inventory held toward the finished goods level means shorter delivery time, but higher holding costs.

d. Example: In the video, R.R. Donnelley positions inventory toward the raw materials level.

7. ABC analysis

a. Step 1: Divide into 3 classes, according to annual dollar usage. Look for natural changes, because dividing lines not exact.

b. Step 2: Have close control over "A" items. Use levers, review frequently, centralized buying, inventory record accuracy.

B. Economic Order Quantity

1. Five assumptions

a. The demand rate is known and constant.

- Therefore the depletion of inventory results in a straight line with slope equal to the negative of the demand rate.

b. Replenishments arrive in a batch equal to the order quantity rather than piecemeal. There are no limitations on lot size.

- The replenishment results in a *vertical* line on the graph, rather than a line with a positive finite slope.

c. Annual holding cost and annual ordering cost are the *only* costs which are relevant to the *order quantity* decision.

- There are no quantity discounts, so per-unit price is irrelevant.

d. Replenishment decisions for one item (say doughnuts) are made independently from replenishment decisions for other items, (say coffee).

- Model enhancements are required to consider situations where several items are purchased from the same supplier, or several items belong to a product family that can share the same setup.

e. There is no uncertainty in lead time or supply.

- Therefore, replenishment orders can be timed so that no stockouts occur. Since none occur, stockout costs are irrelevant to the decision.

- The minimum inventory equals zero, the maximum inventory equals the *EOQ*, and the average cycle inventory equals *EOQ*/2.

These five assumptions describe an unrealistic situation. However, there are other models, and the *EOQ* often is a reasonable first approximation when the actual situation is only somewhat similar to the one stated by the assumptions.

2. Calculating the EOQ

    a. Annual holding cost

    $$\text{Annual holding cost} = \frac{Q}{2}(H)$$

    where

    > $Q/2$ = average inventory in cycle stock, and
    > H = cost of holding one unit in inventory for a year.
    > $H = iP$ (if expressed as a proportion of the item's value, where $\underline{P}$ = item's value)

    b. Annual ordering cost

    - With Q in the denominator, the annual ordering cost varies inversely with Q.

    $$\text{Annual ordering cost} = \frac{D}{Q}(S)$$

    where

    > D = *annual* demand
    > D/Q = number of (purchase/work) orders placed in one year
    > S = average cost of placing one (purchase/work) order
    > (In manufacturing, this cost is called setup.)
    > Since these are the only relevant costs, the *annual* total of the relevant costs:

    c. Total inventory costs (C)

    $$C = \frac{Q}{2}(H) + \frac{D}{Q}(S)$$

    d. EOQ formula

    - Note that the lowest cost occurs when the ordering cost is approximately equal to holding cost. This is not by accident.

    - A more efficient approach (derived from calculus).

    $$\frac{Q}{2}(H) = \frac{D}{Q}(S)$$

    $$Q = \sqrt{\frac{2DS}{H}} = \text{EOQ}$$

    e. Time between orders (TBO). Sometimes policies are expressed in terms of the time between replenishments. TBO for a lot size is the elapsed time between receiving orders of Q units. If $Q =$ EOQ, the TBO expressed in terms of months, is:

    $$TBO_{EOQ} = \frac{\text{EOQ}}{D}(12 \text{ months/yr})$$

Use **Application 13.2: Finding the EOQ, Total Cost, and TBO (AP 13.2)** to demonstrate the basic inventory equations.

f. Effect of changes

- Change in the demand rate

  Q. What happens to cycle inventory if the demand rate increases?

  A. D is in the numerator of the EOQ equation. EOQ varies directly as the square root of D. If D quadruples, EOQ doubles.

- Change in the setup costs

  Q. What happens to lot sizes if setup costs decrease?

  A. S is in the numerator of the EOQ equation. EOQ varies directly as the square root of S. If S decreases by a factor of 4, EOQ is halved.

- Change in the holding costs

  Q. What happens if interest rates drop?

  A. Interest charged on inventory investment is a component of holding cost. H is in the denominator of the EOQ equation. If the interest rate drops, EOQ increases.

- Errors in estimating D, H, and S.

  Q. How critical are errors in estimating D, H, and S?

  A. Errors such as overestimating ordering cost may be offset by other errors such as overestimating holding cost. The square root also reduces the effect of errors. If one misses a cost or demand estimate by 10%, the effect on total annual cost is often undetectable.

C. Continuous Review (Q) System

Inventory control systems bring together two dimensions—how much and when. Here is one of two systems that we will fully develop.

1. Other names are: reorder point system (ROP), fixed order quantity system, and Q system.

2. Tracks inventory position, which is the item's ability to satisfy future demand.

$$IP = OH + SR - BO$$

where:

IP = inventory position

OH = on-hand inventory

SR = scheduled receipts (open orders)

BO = units backordered

3. Decision rule:

Whenever a withdrawal brings IP down to the reorder point (R), place an order for Q (fixed) units.

Use **Application 13.3: Placing Orders with a Continuous Review System (AP 13.3)** to demonstrate how to place orders with the Q system.

4. Finding R when demand and lead time are certain

   a. Recall that safety stock inventory is inventory used to protect against uncertainties in demand, lead time, and supply. When there are no uncertainties, there is no need for safety stock, and so:

   R = Demand during lead time

5. Finding R when Demand is Uncertain

   a. When there are uncertainties in demand, there is a need for safety stock. We thus make R the largest "reasonable" demand possible during the lead time.

   R = Average demand during the lead time + Safety Stock

   b. The average demand during the lead time is determined by customers. As a management issue, the reorder point decision is really a matter of selecting the safety stock quantity. Safety stock depends on two factors:

   - Service level, or cycle-level policy — the desired probability of <u>not</u> running out in any one cycle

   - Amount of uncertainty in demand — If it is small, then little safety stock needed.

   c. Choosing an appropriate service level policy

   - Weigh benefits of holding safety stock against the cost of holding it.

   - Variability in demand during lead time measured by probability distributions. We consider two: normal and discrete.

6. Finding safety stock by using a normal probability distribution

   a. The concept: Average demand during lead time L is the mean of the distribution. The safety stock is the distance between the mean and R.

   Safety stock = $z\sigma_L$

   where:

   z = number of standard deviations from the mean to implement desired cycle service level

   σ_L = standard deviation of demand during lead time probability distribution

Use **Application 13.4: Selecting the Safety Stock and R (AP 13.4)** to demonstrate the calculations for safety stock and R in a Q system.

   b. Computing σ_L

   - Sometimes we have estimates of the standard deviation of demand over a time interval t that is different from the lead time L. Reasons are that demand and lead time are from different sources, and the demand rate is usually collected for a time period t, which is different than the lead time L.

   - A conversion from the standard deviation of demand during some other time period t to the standard deviation of demand during the lead time L can be made if we assume independence between the demands occurring in each time period t. Making that assumption, variances σ_t^2 can be added. To convert:

   $$\sigma_L = \sigma_t \sqrt{L}$$

   where:

   σ_t = known standard deviation over some time interval t

   σ_L = standard deviation of demand during lead time (which must be calculated in order to find *safety stock*)

   - Both L and t must be in same time units.

Use **Application 13.5: Continuous Review System: Putting It All Together (AP 13.5)** to demonstrate the complete specification of a Q system.

D. Periodic Review (P) System

1. Other names are: fixed interval reorder system or periodic reorder system.

2. Decision rule

   Review the item's inventory position IP every P time periods (not continuously). Place an order equal to $(T - IP)$, where T is the target inventory, that is, the desired IP just after placing a new order.

3. Here Q varies, and time between orders (TBO) is fixed. Same four assumptions, but again allow for uncertain demand.

Use **Application 13.6: Placing Orders with a Periodic Review System (AP 13.6)** to demonstrate how to place orders with a P system.

4. Finding P: two options

   a. Administratively convenient

   b. Approximation of EOQ. The order interval P is determined by substituting EOQ for Q in the formula for average time between orders:

   $$P = \frac{EOQ}{D}$$

   This result will have the units of "years" and may easily be converted to months, weeks, or days by the usual conversion factors.

5. Finding T

   a. The new order must be large enough to make the inventory position, IP, last beyond the next review, which is P periods from now, but also for one lead time (L) after the next review. IP must be enough to cover demand over a "protection interval" of $P + L$.

   b. $T = $ Average demand during protection interval $+$ Safety stock for protection interval

   where:

   $$\text{Safety stock} = z\sigma_{P+L}$$

   $$\sigma_{P+L} = \sigma_t\sqrt{P + L}$$

Use **Application 13.7: Periodic Review System: Putting It All Together (AP 13.7)** to show how to construct a P-system and compare it to a Q-system.

E. Comparative Advantages

- Advantages of one system are implicitly disadvantages of the other one.

1. Periodic review system

   a. Fixed replenishment intervals

      - Administration is convenient.

      - Standardized routes for transportation systems.

   b. Easier to combine orders to same supplier

      - May help with price break or paperwork.

- May reduce supplier's shipping costs.

   c. **Perpetual inventory system** not mandatory

     - Moot point if computerized

2. Continuous review system

   a. Can individualize the replenishment intervals

     - Tailoring Q to costs for each item

   b. Easier for quantity discounts or capacity limitations

     - Physical limits on container size or furnace capacities

   c. Less safety stock

F. Hybrid Systems

1. Optional replenishment system.

   - The optional replenishment system reviews the inventory position at fixed time intervals and, if the position has dropped to (or below) a predetermined level, places a variable-sized order to cover expected needs.

   - This ensures that a reasonably large order is placed.

2. Base stock system

   - A replenishment order is issued each time a withdrawal is made.

   - Order quantities vary to keep the inventory position at R at all times.

   - Minimizes cycle inventory, but increases ordering costs.

   a. Modifications for distribution system

   b. Modifications for kanban system

3. Special cases of the Q and P systems

   - Inventory position records are not kept.

   - Used with low value items that have steady demand.

   - Overstocking is common, but these are "C" items in the ABC classification. Little money is tied up by overstocking.

   a. Single-bin system

     - Essentially a P system

     - Target inventory T and current inventory position IP are established visually.

   b. Two-bin system

     - Essentially a Q system

     - When the first bin is empty, it triggers the replenishment order.

     - The second bin contains an amount equal to R, or the average demand during lead time + Safety stock.

G. Approaches for Inventory Record Accuracy

1. Focused responsibility: Assign responsibility for reporting inventory transactions to specific employees.

2. Closed stores: Secure inventory in locked storage areas.

3. Cycle counting: Use cycle counts to frequently check records against physical inventory.

4. Logic error checks: Catch errors in inventory transactions and investigate discrepancies.

   - Examples: Receipt when no scheduled receipt; receipt different than amount of scheduled receipt; disbursement larger than on-hand balance

   - If inventory records prove to be accurate over several years' time, the annual physical count can be avoided. The annual physical count is disruptive and costly, it adds no value to the products, and it often introduces as many errors into the records as it removes.

Supplement G: Special Inventory Models

Covers some realistic situations which relax one or more assumptions of the EOQ: noninstantaneous replenishment, quantity discounts, and one-period decisions.

A. Noninstantaneous Replenishment

1. Maximum cycle inventory

    - Item used or sold as they are completed, without waiting for a full lot to be completed

    - Usual case is where production rate, p, exceeds the demand rate, d, so there is a buildup of $(p-d)$ units during time when both production and demand occur.

    - Both p and d expressed in same time interval.

    - Buildup continues until Q units produced, so maximum cycle inventory is:

    $$I_{max} = \frac{Q}{p}(p-d) = Q\left(\frac{p-d}{p}\right)$$

    where:

    p = production rate

    d = demand rate

    Q = lot size

2. Total cost = Annual holding cost + Annual ordering or setup cost

    - Setting up total cost equation, where D is annual demand and d is daily demand:

    $$C = \frac{I_{max}}{2}(H) + \frac{D}{Q}(S) = \frac{Q}{2}\left(\frac{p-d}{p}\right)(H) + \frac{D}{Q}(S)$$

3. Economic Production Lot Size (ELS): optimal lot size

    - Derived by calculus

    - Second term is greater than 1, so ELS is larger than EOQ.

    $$\text{ELS} = \sqrt{\frac{2DS}{H}}\sqrt{\frac{p}{p-d}}$$

    - Use **Application G.1: Noninstantaneous Replenishment (AP G.1)** to show the difference between the ELS model and the EOQ model.

    a. What is the economic lot size?

    b. How long is the production run?

    $$\frac{Q}{p} = \frac{1555}{60} = 25.91, \quad \text{or 26 production days}$$

    c. What is the average quantity in inventory?

    $$\frac{I_{max}}{2} = \frac{Q}{2}\left(\frac{p-d}{p}\right) = \frac{1555}{2}\frac{(60-35)}{60} = 324 \text{ engines}$$

d. What is the total of the annual relevant costs?

$$C = \frac{Q}{2}\left(\frac{p-d}{p}\right)(H) + \frac{D}{Q}(S)$$

$$= \frac{1555}{2}\left(\frac{60-35}{60}\right)\$2000 + \frac{10,080}{1555}(\$100,000)$$

$$= \$647,917 + \$648,231$$

$$= \$1,296,148$$

B. Quantity Discounts

1. Quantity discount schedules

   • Quantity discounts are price incentives to purchase large quantities.

   • The item's price is no longer fixed, so a new approach that considers three costs is needed.

   a. Price break: minimum purchase quantity to get a certain discount rate

   b. Total annual cost

   $$C = \frac{Q}{2}(H) + \frac{D}{Q}(S) + PD$$

   • Unit holding cost H is usually expressed as a percentage of unit price. The lower P is, the lower H is.

   c. Discontinuities and **feasible** price-quantity combinations

   • There are cost curves for each price level.

   • The feasible total cost begins with the top curve, then drops down, curve by curve, at the price breaks.

   • EOQs do not necessarily produce the best lot size. [**Discuss why this may be the case.**]

2. Solution procedure

   a. **Step 1.** Beginning with **lowest** price, calculate the EOQ for each price level until a feasible EOQ is found. It is feasible if it lies in the range corresponding to its price. Each subsequent EOQ is smaller than the previous one, because P, and thus H, gets larger and because the larger H is in the denominator of the EOQ formula.

   b. **Step 2.** If the first feasible EOQ found is for the **lowest** price level, this quantity is the best lot size. Otherwise, calculate the total cost for the first feasible EOQ and for the larger price break quantity at each **lower** price level. The quantity with the lowest total cost is optimal.

Use **Application G.2: Quantity Discounts (AP G.2)** to demonstrate the steps for recognizing quantity discounts in making lot size decisions.

C. One-Period Decisions

1. Example

   • Retailers who handle seasonal goods. Can't sell at full markup after season, and can't rush through a seasonal order to cover high demand.

- Newsboy problem

2. Selecting the best purchase quantity

   a. List different demand levels and probabilities

   b. Develop a payoff table, where each new row represents a different order quantity and each column represents a different demand. The payoff is:

   $$\text{Payoff} = \begin{cases} pQ & \text{if } Q \le D \text{ (all units sold at full markup)} \\ pD - l(Q-D) & \text{if } Q > D \text{ (purchase quantity exceeds demand)} \end{cases}$$

   where:

   p = profit per unit sold during the season

   l = loss per unit disposed of after the season

   Q = purchase quantity

   D = demand level

   c. Calculate the **expected** payoff of each Q. For a specific Q, first multiply each payoff by its demand probability, and then add the products.

   d. Choose the order quantity Q with the highest expected payoff.

Use **Application G.3: One-Period Decisions (AP G.3)** to demonstrate the use of a pay-off table to make one-period inventory decisions.

3. One-time decisions in manufacturing

   a. When customized items are made (or purchased) for a single order, *and* scrap quantities are high.

   b. Conflicting goals of no inventory and satisfying order in one run.

Chapter 14: Aggregate Planning

A. Problem Context

1. Production plan (manufacturing)

   a. A statement of time-phased production rates, work-force levels, and inventory holdings based on customer requirements and capacity limitations

   b. Intermediate link between strategic goals and plans for individual items and components

2. Staffing plan (service firm)

   a. A statement of time-phased staff sizes and labor-related capacities, based on customer requirements and machine-limited capacities

   b. Intermediate link between annual plan and work-force schedule

3. Examples

   - Illustrate with Whirlpool, auto manufacturers, delivery services, or Intel.

   Conclusions:

   - Top management is involved.

   - Uneven demand (or supply), and how it is handled, has a big profit impact.

4. Aggregation

   - Useful because it is general; problems too big to solve all at once

   - Based on aggregate quantities for similar products and services

   - Three dimensions: products (or services), labor, and time. Aggregate along all three.

   a. Product families

   - Have similar markets and manufacturing processes

   - Share relevant units of measurement: units, barrels, tons, dollars, standard hours

     — In post office: hours or feet of mail

   b. Labor

   - Aggregation depends on degree of work-force flexibility

   - May be considered a single aggregate group if work force is flexible or entire work force produces every product family

   - Aggregated on a product family basis if

     — Different parts of the work force are used in the production of different product families

     — Different product families are produced in different plants at scattered locations

   c. Time

   - Updated monthly or quarterly

   - Planning periods are months or quarters, not weeks or days

5. Relationship to other plans

- Accompanied by
  - — Budgets
  - — Projected balance sheet
  - — Projected cash flow
- Brings together operations, finance, and marketing plans
- The business plan is analogous to the annual plan for nonprofit services.

a. Manufacturing

Business plan (upper)

- Provides the overall framework of demand projections, functional area inputs, and capital budget
- Guides and constrains the aggregate plan

Production plan (intermediate)

- Specifies corresponding product family
  - — Production rates
  - — Inventory levels
  - — Work-force levels
- Guides and constrains master production schedule

Master production schedule (lower)

- Specifies timing and size of production quantities for each product in the product family

b. Service sector

Annual plan (upper)

- Sets the organization's direction and objectives
- Provides the framework for the staffing plan and the work-force schedule

Staffing plan (intermediate)

- Presents the number and types of employees required to meet objectives stated in the annual or business plan

Work-force schedule (lower)

- Details specific work schedule for each employee category.

c. Information flows

- Not just top down (see arrows). Infeasibilities lead to upper-level changes.

B. Managerial Importance of Aggregate Plans

1. Managerial inputs to help synchronize the flow of materials, services, and information through the supply chain.

- Create a committee of functional-area representatives.
- Committee chaired by a general manager having overall responsibility
- Each representative furnishes information essential to development of the aggregate plan.

2. Typical objectives

- Involves cost trade-offs and consideration of qualitative factors.

- Objectives include:
  — Costs and profits
  — Customer service
  — Inventory investment
  — Changes in production rates
  — Changes in work-force levels
  — Utilization

C. Reactive Alternatives

Accept demand forecast as a given. React to fluctuations in demand.

1. Work-force adjustment

- Hiring and firing. Varies by industry, training requirements, labor pool

a. Example

b. Limitations **[Ask students to describe.]**
  — Labor supply
  — Economic conditions
  — Cost
  — Skill requirements
  — Union contract
  — Productivity

2. Work-force utilization (overtime and undertime)

- Overtime means that work longer than regular workday or workweek and paid extra (if nonexempt).

- Undertime means that don't work productively for the regular-time workday or workweek. Undertime can be paid or unpaid.

- Excessive overtime leads to declining quality and productivity. To retain skilled employees in a slack business period, undertime is preferable to layoffs.

a. Example

b. Limitations
  — Wage premium
  — Productivity
  — Legal limit

3. Vacation schedules

- Schedule vacations to decrease output when inventories are high, or when replacement labor is available.

a. Example

b. Limitations
  — Union contract
  — Availability of seasonal workers

4. Anticipation inventory

- Build inventory in slack periods to be used in peak demand periods and level demand on operations.

- This option is generally not available to services because services can not be stored.

a. Example

b. Limitations
 — Inventory holding cost
 — Shelf life
 — Financial constraints
 — Product customization
 — Services

5. Subcontractors (outsourcing)

- A common approach in aerospace and auto industries.

- Subcontractors provide extra capacity, but scheduling, quality, and labor relations issues are more difficult to control.

a. Example

b. Limitations
 — Cost
 — Subcontractor capability

6. Backlogs, backorders, and stockouts

- Backlog—an accumulation of customer orders promised for a future date. Backlogs are used when customers expect to wait some defined time period for delivery as a normal course of business.

- A backorder is an *order* that the customer expected to be filled immediately; the customer reluctantly asks for delivery as soon as possible.

- A stockout is an inability to satisfy demand for a *stock* item at the time it occurs, leading the customer to go elsewhere.

a. Example

b. Limitations: lost sales, competition, and competitive priorities

D. Aggressive Alternatives

Adjust the demand pattern to achieve efficiency and reduce costs.

These actions are typically specified in the marketing (sales) plan.

1. Complementary products

- Peak demand occurs at different times, leveling demand on production facilities.

a. Example

b. Limitations

  - Resource flexibility

  - Maintaining focus

2. Creative pricing

- Gives customers an incentive to shift demand from peak times.

a. Example

b. Limitation: squeezes the contribution margin

E. Planning Strategies

Combine alternatives in ways to find acceptable plan. For rest of today, assume limited to reactive alternatives.

1. Chase strategy:

   a. Matches demand during planning horizon by varying with the work-force level or the output rate. When uses the first method, varying the work-force level to match demand, it relies just on one reactive alternative (work-force variation) and just uses hiring and layoffs to match demand. Other ways to implement chase strategy can make use of

      - Overtime in peak periods

      - Undertime in slack periods

      - Vacations in slack periods

      - Subcontracting in peak periods

   b. Mix of alternatives to implement a chase strategy does not include building anticipation inventory.

   c. Advantages

      + Minimal inventory investment

   d. Disadvantages

      − Expense of adjusting output rates and/or work force

      − Alienation of the work force, loss of productivity, and lower quality

2. Level strategy:

   a. Maintains either (1) constant work-force level or (2) constant output rate during the planning horizon. When a level strategy uses the first method, maintaining a constant work-force level, it might consist of:

      - Not hiring or laying off workers (except at the beginning of the planning horizon),

      - Overtime in peak periods

      - Undertime in slack periods

      - Vacations in slack periods

      - Subcontracting in peak periods

      - Building anticipation inventories in slack periods

   b. When using only the first three alternatives, the smallest possible work-force level that minimizes undertime is the one that meets demand with the full allowance of overtime in the peak period. Of course, other constant work-force levels are also possible that uses less overtime.

   c. Advantages

      + Level output rates

      + Stable work force

   d. Disadvantages

      − Increased inventory investment

      − Increased undertime and overtime expense

3. Mixed strategy

A range of strategies that follow neither a pure level or pure chase strategy. The work force (or output rate) is not exactly level, and yet it does not exactly match demand on a period-by-period basis.

4. Fitting the situation

The best strategy must fit a company's environment and competitive priorities. Often the best strategy is easy to spot.

    a. Infant food producer

- Capital intensive and top priority on good work-force relations

- Limited shelf life and storage space

- Choice:
  Because capacity utilization is so important, a level strategy is appropriate. Without ability to use of anticipation inventory, the choice is to use overtime and variable shift length.

    b. Container plant (for beverage industry)

- Quick delivery times mandatory; bulky product at third stage but not at final stage

- Capital intensive

- Choice:
  Anticipation inventory helps to achieve fast delivery times and capital intensity argues for a level strategy. However, the bulky nature of the product rules out a level strategy for the third stage where product becomes so bulky, but not in first two stages.

F. The Planning Process

Update periodically, dynamically, with new information and opportunities.

1. Determining demand requirements

- For staffing plans in services, forecast demand based on historical usage, judgment, and existing backlogs.

- For manufacturing, future requirements for finished goods are derived from backlogs or forecasts for product families.

2. Identifying alternatives, constraints, and costs

Here, focus on constraints and costs, because already examined alternatives.

    a. Physical and policy constraints

- Training may limit rate of new hiring.

- Machine capacity may limit output.

- Storage space, investment costs, and customer service may limit inventory.

- Customer service may limit back orders.

- Quality, delivery uncertainty, or cost may limit subcontracting.

- Cost or diminishing return may limit overtime.

- Union contracts may limit undertime.

b. Types of Costs

Must Estimate Relevant Costs.

- Regular-time costs

  — wages

  — benefits

  — social security

  — vacations

- Overtime costs—typically 150 – 200% of regular-time rate

  — significant amounts of overtime cannot be sustained without incurring diminishing returns

- Hiring and layoff costs

  — severance

  — loss of productivity and morale

  — retraining

- Inventory holding costs

  — interest or opportunity costs of capital

  — storage, utilities

  — pilferage and obsolescence

  — insurance and taxes

- Backorder and stockout costs (More difficult to assess. Varies by situation.)

  — expediting

  — potential cost of lost sales

  — potential loss of goodwill

3. Preparing an acceptable Plan

An Iterative Process

- Develop a prospective plan (trial balloon)—specify monthly or quarterly

  — production rates

  — inventory and backlog accumulations

  — subcontracted production

  — work-force levels

  — overtime and undertime

- Check prospective plan against constraints and cost objectives. If not acceptable, return to step 1; otherwise proceed to step 3.

- Top managers of finance, marketing, and operations and the planning committee general manager authorize the plan.

- Implementation can begin.

4. Implementing and updating the plan

- Requires the commitment of top management (refer to step 3 in the iterative process above).

- Commitment begins with creation of a planning committee.

  - commitment expands with input from its members

  - recommend changes to better balance conflicting objectives

- A commitment to work toward achieving the plan, whether the manager totally agrees with it or not.

G. Aggregate Planning with Spreadsheets

Here we will use the spreadsheet approach of stating a strategy, developing a plan, identifying high cost elements for clues for improvement, and modifying until satisfied. Components of a spreadsheet are input values, derived values, and calculated costs. Here we examine the level and chase strategies.

1. Level strategy

   a. One possible level strategy, which uses a constant work force, is determined by using the maximum of overtime in the peak period. Undertime is used in slack periods. The work-force level doesn't change, except possibly for hiring or layoffs at the beginning of the first period.

   b. Use **Application 14.1: Level Strategy with Overtime and Undertime (AP 14.1)** for an in-class example of using spreadsheets to formulate a level strategy plan and determine its costs.

2. Chase strategy

   a. One possible chase strategy adjusts work-force levels as needed to achieve requirements without using overtime, undertime, or subcontractors. Only hiring and layoffs are used to match demand.

   b. Use **Application 14.2: Chase Strategy with Hiring and Layoffs (AP 14.2)** for an in-class exercise using spreadsheet logic to formulate a chase strategy plan, and to calculate its costs for the same example.

3. Mixed strategies

   a. Used alone, the chase and level strategies are unlikely to produce the best acceptable aggregate plan. Improvements likely by considering plans that are neither a pure level or pure chase strategy.

   b. Use **Application 14.3: Mixed Strategy (AP 14.3)** to finish the in-class exercise on Barberton Municipal Division, deviating from the chase plan.

H. Aggregate Planning with Mathematical Methods

1. Transportation method of production planning

   For a *given* demand forecast and a *given* capacity plan (no hires or layoffs) with constraints on regular time, overtime, and subcontractor production for each period of the planning horizon, and *assuming* production costs, holding costs, and backorder costs are linear, *and assuming* there are no costs for unused capacity, *then* the transportation method will identify the minimum cost production plan that satisfies demand.

   a. For given capacity plan, finds best amount of anticipation inventory, overtime, and subcontracting.

   - Each row represents an alternative source of production output and the associated time period. The constraint on each production source is the last number in each row.

- Each column represents a demand and the timing of that demand. The total demand for each period appears at the bottom of its column.

- The numbers in the small boxes are the *total of all* costs associated with producing one unit using the source represented by that row to satisfy a demand represented by that column.

- Demand may be satisfied from existing inventory, or regular time, overtime, or subcontracted production.

- Production might not occur during the same time period as demand. If produced before demand, a holding cost is added. If backorders are allowed and occur, a backorder cost is added.

- Handling backorders

b. Notation

h = holding cost per unit per period
r = regular-time cost per unit
c = overtime cost per unit
s = subcontracting cost per unit
u = undertime cost per unit
b = backorder cost per unit
U = total unused capacity
I_0 = beginning inventory
I_4 = desired inventory at end
R_t = regular-time capacity in period t
O_t = overtime capacity in period t
S_t = subcontracting capacity in period t
D_t = forecasted demand in period t

c. Solution Method

- Select a work-force adjustment plan. Identify the capacity constraints, and on-hand inventory currently available. Input these values for the last column of the transportation tableau.

- Input cost parameters for different cells.

- Forecast demand for future periods, and input for tableau's last row. Last period's requirement should be increased to account for desired ending inventory. Unused capacity cell in last row.

- Solve with a computer routine, and interpret results. A check: The sum of entries in row must equal total capacity, and the sum of entries in a column must equal the column's requirements.

- Return to first step and try other staffing plans.

d. Use **Application 14.4: Transportation Method of Production Planning (AP 14.4)** to formulate the tableau, calculate the costs of a solution, and interpret the results.

e. Additional capacity plans

- Tableau method finds the optimal solution *for a given capacity plan.*

- Adjusting the work-force level by hires and layoffs changes the capacity plan, resulting in better or worse solutions.

f. Incorporating backorders

- If appropriate penalty costs for backorders can be determined, they are placed in the boxes in the lower left area of the tableau. In that region, production occurs *after* demand... a backorder situation. The same solution method applies, but now alternatives involving backorders are also considered in finding the optimal solution.

2. Linear programming for production planning

- The transportation method is a specialized form of linear programming.

- Linear programming models can determine optimal

  - Hires and layoffs (not possible with transportation method)

  - Inventory levels

  - Back orders

  - Subcontractor quantities

  - Production quantities

  - Overtime

- Major drawbacks

  - All variables must be linear.

  - Optimal values may be fractional. (For example, the optimal solution may require firing part of a person.)

  [Use Application H.10: Production Planning (AP H.10) on Bull Grin if you want students to learn this formulation.]

3. Managerial considerations

- Mathematical techniques are useful aids to the planning process.

- Planning process is dynamic and complicated by conflicting objectives.

- Managers—not techniques—make the decisions.

Supplement H: Linear Programming

A technique for allocating scarce resources among competing demands. Resources may be time, money or materials. Seeks best allocation solution.

A. Basic concepts

1. Linear programming is an optimization process.

   - A single *objective function* states mathematically what is being maximized or minimized.
   - *Decision variables* represent choices that the decision maker can control. Solving the problem yields their optimal values. Assume continuous variables.
   - *Constraints* are limitations that restrict the permissible choices for the decision variables. Can be ≤, =, or ≥ constraints.
   - The *feasible region* includes all of the combinations of the decision variables which satisfy the given constraints. Usually an infinite number of possible solutions.
   - A *parameter* is a value that the decision maker cannot control and that does not change when the solution is implemented. Assumed to be known with certainty.
   - The objective function and constraints are assumed to be *linear*, that is there can be no products or powers of decision variables. Implies proportionality and additivity.
   - We assume the model to exhibit nonnegativity, the decision variable must be positive or zero.

2. Formulating a problem

   - Linear programming applications begin with the formulation of a model of the problem using the general characteristics above.

   a. Step 1. Define the decision variables.

      - What must be decided?
      - Define each decision variable specifically, remembering that the definitions used in the objective function must be equally useful in the constraints.

   b. Step 2. Write out the objective function.

      - What is to be maximized or minimized?
      - Write out an objective function to make what is being optimized a linear function of the decision variables.

   c. Step 3. Write out the constraints.

      - What limits the values of the decision variables?
      - Identify the constraints and the parameters for each decision variable in them. To be formally correct, also write out the nonnegativity constraints.

   d. Consistency check: Make sure the same measure is being used on both sides of each constraint and in the objective function.

3. Use **Application H.1: Problem Formulation for Crandon Manufacturing (AP H.1)** as an in-class exercise for problem formulation.

B. Graphic Analysis

1. Purpose: to gain insight into the meaning of linear computer programming output; not a practical technique for three or more decision variables

2. Steps

    a. Plot constraints, disregarding the inequality portion.

        - Find *axis intercepts*. Set one variable equal to zero and solve the constraint equation for the second variable. Repeat to get both intercepts.

        - Once both of the *axis intercepts* are found, draw a line connecting the two points to get the constraint equation.

    b. Identify the feasibility region.

        - The feasible region is the area on the graph that contains the solutions which satisfy all of the constraint equations.

        - Locate the area that satisfies each of the constraints.

            1. For the = constraint, only the points on the line are feasible solutions.

            2. For the ≤ constraint, the points on the line and the points below and/or to the left are feasible solutions.

            3. For the ≥ constraint, the points on the line and the points above and/or to the right are feasible solutions.

        - Locate the area that satisfies all of the constraints.

        - Use the first part of **Application H.2: Graphical Solution for Crandon Manufacturing (AP H.2)** as an in-class exercise for drawing constraints and identifying the feasible region.

    c. Plot an objective function line.

        - Limit search for solution to the corner points.

        - A corner point lies at the intersection of two (or possibly more) constraint lines on the boundary of the feasible region.

        - Interior points need not be considered because at least one corner point is better than any interior point.

        - Other points on the boundary of the feasible region may be ignored for the same reason.

        - Plot an iso-profit line by setting the objective function equal to some arbitrary value and graphing the function.

        - Any point on the iso-profit line will the same objective value.

    d. Find the visual solution, limiting your search to corner points.

        - For maximization problems, the best solution is either on or to the right of the iso-profit line and farthest from the origin.

        - For minimization problems, the best solution is either on or to the left of the iso-profit line closest to the origin.

        - Use the next part of **Application H.2: Graphical Solution for Crandon Manufacturing (AP H.2)** as an in-class exercise for drawing objective function line.

    e. Find the algebraic solution.

        - Used when optimal corner point is found on graph.

- Find coordinates of optimal solution by algebraically solving the constraint equations.

- Find the value of the objective function by inserting coordinate values into equation.

- Use the next part of **Application H.2: Graphical Solution for Crandon Manufacturing (AP H.2)** as an in-class exercise for finding the algebraic solution.

f. Slack and Surplus Variables

- A binding constraint is a resource which is completely exhausted when the optimal solution is used. It limits the ability to improve the objective function.

- Insert the optimal solution into a constraint equation and solve it. If the number on the left-hand side and the number on the right-hand side are equal, then the constraint is binding.

- Relaxing a constraint means increasing the right-hand side for a $\leq$ constraint and decreasing the right-hand side for a $\geq$ constraint. Relaxing a binding constraint means a better solution is possible. No improvement in the objective function is possible if the constraint is not binding.

- Slack is the value needed to be added to the left-hand side of a $\leq$ constraint to make both sides equal. Surplus is the amount to subtract from the left hand side of a $\geq$ constraint to make both sides equal.

- Use the last part of **Application H.2: Graphical Solution for Crandon Manufacturing (AP H.2)** as an in-class exercise for finding the slack variables in each constraint.

C. Sensitivity Analysis

- Parameters in the objective function and constraints are often not known with high certainty.

- Usually parameters are just estimates which don't reflect uncertainties such as absenteeism or personal transfers.

- Sensitivity analysis determines how much the optimal values of the decision variables and the objective function value would be affected if certain parameters had different values. It is better than the brute-force method of changing one or more parameter values and resolving the entire problem. Sensitivity information is routinely available through software packages.

1. Objective function coefficients
   a. Write the objective function in the form of $x_2 = -\dfrac{c_1 x_1}{c_2} + \dfrac{Z}{c_2}$, where c_1 and c_2 are the objective function coefficients. If c_1 increases, slope becomes more negative (steeper) and rotates clockwise.

   b. Range of Optimality

   - If the slope of the objective function is greater than the slope of one constraint equation but less than the slope of the other constraint equation, then the previously found optimal point remains the best solution.

   - The range of c_1, which will continue to produce the same optimal solution, can be found by solving the following equation for c_1: $m_1 \leq -\dfrac{c_1}{c_2} \leq m_2$ where m_1 and m_2 are the slopes for the two constraint equations in terms of $\dfrac{c_1}{c_2}$.

   - Use **Application H.3: Range of Optimality for Crandon Manufacturing (AP H.3)** as an in-class exercise for finding the range of optimality for the c_1 coefficient in the Crandon problem.

c. Coefficient sensitivity

- Measures how much the objective function coefficient of a decision variable, currently in solution as 0, must improve (increase for maximization or decrease for minimization) before the optimal solution changes and the decision variable becomes some positive number.

- The coefficient sensitivity for c_1 can be found in the following manner:

    Step 1.
    — Identify direction of rotation (clockwise or counterclockwise) of iso-profit (or iso-cost) line that improves c_1.

    — Rotate iso-profit(or iso-cost) line in this direction until it reaches a new optimal corner point that makes x_1 greater than 0. (See orange line. New point is C.)

    Step 2.
    — Determine which binding constraint has the same slope as the rotated iso-profit (or iso-cost) line at this new point.

    — Solve for the value of c_1 that makes the objective function slope equal to the slope of this binding constraint.

    Step 3.
    — Set the coefficient sensitivity equal to the difference between this value and the current value of c_1.

2. Right-hand-side parameters

    a. Shadow prices

    - Indicates the amount by which the objective function value changes given a unit increase in the RHS value of the constraint.

    - The shadow price can be found by increasing the RHS value by one and solving the constraint equations for the new optimal point. The shadow price is the difference between the old optimal objective function value (using the old optimal point) and the new objective function value (using the new optimal point).

    b. Use **Application H.4: Shadow Prices for Crandon Manufacturing (AP H.4)** as an in-class exercise for finding the shadow price for one of the Crandon Manufacturing constraints.

    c Range of feasibility

    - The interval over which the right-hand-side parameter can vary while its shadow price remains valid.

    - If right-hand side is increased beyond the upper limit or reduced beyond the lower limit, at least one other constraint becomes binding, which changes the rate of change of Z.

    - These two limits are established when, as the constraint line is tightened or relaxed, a new corner point on the feasible region is reached that makes a different constraint binding.

D. Computer Solution

1. Simplex method

    - The simplex method is an iterative algebraic procedure.

    - Graphic analysis gives insight into the logic of the simplex method.

    - The initial feasible solution of the simplex method usually starts out at an initial corner point. Each subsequent iteration results in an improved intermediate solution which we have represented graphically by the intersection of two linear constraints. In general, a corner point has variables greater than 0, where m is the number of constraints.

- When no further improvement is possible, the optimal solutions have been found and the algorithm stops.

2. Computer Output

- Most real-world linear programming problems are solved on a computer.

- Contained within the final (optimal) tableau are the shadow price, feasibility range, coefficient sensitivity and other information useful to the decision analyst.

- Use the last transparency for **Application H.4: Shadow Prices for Crandon Manufacturing (AP H.4)** for the display of the output for the Crandon Manufacturing problem, or if the classroom is equipped, demonstrate with the OM5 Software.

E. Other Applications

1. Examples in operations management

- Aggregate planning

- Distribution

- Inventory

- Location

- Process management

- Scheduling

2. Use the following six applications to further teach the problem formulation process. You might assign each one to a different team and have the teams write down their formulations on transparencies and present them to the class.

- **Application H.5: Product mix problem (AP H.5)**

- **Application H.6: Process design (AP H.6)**

- **Application H.7:Blending Problem (AP H.7)**

- **Application H.8: Portfolio selection (AP H.8)**

- **Application H.9: Shift scheduling (AP H.9)**

- **Application H.10: Production planning (AP H.10)**

Chapter 15: Material Requirements Planning

A. Dependent Demand

1. Independent versus dependent demands

2. Definitions [**Explain the example in Fig. 15.1 on page 676 of the text.**]
   a. Independent demands
   b. Dependent demands
   c. Parents and components

B. Benefits of MRP

1. Reduction of forecast errors [**Mention Plasco, Inc. in MP 15.1.**]

2. Information for planning capacities and estimating financial requirements

3. Automatic updates of material replenishment changes

C. Inputs to Material Requirements Planning

1. Bill of materials
   - Usage quantity
   - End item
   - Intermediate item
   - Subassembly
   - Purchased item
   - Part commonality

2. Master production schedule
   a. Definition
      - The MPS is a detailed plan that states how many end items will be produced within specified periods of time.
   b. Purposes
      - Set due dates and lot sizes for production orders of end items.
      - Provide a more accurate picture of the resources and materials needed to support the production plan.
   c. Typical constraints
      - Sum of MPS quantities equals production plan
      - Efficient allocation, recognizing setup costs and inventory holding costs
      - Capacity limitations

3. Inventory record

   a. Top of record

     • Part identification

     • Time buckets

   b. Deriving gross requirements (i.e., the dependent demand from parents at MPS level and lower levels)

   c. Scheduled receipts (or "open orders") and current on-hand inventory

     • Possible stages **[ordered by a buyer, processed by a supplier, transported to the buyer, or being inspected by the buyer]**

     • Keeping up-to-date information

   d. Projected on-hand inventory:

$$\begin{array}{c}\text{Projected on-hand} \\ \text{inventory balance} \\ \text{at end of period } t\end{array} = \begin{array}{c}\text{Inventory on} \\ \text{hand at end of} \\ \text{period } t\text{–}1\end{array} + \begin{array}{c}\text{Scheduled or} \\ \text{planned} \\ \text{receipts due} \\ \text{in period } t\end{array} - \begin{array}{c}\text{Gross} \\ \text{requirements} \\ \text{in period } t\end{array}$$

   e. Planned receipts

     • A new order—not yet released—for an item. It keeps projected on-hand balance from dropping below the desired safety stock level.

     • Planned receipts can change.

   f. Planned order release

     • Indicates when a planned order will be released — not received

     • Uses midpoint convention and offsetting for the lead time

     • Derives gross requirements for its components from this planned order release row; additional time offsets are needed

Use **Application 15.1: MRP Record with FOQ Rule (AP 15.1)** to show the logic of the MRP record.

D. Planning Factors

1. Planning lead time

   a. Time elements of planning lead times

   b. Implications of inaccurate planning lead times

2. Lot-sizing rules

   a. Static lot-sizing rules

     • Maintain same order quantity each time an order is issued

     • **Fixed order quantity (FOQ) rule**

     • Quantity discounts, truckload capacity, minimum purchase quantity, or *EOQ*

   b. Dynamic lot-sizing rules

     • Each order large enough to prevent shortages (falling below the desired safety stock) — but no larger—over a specified number of weeks

- **Periodic order quantity (POQ) rule:** Restores safety stock and exactly covers P weeks' worth of gross requirements

- **Lot for lot (L4L) rule:** Special case of POQ, where $P = 1$. Minimizes inventory.

c. Comparison of rules

- Average projected on-hand inventory **[L4L is best but requires more orders.]**

- Remnants: the good and the bad **[FOQ has remnants, or excess inventory, but the remnants can be used for unexpected requirements.]**

Use **Application 15.2: MRP Record with POQ Rule (AP 15.2)** and **Application 15.3: MRP Record with L4L Rule (AP 15.3)** to show the differences between the POQ and L4L rules.

3. Safety stock

a. More complex for dependent-demand items

b. Usual policy **[Use for end items and purchased items.]**

E. Outputs from MRP

1. MRP explosion

a. Explosion process **[This material is critical to understanding MRP. Often students think they understand but do not.]**

Gross requirements modified by usage quantities are derived from

- MPS for immediate parents that are end items

- Planned order releases for parents below MPS level

- Requirements not originating in the MPS

b. Explosion generates requirements for all subassemblies, components, and raw materials.

2. Action notices

a. Material requirements plan: the need for a management-by-exception approach

b. A computer-generated memo indicating the need to release a new order or adjust the due date of a scheduled receipt

- **Release new orders:** if a planned order release is in the first week's entry (i.e., the " action bucket")

- **Adjusting the due dates of scheduled receipts:**

  — **Arriving too early:** when subtracting the scheduled receipt from projected on-hand inventory does not reduce inventory below desired safety stock.

  — **Arriving too late:** when projected on-hand balance for week **prior** to its arrival is not enough.

c. Making decisions

- Planner decides, not computer

- Inventory transactions are inputs to the MRP system.

3. Capacity reports

a. Capacity requirements planning (CRP): projects time-phased labor requirements for critical work stations; uses scheduled receipts and planned order releases for all produced items

- Planned hours
- Actual hours

b. Finite capacity scheduling—recognizing constraints

c. Input–output control: compares planned input with actual input and planned output with actual output

- Insufficient inputs
- Insufficient capacity

Use **Application 15.4: Material Requirements Planning for Single Product Case (AP 15.4)** to demonstrate the explosion process using a simple problem at the level of difficulty of the one we used in the text.

Use **Application 15.5: Material Requirements Planning for Multiple Product Case (AP 15.5)** for a rich example of the explosion process with two end items.

F. Resource Planning

1. Manufacturing resource planning (MRP II)

a. Ties MRP to the firm's financial system

b. The basis of the information is the master production plan, which (after exploded by MRP) can be used to project capacity problems, dollar value of shipments, product costs, overhead allocations, inventories, backlogs, profits and cash flows.

c. MRP II can be used by managers in manufacturing, purchasing, marketing, finance, accounting, and engineering.

2. Resource planning for services

a. The basics of MRP can be used by service providers.

b. The concept of a BOM changes to a bill of resources (BOR), which identifies the type of resource and the quantity needed for a given service that is provided.

c. The BOR can be complex. **[Discuss the BOR for a hospital as provided in the text.]**

3. Enterprise resource planning (ERP)

a. ERP goes beyond MRP II to encompass the customers and suppliers of a firm.

b. ERP has capabilities for quality management, field service, maintenance management, distribution, marketing, and supplier management.

c. The focus is on the external supply chain, allowing firms to operate as if their suppliers were actually a part of their own processes.

d. ERP allows customers access to the firm's production schedules to see when a particular order is expected to be completed. **[Mention Landa, Inc. in MP 15.2]**

e. ERP is a complex system still in its infancy stage of implementation.

G. Implementation Issues

1. Prerequisites

    a. Management support

    b. Computer support

    c. Accurate and realistic inputs

    - MPS

    - BOMs

    - Inventory records

2. Favorable environments

    a. Many BOM levels

    b. Large lot sizes

    c. Less volatility

    d. Manufacturing's positioning strategy (between line flow and flexible flow)

Supplement I: Master Production Scheduling

A. Master Production Scheduling Process

- The MPS is a detailed plan that states how many end items will be produced within specified periods of time.

1. Purposes

   - sets due dates and lot sizes for production orders of end items
   - provides a more accurate picture of the resources and materials needed to support the production plan

2. Process

   a. Create a prospective MPS.

   b. Test to see whether it meets the schedule within the allowable resources.

   c. If it does not, the MPS or the production plan must be revised.

   d. If agreeable, the MPS is authorized and used as an input to the MRP system.

B. Functional Interfaces

1. Marketing—impact of product mix changes on resource needs and customer schedules

2. Finance—estimate cash flows and the impact of production schedules on budgets

3. Manufacturing—estimate capacity requirements and the effects of order quantity changes on the schedules of other orders

C. Developing a Prospective MPS

- *Step* 1: Calculate projected on-hand inventory:

$$\begin{array}{c}\text{Projected on-hand} \\ \text{inventory at end of} \\ \text{this period}\end{array} = \begin{array}{c}\text{On hand} \\ \text{inventory} \\ \text{last period}\end{array} + \begin{array}{c}\text{MPS quantity} \\ \text{due this} \\ \text{period}\end{array} - \begin{array}{c}\text{Projected} \\ \text{requirements} \\ \text{this period}\end{array}$$

- *Step* 2: Determine the timing and size of MPS quantities. Time the orders so that you maintain a non-negative on-hand inventory, or at least the level of safety stock if one is specified.

D. Available-To-Promise Quantities

1. *Concept*: ATP shows amount of MPS that can still be used to meet new booking requests, considering **current** on-hand inventory, the MPS scheduled to arrive this period, and the customer orders booked until the next MPS arrival.

   a. *First period*: Current on-hand inventory plus the MPS scheduled to arrive in the first period (if any), minus the cumulative booked orders up to the period when the next MPS quantity arrives.

   b. *Subsequent periods*: Only for periods when MPS quantity arrives. Same calculation, except don't include projected on-hand inventory.

Use **Application I.1: Developing a Master Production Schedule (API.1)** to demonstrate the construction of an MPS and the use of the ATP quantities.

E. Freezing the MPS

1. Demand time fence

2. Planning time fence

3. Examples **[Mention Ethan Allen, Black & Decker.]**

Chapter 16: Just-In-Time Systems

A. Characteristics of Just-In-Time Systems

[Relate this discussion to topics previously covered in the course.]

1. Pull method of material flow

   a. What is a **push** system?

   b. How does the **pull** method differ from the push method?

   c. Examples **[Relate to MRP or ROP; bring in fast food production.]**

2. Consistently high quality

3. Small lot sizes

4. Uniform workstation loads **[This point usually requires a little more time.]**

   a. Assembly schedule must generate stable workload. Assemble same type and number of units each day.

   b. Establish production cycle and number of each product in cycle: mixed-model assembly.

5. Standardization of components and work methods: part commonality

6. Close supplier ties **[Mention Saturn, Harley-Davidson, NUMMI.]**

7. Flexible work force

8. Line flow strategy

9. Automated production

10. Preventive maintenance

B. Continuous Improvement With Just-In-Time Systems

1. Philosophy **[Relate to topics covered earlier in the course.]**

   a. Water level represents inventory level (or resource such as labor hours in a service setting).

   b. Rocks represent problems.

2. Inventory reduction as a catalyst in manufacturing **[Use T15.5 as an example.]**

3. Workforce reduction as a catalyst in services **[The water level is workforce capacity.]**

C. The Kanban System

1. Coordination

   a. Using process comes to the producing process to withdraw parts or materials in the quantity needed at the time needed.

   b. Producing process produces only the exact quantity withdrawn by the using process.

2. Kanban

    a. A Japanese word for "card" or "visible record"

    b. Information included: item, quantity, and storage location

3. General operating rules **[Discuss the operation of a single-card system. Use MP 16.1 for an example.]**

    a. Use one and only one card for each container.

    b. Assembly line must go to fabrication cell to get materials needed.

    c. Containers can be moved only with a card.

    d. Containers must have exact quantity of good parts.

    e. Defective parts should never be passed along to the using process.

    f. Total production should not exceed the quantity specified on the card.

4. Determining the number of containers

    a. Formula

$$k = \frac{\text{Average demand during lead time plus safety stock}}{\text{Number of units per container}}$$

$$= \frac{d(\overline{w} + \overline{p})(1 + \alpha)}{c}$$

where

    k = number of containers for a part

    d = expected daily demand for the part, in units

    $\overline{w}$ = average waiting and materials handling time per container

    $\overline{p}$ = average processing time per container

    c = quantity in a standard container

    α = efficiency policy variable

Use **Application 16.1: Determining the Number of Containers (AP 16.1)** to demonstrate the model.

5. Other kanban signals **[Discuss examples or situations where each could be used.]**

    a. Container system

    b. Containerless system

D. JIT II

1. In-plant representative

2. Benefits to the customer

3. Benefits to the supplier

E. Just-In-Time Systems in Services

1. Likely environments

2. JIT concepts useful for service providers
   - Consistently high quality
   - Uniform facility loads
   - Standardized work methods
   - Close supplier ties
   - Flexible work force
   - Automation
   - Preventive maintenance
   - Pull method
   - Line flow strategy

F. Strategic Implications of Just-In-Time Systems

1. Competitive priorities

2. Flow strategy

3. Operational benefits
   - Space
   - Inventory
   - Lead times
   - Productivity
   - Equipment utilization
   - Paperwork
   - Valid priorities
   - Workforce participation
   - Quality

G. Implementation Issues

1. Organizational considerations
   a. Human costs
   b. Cooperation and trust
   c. Reward systems and labor classifications **[Use GM in MP 16.2 as an example.]**

2. Process considerations

3. Inventory and scheduling

   a. MPS stability

   b. Setups

   c. Purchasing and logistics

H. Choosing a Production and Inventory Management System

1. ROP versus MRP

2. MRP versus JIT

I. Shaping the Manufacturing Environment

[Pose the following questions and bring out the points on pages 754–755 in the text.]

1. Does any system fit all environments?

2. What are the keys for improved manufacturing performance?

Chapter 17: Scheduling

[Define the term "scheduling."]

A. Scheduling in Manufacturing

1. Operations schedules

    a. Assign people to jobs or jobs to machines—a complex problem

    b. Focus on how best to use a given capacity

    c. Deal primarily with technical constraints related directly to production

    d. Job shop vs. flow shop

2. Gantt charts

    a. Progress chart

    b. Machine chart

3. Performance measures

    a. Job flow time **[Relate to job or customer "cycle" time.]**

    b. Makespan

    c. Past due

    d. Work-in-process inventory **[Mention that it may not always be best to minimize this measure.]**

    e. Total inventory **[This measure penalizes early completion of orders.]**

    f. Utilization **[Mention that maximizing this criterion may not be best in all cases.]**

4. Job shop dispatching

    a. The decision about which job to process next (or let the station remain idle) is made when the work station is available for further processing. **[Mention that there are other ways to develop a schedule.]**

    b. Priority sequencing rules

    - Critical ratio (CR)

    - Slack per remaining operation (S/RO)

    - Earliest due date (EDD)

    - First come, first served (FCFS)

    - Shortest processing time (SPT)

5. Sequencing operations for one machine

    a. Single-dimension rules: EDD, FCFS, SPT

Use **Application 17.1: Scheduling at One Operation Using SPT (AP 17.1)** to demonstrate the use of the shortest processing time rule.

b. Comparison of SPT to EDD **[Consider comparing the SPT schedule to the EDD schedule for the data in the application.]**

- SPT has lower work-in-process and lower average flow times.

- EDD has lower average hours past due and lower maximum hours past due.

c. Multiple-dimension rules

Use **Application 17.2: Scheduling at One Operation Using CR and S/RO (AP 17.2)** to demonstrate the critical and slack per remaining operation rule.

6. Multiple-workstation scheduling **[Discuss how the single-machine priority rules can be used to develop a schedule for many machines or operations.]**

7. Two-station flow shop: Johnson's rule

Step 1: Scan the process times at each work station and find the shortest process time among those not yet scheduled. Arbitrarily break ties.

Step 2: If the shortest process time is on work station 1, schedule the corresponding job as early as possible. If the shortest process time is on work station 2, schedule the corresponding job as late as possible.

Step 3: Eliminate the last job scheduled from further consideration. Repeat steps 1 and 2.

Use **Application 17.3: Sequencing Jobs at a Two-Station Flow Shop Using Johnson's Rule (AP 17.3)** to show how to sequence five jobs so as to minimize the makespan.

8. Labor-limited environments

9. Theory of constraints

a. The theory of constraints (TOC), or the drum-buffer-rope method, is an approach to management that focuses on whatever impedes progress towards the goal of maximizing the flow of total value added funds (that is, sales less discounts and variable costs).

b. Bottlenecks are scheduled to maximize their throughput of products or services while adhering to promised completion dates.

c. There are five steps to TOC:

- Identify the system bottlenecks

- Exploit the bottlenecks

- Subordinate all other decisions to step 2

- Elevate the bottlenecks—add capacity if necessary

- Don't let inertia set in

d. Examples **[Mention the use of TOC at Dixie Iron Works in MP 17.1]**

B. Scheduling in Services

[The video segment "Scheduling Services at Air New Zealand" is a good introduction here.]

1. Scheduling customer demands

    a. Appointments

    b. Reservations

    c. Backlogs

2. Scheduling the work force

    - Translates the staffing plan into specific schedules of work for each employee

    - Must satisfy work-force requirements

    - Must reallocate employees if requirements change

    a. Constraints

        - Technical constraints

        - Legal and behavioral considerations

        - Schedule types fixed and rotating

    b. Developing a work-force schedule for two consecutive days off

        Step 1: Find the unique pair of days off that exclude the maximum daily requirements and have the lowest total for the two days. If all pairs include the maximum daily requirement, select the pair with the lowest total requirements.

        Step 2: Break ties consistent with provisions in the labor contract.

        Step 3: Assign the employee the selected pair of days off. Reduce the net requirements for the days the employee will work.

        Step 4: Repeat steps 1–3 until all requirements have been satisfied or all employees have been scheduled.

Use **Application 17.4: Developing a Work-Force Schedule (AP 17.4)** to demonstrate the heuristic.

Chapter 18: Managing Projects

A. Project Management

- A project is an interrelated set of activities that has definite starting and ending points and that results in a unique product or service.

1. Elements of project management

    a. Project manager—has the responsibility to integrate the efforts of people from various functional areas to achieve specified project goals

    b. Project team—a group of people that often represent different functional areas or organizations

    c. Project management system—consists of an organizational structure (functional or matrix) and an information system (network planning system)

2. Appropriate use of the project management approach: six situations

    a. The magnitude of the effort requires substantially more resources than are available in a particular functional area or department.

    b. The need for coordination among functional areas or other organizations is overwhelming.

    c. There is unfamiliarity with respect to certain tasks in the project and employees with appropriate expertise need to be brought together to carry out the project.

    d. The environment is rapidly changing and the firm needs to be flexible to adapt to changing needs.

    e. Functional areas working independently focus on their own situations rather than the organization's goals.

    f. Project success is crucial to the organization.

B. Network Planning Methods

- PERT and CPM are in common use today.
- Network planning has benefits that include (i) forcing managers to organize data and express critical relationships; (ii) managers can estimate the completion time of a project; (iii) reports highlight the activities that are crucial to the completion of the project on time; and (iv) managers can analyze the time/cost implications of resource trade-offs.

1. Describe the project.

    a. Activities

    b. Immediate predecessors

2. Diagram the network.

    a. Nodes (circles) and arcs (arrows)

    b. Activity-on-arc (AOA) network

    - Arcs are activities and nodes are events.

- Event: any point at which one or more activities are to be completed and one or more other activities are to begin

- An event consumes neither time nor resources.

- Event-oriented

c. Activity-on-node (AON) network

- Nodes are activities and arcs show precedence relationships.

- Activity-oriented

Use **Application 18.1: Diagramming the Network (AP 18.1)** to demonstrate network modeling.

3. Estimating time of completion

a. Probabilistic (uncertain)

b. Deterministic (certain)

c. The critical path: sequence of activities between a project's start and finish that takes the longest time to complete

- Use **Application 18.2: Estimating the Time of Completion (AP 18.2)** to show how to find the critical path of the hospital project.

d. Earliest start and earliest finish times

- Earliest finish time (EF)

$$EF = ES + t$$

- Earliest start time (ES)

ES = Max **[EF times of all immediately preceding activities]**

- Use **Application 18.3: Earliest Start and Earliest Finish Times (AP 18.3)** to demonstrate the technique for determining ES and EF for the hospital project.

e. Latest start and latest finish times

- Latest start time (LS)

$$LS = LF - t$$

- Latest finish time (LF)

LF = Min [LS times for all immediately following activities]

- Use **Application 18.4: Latest Start and Latest Finish Times (AP 18.4)** to demonstrate the technique for determining LS and LF for the hospital project.

f. Activity slack: maximum time an activity can be delayed without delaying the entire project

g. Critical path: sequence of activities with zero slack

- Use **Application 18.5: Activity Slacks (AP 18.5)** to show the value of computing activity slacks in a project.

4. Monitoring project progress

C. Probabilistic Time Estimates

1. Calculating time statistics

   a. **Optimistic time (a):** shortest time an activity can be completed

   b. **Most likely time (m):** best estimate of average time

   c. **Pessimistic time (b):** longest time an activity can take

   d. **Activity's mean time (t_e)** and **variance (σ^2)** with beta distribution

   $$t_e = \frac{a + 4m + b}{6}$$

   $$\sigma^2 = \left(\frac{b - a}{6}\right)^2$$

   e. Use **Application 18.6: Calculating Time Statistics (AP 18.6)** to demonstrate the calculation of the mean and variance for each activity in the hospital project.

2. Analyzing probabilities

   a. Using the z-transformation formula:

   $$Z = \frac{T - T_E}{\sqrt{\sigma^2}}$$

   where:

   T = due date of project

   T_E = earliest expected completion date

   σ^2 = sum of variances on the critical path

   b. Use **Application 18.7: Analyzing Probabilities (AP 18.7)** to determine the probability of completing the hospital project in 75 weeks.

D. Cost Considerations

1. Analyzing costs

   a. Direct costs and times

   Normal time (NT)

   Normal cost (NC)

   Crash time (CT)

   Crash cost (CC)

   b. Cost assumptions

   $$\text{Crash cost per week} = \frac{CC - NC}{NT - CT}$$

c. Indirect and penalty costs

d. Minimum-cost schedule **[As this is a complicated analysis, we do not suggest making this an application to be completed by the students in class. It is usually best to walk them through the procedure.]**

Start with normal time schedule and crash least-expensive activities along the critical path. Continue until (a) it cannot be further crashed, (b) another path becomes critical, or (c) added crash costs will be less than savings in indirect and penalty costs. When there is more than one path, it may be necessary to crash several activities simultaneously.

E. Computerized Project Scheduling and Control

1. Gantt charts and network diagrams

2. Project status reports

3. Tracking reports

Applications & Transparency Masters Correlative Table of Contents

Chapter / Supplement	Application & Title	Corresponding Transparencies	Comments
1	AP 1.1: Productivity Calculations	TM 1.1a-1.1b	source is past Chrysler financial statement
2	NONE		
A	AP A.1: Break-Even Analysis for Evaluating Products or Services	TM A.1a-A.1f	
	AP A.2: Break-Even Analysis for Evaluating Processes	TM A.2a-A.2b	
	AP A.3: Preference Matrix	TM A.3a-A.3b	
	AP A.4: Decision Making Under Uncertainty	TM A.4a-A.4d	patterned after Problem 16 in text
	AP A.5: Decision Making Under Risk	TM A.5	
	AP A.6: Decision Trees	TM A.6a-A.6b	same as Problem 18 in text
3	AP 3.1: Break-Even Analysis in Process Choice	TM 3.1	
4	NONE		
B	NONE		
5	AP 5.1: Time Study Method	TM 5.1a-5.1b	
	AP 5.2: Work Sampling Method	TM 5.2a-5.2c	
C	AP C.1: Estimating Direct Labor Requirements	TM C.1	
	AP C.2: Estimating Cumulative Labor Hours	TM C.2a-C.2b	same as part of solved Problem in Supplement C
6	AP 6.1: Reliability Analysis	TM 6.1	
7	AP 7.1: Control Charts for Variables	TM 7.1a-7.1c	
	AP 7.2: p-Chart for Attributes	TM 7.2a-7.2b	
	AP 7.3: c-Chart for Attributes	TM 7.3	
	AP 7.4: Process Capability Analysis	TM 7.4	
D	AP D.1: Drawing the OC Curve	TM D.1a-D.1d	
	AP D.2: Average Outgoing Quality	TM D.2	
8	AP 8.1: Estimating Capacity Requirements	TM 8.1	same as solved Problem 1
	AP 8.2: Identifying Capacity Gaps	TM 8.2	same as Example 8.3
	AP 8.3: Developing Capacity Alternatives	TM 8.3	same as solved Problem 2
E	AP E.1: Single-Server Model	TM E.1a-E.1b	
	AP E.2: Analyzing the Service Rate	TM E.2	
	AP E.3: Multiple-Server Model	TM E.3a-E.3b	
	AP E.4: Finite-Source Model	TM E.4a-E.4b	
	AP E.5: Hilltop Produce	TM E.5	
F	AP F.1: Monte Carlo Simulation	TM F.1a-F.1b	
9	AP 9.1: Preference Matrix	TM 9.1	
	AP 9.2: Distance Measures	TM 9.2	
	AP 9.3: Load-Distance Method	TM 9.3	
	AP 9.4: Center of Gravity	TM 9.4	
	AP 9.5: Break-Even Analysis	TM 9.5a-9.5b	
	AP 9.6: The Transportation Method	TM 9.6a-9.6b	
10	AP 10.1: Process Layout	TM 10.1a-10.1c	Problem 4 in book; new application
	AP 10.2: Warehouse Layout	TM 10.2a-10.2b	
	AP 10.3: Product Layout	TM 10.3a-10.3f	
11	AP 11.1: Inventory Turnover	TM 11.1	
12	AP 12.1: Estimating the Average	TM 12.1a-12.1c	
	AP 12.2: Forecasting Using Trend-Adjusted Exponential Smoothing	TM 12.2a-12.2b	
	AP 12.3: Forecasting Using the Multiplicative Seasonal Method	TM 12.3a-12.3b	
	AP 12.4: Calculating Measures of Forecast Error	TM 12.4a-12.4b	
13	AP 13.1: Estimating Inventory Levels	TM 13.1	

APPLICATIONS

Chapter 1: Operations as a Competitive Weapon

Application 1.1: Productivity Calculations

	This Yr.	Last Yr.	Year Before Last
Factory unit sales	2,762,103	2,475,738	2,175,447
Employment	112,000	113,000	115,000
Sales of manufactured products	$49,363	$40,831	—
Total manufacturing cost of sales	$39,000	$33,000	—

- Calculate the year-to-year percentage in labor productivity.

- Calculate the multifactor productivity.

Supplement A: Decision Making

Application A.1: Break-Even Analysis for Evaluating Products or Services

The Denver Zoo must decide whether to move twin polar bears to Sea World or build a special exhibit for them and the zoo. The expected increase in attendance is 200,000 patrons. The data are:

Revenues per Patron for Exhibit
Gate receipts	$4
Concessions	$5
Licensed apparel	$15

Estimated Fixed Costs
Exhibit construction	$2,400,000
Salaries	$220,000
Food	$30,000

Estimated Variable Costs per Person
Concessions	$2
Licensed apparel	$9

Is the predicted increase in attendance sufficient to break even?

Denver Zoo Graphical Solutions Axes

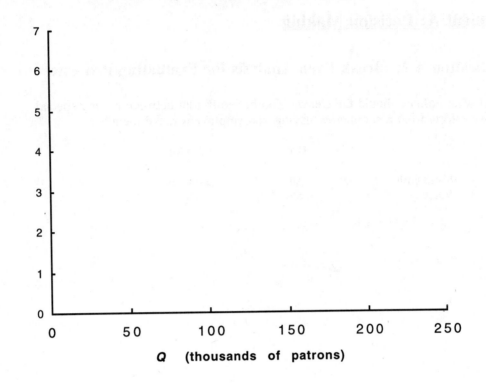

Cost and revenue (millions of dollars)

Q (thousands of patrons)

a. Graphical solution of Denver Zoo problem

Q(M)	TR(MM)	TC(MM)
0		
100		

b. Algebraic solution of Denver Zoo problem

$$pQ \; = \; F + cQ$$

$$24Q \; =$$

$$13Q \; = \; 2,650,000$$

$$Q \; = \; 203,846$$

c. Sensitivity analysis and total profit contribution

- How low must the variable cost per patron be to break even?

- How low must be the fixed cost to break even?

- At what admission price would the attraction break even?

Supplement A: Decision Making

Application A.2: Break-Even Analysis for Evaluating Processes

At what volume should the Denver Zoo be indifferent between buying special sweatshirts from a supplier or having zoo employees make them?

	Buy	Make
Fixed costs	$0	$300,000
Variable costs	$9	$7

$$Q = \frac{E_m - F_b}{c_b - c_m}$$

Supplement A: Decision Making

Application A.3: Preference Matrix

The concept of a weighted score. Here we evaluate the advisability of adding a new service to our product line.

Performance Criterion	Weight	Score	Weighted Score
Market potential	10	5	
Unit profit margin	30	8	
Operations compatibility	20	10	
Competitive advantage	25	7	
Investment requirements	10	3	
Project risk	5	4	_____
		Total weighted score =	_____

Repeat this process for each alternative — pick the one with the largest weighted score.

Supplement A: Decision Making

Application A.4: Decision Making Under Uncertainty

Fletcher (a realist), Cooper (a pessimist), and Wainwright (an optimist) are joint owners in a company. They must decide whether to make Arrows, Barrels, or Wagons. The government is about to issue a policy and recommendation on pioneer travel that depends on whether certain treaties are obtained. The policy is expected to affect demand for the products, however it is impossible at this time to assess the probability of these policy "events." The following data are available:

Payoffs (Profits)

Alternative	Land Routes No treaty	Land Routes Treaty	Sea Routes only
Arrows	$840,000	$440,000	$190,000
Barrels	$370,000	$220,000	$670,000
Wagons	$25,000	$1,150,000	($25,000)

- Which product would be favored by Fletcher?

- Which product would be favored by Cooper?

- Which product would be favored by Wainwright?

- What is the minimax regret solution?

Supplement A: Decision Making

Application A.5: Decision Making Under Risk

For CF&W, find the best decision using the expected value rule and the value of perfect information. The probabilities for the events are given below.

- Expected value decision

Alternative	Land routes, No Treaty(0.50)		Land Routes, Treaty Only (0.30)		Sea routes, Only (0.20)		Expected Value
Arrows	(0.50)(	) +	(0.30)(	) +	(0.20)(	) =	
Barrels	(0.50)(	) +	(0.30)(	)	(0.20)(	) =	
Wagons	(0.50)(	) +	(0.30)(	) +	(0.20)(	) =	

- Expected value of perfect information

$$(0.50)(\quad\quad) + (0.30)(\quad\quad) + (0.20)(\quad\quad) =$$

$$EVPI \quad = (\quad\quad) - (\quad\quad) =$$

Supplement A: Decision Making

Application A.6: Decision Trees

- Draw the decision tree for the CF&W problem.

- What is the expected payoff for the best alternative in the decision tree below?

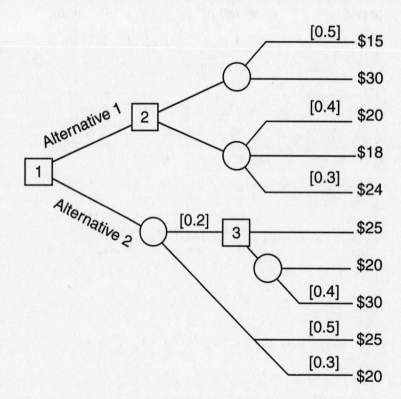

Chapter 3: Process Management

Application 3.1: Break-Even Analysis in Process Choice

BBC is deciding whether to weld bicycle frames manually or to purchase a welding robot. If welded manually, investment costs for equipment are only $10,000. The per-unit cost of manually welding a bicycle frame is $50.00 per frame. On the other hand, a robot capable of performing the same work costs $400,000. Robot operating costs including support labor are $20.00 per frame. At what volume would BBC be indifferent to these alternative methods?

Chapter 5: Work-Force Management

Application 5.1: Time Study Method

Lucy and Ethel have repetitive jobs at the candy factory. Management desires to establish a time standard for this work for which they can be 95% confident to be within ± 6% of the true mean. There are three work elements involved:

Step 1: Selecting work elements.

#1: Pick up wrapper paper and wrap one piece of candy.

#2: Put candy in a box, one at a time.

#3: When the box is full (4 pieces), close it and place on conveyor.

Step 2: Timing the elements.
Select an *average* trained worker: Lucy will suffice.

Element	Initial Observation Cycle Number, Minutes									Select Time, $\bar{t}$
	1	2	3	4	5	6	7	8	9	
Wrap #1:	.10	.08	.08	.12	.10	.10	.12	.09	.11	
Pack #2:	.10	.08	.08	.11	.06	.98*	.17	.11	.09	
Close #3:	.27	...	...	...	.34	...	...	...	.29	

* Lucy had some rare and unusual difficulties; don't use this observation.

Step 3: Determine sample size. Assuming a 95% confidence interval, $z = 1.96$. The precision interval of ± 6% of the true mean implies $p = 0.06$. Calculate $\bar{t}$ for each element in Step 2.

Step 4: Setting the standard.

    a. The analyst subjectively assigns a rating factor. (shown below)

    b. Determine the normal time (NT) for each work element.

Element	Select Time, $\overline{t}$	Frequency	Rating Factor	Normal Time
Wrap #1:		1.00	1.2	
Pack #2:		1.00	0.9	
Close #3:		0.25	0.8	

For the third element, the frequency is 0.25 because closing the box occurs only once every four cycles.

    c. Determine the normal time for the cycle.

    d. Subjectively determine the proportion of the normal time to be added for allowance, then calculate standard time, ST. The allowances are 18.5% of the normal time.

Chapter 5: Work-Force Management

Application 5.2: Work Sampling Method

Major League Baseball (MLB) is concerned about excessive game duration. Batters now spend a lot of time between pitches when they leave the box to check signals with coaches, and then go through a lengthy routine including stretching and a variety of other actions. Pitching routines are similarly elaborate. In order to speed up the game, it has been proposed to prohibit batters from leaving the box and to prohibit pitchers from leaving the mound after called balls and strikes. MLB estimates the proportion of time spent in these delays to be 20% of the total game time. Before they institute a rules change, MLB would like to be 95% confident that the result of a study will show a proportion of time wasted that is accurate within ±4% of the true proportion.

Steps 1 and 2.   Define the activities and design the observation form.

Step 3.   Determine the length of the study. Suppose that ten games (or 32 hours) is appropriate.

Step 4.   Determine the initial sample size.

$$n = \left(\frac{}{} \right)^2 0.20(1 - 0.20) =$$

Steps 5 and 6.   Determine the observer schedule.

Step 7.   Observe the activities and record the data.

Step 8.   Check to see whether additional sampling is required.

For pitchers:

$$n = \left(\frac{}{} \right)^2 ()(1 -) =$$

For batters:

$$n = \left(\frac{}{} \right)^2 ()(1 -) =$$

Conclusion?

Supplement C: Learning Curves

Application C.1: Estimating Direct Labor Requirements

The first unit of a new product is expected to take 1000 hours to complete. If the rate of learning is 80 percent, how much time should the 50th unit take?

Supplement C: Learning Curves

Application C.2: Estimating Cumulative Labor Hours

A company has a contract to make a product for the first time. The total budget for the 38-unit job is 15,000 hours. The first unit took 1000 hours, and the rate of learning is expected to be 80 percent.

- Do you think the job can be completed within the 15,000-hour budget?

- How many hours would you need for a second job of 26 units?

Chapter 6: Total Quality Management

Application 6.1: Reliability Analysis

In order to start an old car, we need keys, fuel, and a charged battery. Lacking any of these, the car will not start. In order to start a new car, we need keys, fuel, a charged battery, and a computer system.

Which is more likely to start?

For our example, say the probability of remembering the keys is 95%, the chances of fuel being in the tank is 80%, and the probability of a charged battery is 98%.

What is the reliability of the old car?

The reliability of a system with N components *in series* is equal to the probability of the simultaneous occurrence of independent events.

$$r_s \quad =$$

Now let's say the probability of the computer functioning in the new car is 92%.
This estimate is very low, but suits the purposes of our example.

What is the reliability of starting the new car?

$$r_s \quad =$$

Chapter 7: Statistical Process Control

Application 7.1: Control Charts for Variables

Webster Chemical Company produces mastics and caulking for the construction industry. The product is blended in large mixers and then pumped into tubes and capped.

Webster is concerned whether the filling process for tubes of caulking is in statistical control. The process should be centered on 8 ounces per tube. Several samples of eight tubes are taken and each tube is weighed in ounces.

Sample	Tube Number 1	2	3	4	5	6	7	8	Avg	Range
1	7.98	8.34	8.02	7.94	8.44	7.68	7.81	8.11		
2	8.23	8.12	7.98	8.41	8.31	8.18	7.99	8.06		
3	7.89	7.77	7.91	8.04	8.00	7.89	7.93	8.09		
4	8.24	8.18	7.83	8.05	7.90	8.16	7.97	8.07		
5	7.87	8.13	7.92	7.99	8.10	7.81	8.14	7.88		
6	8.13	8.14	8.11	8.13	8.14	8.12	8.13	8.14	___	___
								Avgs	$=$	$=$

Assuming that taking only 6 samples is sufficient, is the process in statistical control?

Conclusion on process variability?

UCL_R =

LCL_R =

Conclusion on process average?

UCL_x =

LCL_x =

Chapter 7: Statistical Process Control

Application 7.2: p - Chart for Attributes

A sticky scale brings Webster's attention to whether caulking tubes are being properly capped. If a significant proportion of the tubes aren't being sealed, Webster is placing their customers in a messy situation. Tubes are packaged in large boxes of 144. Several boxes are inspected and the following number of leaking tubes are found:

Sample	Tubes	Sample	Tubes	Sample	Tubes
1	3	8	6	15	5
2	5	9	4	16	0
3	3	10	9	17	2
4	4	11	2	18	6
5	2	12	6	19	2
6	4	13	5	20	1
7	2	14	1	Total =	72

Calculate the p-chart three-sigma control limits to assess whether the capping process is in statistical control.

UCL =

LCL =

Chapter 7: Statistical Process Control

Application 7.3: c-Chart for Attributes

At Webster Chemical, lumps in the caulking compound could cause difficulties in dispensing a smooth bead from the tube. Even when the process is in control, there will still be an average of 4 lumps per tube of caulk. Testing for the presence of lumps destroys the product, so Webster takes random samples. The following are results of the study:

Tube #	Lumps	Tube #	Lumps	Tube #	Lumps
1	6	5	6	9	5
2	5	6	4	10	0
3	0	7	1	11	9
4	4	8	6	12	2

Determine the c-chart two-sigma upper and lower control limits for this process.

$$c \quad = \qquad\qquad\qquad\qquad \sigma_c \quad =$$

$$UCL_c \quad = \qquad\qquad\qquad\qquad LCL_c \quad =$$

Chapter 7: Statistical Process Control

Application 7.4: Process Capability Analysis

Webster Chemical's nominal weight for filling tubes of caulk is 8.00 ounces ± 0.60 ounces. The target process capability ratio is 1.33. The current distribution of the filling process is centered on 8.054 ounces with a standard deviation of 0.192 ounces. Compute the process capability ratio and process capability index to assess whether the filling process is capable and set properly.

- Process capability ratio:

  $$C_p \quad =$$

- Process capability index:

  $$C_{pk} \quad =$$

  $$C_{pk} \quad =$$

- *Conclusion:*

Supplement D: Acceptance Sampling

Application D.1: Drawing the OC Curve

A sampling plan is being evaluated where $c = 10$ and $n = 193$. If $AQL = 0.03$ and $LTPD = 0.08$. What are the producer's risk and consumer's risk for the plan? Draw the OC curve.

- Finding α (probability of rejecting AQL quality)

    $p \ =$

    $np =$

    $P_a =$

    $\alpha \ =$

- Finding β (probability of accepting LTPD quality)

    $p \ =$

    $np =$

    $P_a =$

    $\beta \ =$

Supplement D: Acceptance Sampling

Application D.2: Average Outgoing Quality

Management has selected the following parameters:

$AQL = 0.01$ $\alpha = 0.05$
$LTPD = 0.06$ $\beta = 0.10$
$n = 100$ $c = 3$

What is the AOQ if $p = 0.05$ and $N = 3000$?

$$p \quad =$$

$$np \quad =$$

$$P_a \quad =$$

$$AOQ \quad = \quad \frac{(\quad\quad)(\quad\quad\quad)2900}{3000} \quad =$$

Application 8.1: Estimating Capacity Requirements

Surefoot Sandal Company operates two 8-hour shifts, five days per week, 50 weeks per year. A capacity cushion of 5 percent will suffice. Time standards, lot sizes, and demand forecasts are:

	Time Standards			
Product	**Processing (hr/pair)**	**Setup (hr/lot)**	**Lot Size (pairs/lot)**	**Demand Forecast (pairs/yr)**
Men's sandals	0.05	0.5	240	80,000
Women's sandals	0.10	2.2	180	60,000
Children's sandals	0.02	3.8	360	120,000

Estimate Capacity Requirements:

$$M = \frac{}{[1-()]}$$

$$M =$$

How much additional capacity does the company need?

Chapter 8: Capacity

Application 8.2: Identifying Capacity Gaps

Demand forecasts (in meals per year) are shown below. The kitchen has a capacity of 80,000 meals, and the dining room a capacity of 105,000. What are the gaps?

Year	Demand (meals)	Gaps (meals)	
		Kitchen	Dining
1	90,000		
2	100,000		
3	110,000		
4	120,000		
5	130,000		

Application 8.3: Developing Capacity Alternatives

One alternative at Grandmother's Chicken is a two-stage expansion. This alternative expands the kitchen at the *end* of year 0 to 105,000 meals, and both the kitchen and dining room to 130,000 at the *end* of year 3. The initial investment would be $80,000 at the end of year 0, and $170,000 at the end of year 3. The pre-tax profit is $2 per meal. What are the before-tax cash flows through year 5, compared to the base case?

Year	Projected demand (meals/yr)	Projected capacity (meals/yr)	Incremental cash flow compared to base case (80,000 meals/yr)	Cash inflow (outflow)
0	80,000			
1	90,000			
2	100,000			
3	110,000			
4	120,000			
5	130,000			

Supplement E: Waiting Line Models

Application E.1: Single-Server Model

Customers arrive at a checkout counter at an average 20 per hour, according to a Poisson distribution. They are served at an average rate of 25 per hour, with exponential service times. Use the single-server model to estimate the operating characteristic of this system.

$$\rho \quad =$$

$$L \quad =$$

$$L_q \quad =$$

$$W \quad =$$

$$W_q \quad =$$

Supplement E: Waiting Line Models

Application E.2: Analyzing the Service Rate

In the checkout counter example, what service rate is required to have customers average only 10 minutes in the system?

$$W = \frac{1}{(\mu - \lambda)} = 0.17 \text{ hr (or 10 minutes)}$$

$$0.17(\mu - \lambda) = 1$$

$$\mu =$$

Supplement E: Waiting Line Models

Application E.3: Multiple-Server Model

Suppose the manager of the checkout system decides to add another counter. The arrival rate is still 20 customers per hour, but now each checkout counter will be designed to service customers at the rate of 12.5 per hour. What is the waiting time in line of the new system?

ρ =

$$P_0 = \cfrac{1}{\left[1+\dfrac{2.0}{12.5}+\dfrac{\left(\dfrac{2.0}{12.5}\right)^2}{2}\left(\dfrac{1}{1-\rho}\right)\right]}$$

L_q =

W_q =

Note that even though the average service rate is the same in the two systems, the average waiting time is less in the multiple-server arrangement.

Supplement E: Waiting Line Models

Application E.4: Finite-Source Model

DBT Bank has 8 copy machines located in various offices throughout the building. Each machine is used continuously and has an average time between failures of 50 hours. Once failed, it takes 4 hours for the service company to send a repair person to have it fixed. What is the average number of copy machines in repair or waiting to be repaired?

$$\lambda = \qquad\qquad \mu =$$

$$P_0 = \cfrac{1}{\displaystyle\sum_{n=0}^{8} \frac{8!}{(8-n)!}\left(\frac{\lambda}{\mu}\right)^n} = 0.44$$

$$\rho = 1 - P_0 = 0.56$$

$$L = 8 - \frac{\mu}{\lambda}(1 - 0.44) =$$

Supplement E: Waiting Line Models

Application E.5: Hilltop Produce

The Hilltop Produce store is staffed by one checkout clerk. The average checkout time is exponentially distributed around an average of two minutes per customer. An average of 20 customers arrive per hour.

a. What is the average utilization rate?

ρ =

b. What is the probability that three or more customers will be in the checkout area?

P_0 =

P_1 =

P_2 =

c. What is the average number of customers in the waiting line?

L_q =

d. If the customers spend an average of 10 minutes shopping for produce, what is the average time customers spend in the store?

W =

Supplement F: Simulation Analysis

Application F.1: Monte Carlo Simulation

1. Car Arrival Distribution (time between arrivals)

Famous Chamois is an automated car wash that advertises that your car can be finished in just 15 minutes. The time until the next car arrival is described by the following distribution.

Minutes	Probability	Minutes	Probability
1	0.01	8	0.12
2	0.03	9	0.10
3	0.06	10	0.07
4	0.09	11	0.05
5	0.12	12	0.04
6	0.14	13	0.10
7	0.14		1.00

2. Random Number Assignment

Assign a range of random numbers to each event so that the demand pattern can be simulated.

Minutes	Random Numbers	Minutes	Random Numbers
1	00–00	8	–
2	01–03	9	–
3	04–09	10	–
4	10–18	11	–
5	19–30	12	–
6	31–44	13	–
7	45–58		

3. Simulation of Famous Chamois Operation

Simulate the operation for 3 hours, using the following random numbers, assuming that the service time is constant at 6 minutes per car.

Random Number	Time to Arrival	Arrival Time	Number in Drive	Service Begins	Departure Time	Minutes in System
50	7	0:07	0	0:07	0:13	6
63						
95						
49						
68						

Random Number	Time to Arrival	Arrival Time	Number in Drive	Service Begins	Departure Time	Minutes in System
11						
40						
93						
61						
48						
82						
09						
08						
72						
98						
41						
39						
67						
11						
11						
00						
07						
66						
00						
29						

Results:

Chapter 9: Location

Application 9.1: Preference Matrix

Management is considering three potential locations for a new cookie factory. They have assigned scores shown below to the relevant factors on a 0 to 10 basis (10 is best). Using the preference matrix, which location would be preferred?

Location Factor	Weight	The Neighborhood	Sesame Street	Peewee's Playhouse
Material Supply	0.1	5	9	8
Quality of Life	0.2	9	8	4
Mild Climate	0.3	10*	6	8
Labor Skills	0.4	3	4	7

Chapter 9: Location

Application 9.2: Distance Measures

What is the distance between (20, 10) and (80, 60)?

- Euclidean distance:

$$d_{AB} = \sqrt{(x_A - x_B)^2 + (y_A - y_B)^2} = \sqrt{(\ -\ )^2 + (\ -\ )^2} = 78.1$$

- Rectilinear distance

$$d_{AB} = |x_A - x_B| + |y_A - y_B| = |\ \ -\ \ | + |\ \ -\ \ | = 110$$

Chapter 9: Location

Application 9.3: Load-Distance Method

Management is investigating which location would be best to position its new plant relative to two suppliers (located in Cleveland and Toledo) and three market areas (represented by Cincinnati, Dayton, and Lima). Management has limited the search for this plant to those five locations. The following information has been collected. Which is best, assuming rectilinear distance?

Location	x,y coordinates	Trips/year
Cincinnati	(11,6)	15
Dayton	(6,10)	20
Cleveland	(14,12)	30
Toledo	(9,12)	25
Lima	(13,8)	40

Calculations:

$$\text{Cincinnati} = 15(\quad) + 20(\quad) + 30(\quad) + 25(\quad) + 40(\quad) \quad =$$

$$\text{Dayton} = 15(\quad) + 20(\quad) + 30(\quad) + 25(\quad) + 40(\quad) \quad =$$

$$\text{Cleveland} = 15(\quad) + 20(\quad) + 30(\quad) + 25(\quad) + 40(\quad) \quad =$$

$$\text{Toledo} = 15(\quad) + 20(\quad) + 30(\quad) + 25(\quad) + 40(\quad) \quad =$$

$$\text{Lima} = 15(\quad) + 20(\quad) + 30(\quad) + 25(\quad) + 40(\quad) \quad =$$

Chapter 9: Location

Application 9.4: Center of Gravity

A firm wishes to find a central location for its service. Business forecasts indicate travel from the central location to New York City on 20 occasions per year. Similarly, there will be 15 trips to Boston, and 30 trips to New Orleans. The x,y-coordinates are (11.0, 8.5) for New York, (12.0, 9.5) for Boston, and (4.0, 1.5) for New Orleans. What is the center of gravity of the three demand points?

$$x^* = [(\quad) + (\quad) + (\quad)] / (\quad) = \underline{\quad}$$

$$y^* = [(\quad) + (\quad) + (\quad)] / (\quad) = \underline{\quad}$$

Chapter 9: Location

Application 9.5: Break-Even Analysis

By chance, the Atlantic City Community Chest has to close temporarily for general repairs. They are considering four temporary office locations:

Property Address	Move-in Costs	Monthly Rent
Boardwalk	$400	$50
Marvin Gardens	$280	$24
St. Charles Place	$350	$10
Baltic Avenue	$60	$60

Use the graph below to determine for what length of lease each location would be favored? Hint: In this problem, lease length is analogous to volume.

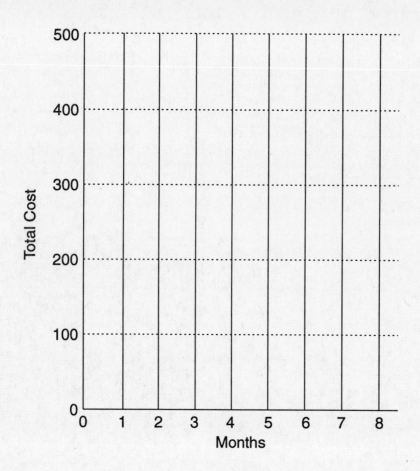

Chapter 9: Location

Application 9.6: The Transportation Method

Fire Brand makes picante sauce in San Antonio and New Yok City. Distribution centers are located in Atlanta, Omaha, and Seattle. The capacities, demands, and shipment costs per case are shown below.

Plant	Capacity (cases)	Distribution Center	Demand (cases)
San Antonio	12,000	Atlanta	8,000
New York City	10,000	Omaha	6,000
Total	22,000	Seattle	5,000
		Total	19,000

	Shipping Cost to Distribution Center (per case)		
Plant	Atlanta	Omaha	Seattle
San Antonio	$4	$5	$6
New York City	$3	$7	$9

Set up the initial tableau for Fire Brand in the table below.

Sources	Destinations			Dummy unused	Capacity
Demand					

Application 10.1: Process Layout

Matthews and Novak Design Company has been asked to design the layout for a newly constructed office building of one of its clients. The trip matrix showing the daily trips between its six department offices is given below.

Department	Trips Between Departments					
	1	2	3	4	5	6
1	—	25	90			165
2		—			105	
3			—		125	125
4				—	25	
5					—	105
6						—

a. Shown below on the right is a block plan that has been suggested for the building. A partially completed table is shown to the left of it, which calculates its load-distance score by assuming rectilinear distance. Finish the table.

Department Pair	Closeness Factor	Distance	Score
1, 6	165	1	165
3, 5	125		
3, 6	125	___	___
2, 5	105	1	105
5, 6	105	1	105
1, 3	90	___	___
1, 2	25	3	75
4, 5	25	1	25
Total			**1030**

```
3 6 1
2 5 4
```

b. Based on the above results, propose a better plan in the space below, and evaluate it in terms of the load-distance score.

Department Pair	Closeness Factor	Distance	Score
1, 6	165	_____	_____
3, 5	125	_____	_____
3, 6	125	_____	_____
2, 5	105	_____	_____
5, 6	105	_____	_____
1, 3	90	_____	_____
1, 2	25	_____	_____
4, 5	25	_____	_____
	Total		_____

Application 10.2: Warehouse Layout

A plant warehouse, consisting of 12 equal sections, stores parts used in a nearby assembly line. It uses an "out-and-back" pattern. Distances, area requirements, and trip frequencies follow. What is the best layout?

Storage Section Data			Parts Data		
Section	Distance to Assembly Line		Part Category	Trips per Day	Number of Sections Needed
1	50		A	150	3
2	60		B	75	1
3	200		C	120	2
4	210		D	150	1
5	220		E	80	2
6	230		F	140	2
7	920		G	25	1
8	930				
9	940				
10	1680				
11	1690				
12	1700				

Working out the solution:

Part	Ratio of Trips to Area	Priority	Sections Assigned
A	50	5	7, 8, 9
B	____	2	____
C	60	4	5, 6
D	____	1	____
E	40	6	10, 11
F	____	3	____
G	25	7	12

Chapter 10: Layout

Application 10.3: Product Layout

A plant manager needs a design for an assembly line to assembly a new product that is being introduced. The time requirements and immediate predecessors for the work elements are as follows:

Work Element	Time (sec)	Immediate Predecessor
A	12	–
B	60	A
C	36	–
D	24	–
E	38	C, D
F	72	B, E
G	14	–
H	72	–
I	35	G, H
J	60	I
K	12	F, J
	Total = **435**	

a.   Draw a precedence diagram for the line by finishing the one that has been started below.

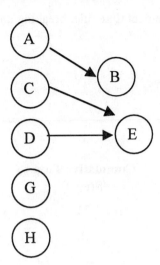

b.   If the desired output rate is 30 units per hour, what are the cycle time and theoretical minimum?

$$c \quad =$$

$$TM \quad =$$

c.   Suppose that we are fortunate enough to find a solution with just four stations. What is the idle time per unit, efficiency, and the balance delay for this solution?

Idle time   =

Efficiency   =

Balance delay   =

d. Find a product layout design using the longest-work-element time rule, breaking any ties with the largest-number-of-followers rule.

Station (Step 1)	Candidate (Step 2)	Choice (Step 3)	Cumulative Time (Step 4)	Idle Time ($c = 120$) (Step 4)
1	A, C, D, G, H	H	72	48
	_____	___	___	___
	_____	___	___	___
2	_____	___	___	___
	_____	___	___	___
	_____	___	___	___
3	E, I	E	38	82
	F, I	F	110	10
4	I	I	35	85
	J	J	95	25
	K	K	107	13

Chapter 11: Supply-Chain Management

Application 11.1: Inventory Turnover

A recent accounting statement showed total inventories (raw materials + WIP + finished goods) to be $6,821,000. This year's "cost of goods sold" is $19.2 million. The company operates 52 weeks per year. How many weeks of supply are being held? What is the inventory turnover?

Weeks of supply =

Inventory turnover =

Chapter 12: Forecasting

Application 12.1: Estimating the Average

We will use the following customer-arrival data in this application.

Month	Customer arrivals
1	800
2	740
3	810
4	790

a. **Simple Moving Average.** Use a three-month moving average to forecast customer arrivals for month 5.

$F_5 \quad =$

Forecast for month 5 $\quad =$

If the actual number of arrivals in month 5 is 805, what is the forecast for month 6?

$F_6 \quad =$

Forecast for month 6 $\quad =$

b. **Weighted Moving Average.** Let $W_1 = 0.50$, $W_2 = 0.30$, and $W_3 = 0.20$. Use the weighted moving average method to forecast arrivals for month 5.

$F_5 \quad =$

Forecast for month 5 $\quad =$

If the actual number of arrivals is 805, compute the forecast for month 6.

$F_6 \quad =$

Forecast for month 6 $\quad =$

c. **Exponential Smoothing Average.** Suppose the value of the series average in month 3 was 783 customers. Use exponential smoothing with $\alpha = 0.20$ to compute the forecast for month 5.

$F_5 \quad =$

Forecast for month 5 $\quad =$

If the actual number of customer arrivals is 805 in month 5, what is the forecast for month 6?

$F_6 \quad =$

Forecast for month 6 $\quad =$

Chapter 12: Forecasting

Application 12.2: Forecasting Using Trend-Adjusted Exponential Smoothing

The forecaster for Canine Gourmet dog breath fresheners estimated (in March) the series average to be 300,000 cases sold per month and the trend to be +8,000 per month. The actual sales for April were 330,000 cases. What is the forecast for May, assuming $\alpha = 0.20$ and $\beta = 0.10$?

A_{Apr} =

T_{Apr} =

Forecast for May =

Suppose you also wanted the forecast for July, three months ahead.

Forecast for July =

Application 12.3: Forecasting Using the Multiplicative Seasonal Method

Suppose the multiplicative seasonal method is being used to forecast customer demand. The actual demand and seasonal indices are shown below.

Quarter	Year 1 Demand	Year 1 Index	Year 2 Demand	Year 2 Index	Average Index
1	100	0.40	192	0.64	0.52
2	400	1.60	408	1.36	1.48
3	300	1.20	384	1.28	1.24
4	200	0.80	216	0.72	0.76
Avg.	250		300		

If the projected demand for Year 3 is 1320 units, what is the forecast for each quarter of that year?

Forecast for Quarter 1 =

Forecast for Quarter 2 =

Forecast for Quarter 3 =

Forecast for Quarter 4 =

Application 12.4: Calculating Measures of Forecast Error

A forecasting procedure has been used for the last 8 months, with the following results. Evaluate how well the procedure is doing, by finishing the following table and then computing the different forecast error measures.

Month	Demand (D_t)	Forecast (F_t)	Error (E_t)	Error Squared (E_t^2)	Absolute Error $(\lvert E_t \rvert)$	Absolute Percent Error $(\lvert E_t \rvert / D_t)100$
1	200	225	___	___	___	___
2	240	220	___	___	___	___
3	300	285	___	___	___	___
4	270	290	___	___	___	___
5	230	250	−20	400	20	8.7
6	260	240	20	400	20	7.7
7	210	250	−40	1600	40	19.0
8	275	240	35	1225	35	12.7
Total			−15	5275	195	81.3%

CFE =

MSE =

σ =

MAD =

MAPE =

Chapter 13: Inventory Management

Application 13.1: Estimating Inventory Levels

Management has decided to establish three DCs in its supply chain, located in different regions of the country, to save on transportation costs. For one of the products, the average weekly demand at **each** DC will be 50 units. The product is valued at $650 per unit. Average shipment sizes into each DC will be 350 units per trip. The average lead time will be two weeks. Each DC will carry one week's supply as safety stock, since the demand during the lead time sometimes exceeds its average of 100 units (50 units/wk × 2 wk). Anticipation inventory should be negligible.

- How many dollars, on the average, of **cycle inventory** will be held at **each** DC?

- How many dollars of **safety stock** will be held at **each** DC?

- How many dollars of **pipeline inventory**, on the average, will be in transit for each DC?

- How much inventory, on the average, will be held at each DC?

- Which type of inventory is your first candidate for reduction?

Chapter 13: Inventory Management

Application 13.2: Finding the EOQ, Total Cost and TBO

Suppose that you are reviewing the inventory policies on an item stocked at a hardware store. The current policy is to replenish inventory by ordering in lots of 360 units. Additional information is:

$D = 60$ units per week, or 3120 units per year

$S = \$30$ per order

$H = 25\%$ of selling price, or $20 per unit per year

a.   What is the EOQ?

$$\text{EOQ} = \sqrt{\frac{(\_)(\underline{\quad})(\_)}{\underline{\quad}}} = 97 \text{ units}$$

b.   What is the total annual cost of the current policy ($Q = 360$), and how does it compare with the cost with using the EOQ?

Current policy	EOQ policy

Current policy

$Q = 360$ units

$C = (\underline{\qquad})(\underline{\quad}) + (\underline{\qquad})(\underline{\quad})$

$C = \underline{\qquad} + \underline{\qquad}$

$C = \$\underline{\qquad}$

EOQ policy

$Q = 97$ units

$C = (\underline{\qquad})(\underline{\quad}) + (\underline{\qquad})(\underline{\quad})$

$C = \underline{\qquad} + \underline{\qquad}$

$C = \$\underline{\qquad}$

c.   What is the time between orders (TBO) for the current policy and the EOQ policy, expressed in weeks?

$\text{TBO}_{360} = \qquad\qquad =$

$\text{TBO}_{EOQ} = \qquad\qquad =$

Application 13.3: Placing Orders with a Continuous Review System

The on-hand inventory is only 10 units, and the reorder point R is 100. There are no backorders and one open order for 200 units. Should a new order be placed?

IP   =

R =

Decision:

Chapter 13: Inventory Management

Application 13.4: Selecting the Safety Stock and R

Suppose instead that the demand during lead time is normally distributed with an average of 85 and $\sigma_L = 40$.

a. Find the safety stock, and reorder point R, for a **95 percent** cycle-service level.

- Safety stock $= z\sigma_L =$ _____ (_____) $=$ _____ , or _____ units

- $R =$ Average demand during lead time $+$ Safety stock

   $R =$ _____ $+$ _____ $=$ _____ units

b. Find the safety stock, and reorder point R, for a **85 percent** cycle-service level.

- Safety stock $= z\sigma_L =$ _____ (_____) $=$ _____ , or _____ units

- $R =$ Average demand during lead time $+$ Safety stock

   $R =$ _____ $+$ _____ $=$ _____ units

Chapter 13: Inventory Management

Application 13.5: Continuous Review System: Putting It All Together

The Discount Appliance Store uses a continuous review system (Q system). One of the company's items has the following characteristics:

>   Demand = 10 units/wk (assume 52 weeks per year)
>
>   Ordering and setup cost (S) = $45/order
>
>   Holding cost (H) = $12/unit/year
>
>   Lead time (L) = 3 weeks
>
>   Standard deviation in weekly demand = 8 units
>
>   Cycle-service level = 70%

a. What is the EOQ for this item?

b. $D =$ _____ (_____) = _____ units

- $EOQ = \sqrt{\dfrac{(\qquad)(\quad)}{}} = 62$ units

b. What is the desired safety stock?

- $\sigma_L =$ _____ $\sqrt{\rule{2cm}{0pt}}$ = _____ units

- Safety stock = $z\sigma_L$ = _____ (_____) = _____ units

c. What is the desired reorder point R?

- R = Average demand during lead time + Safety stock

    = _____ (____) + ___ = _____ units

a. Suppose that the current policy is $Q = 80$ and $R = 150$. What will be the changes in average cycle inventory and safety stock if your EOQ and R values are implemented?

- Cycle inventory reduction: _____ – _____ = _____ units

- Safety stock reduction: _____ – _____ = _____ units

Chapter 13: Inventory Management

Application 13.6: Placing Orders with a Periodic Review System

The on-hand inventory is 10 units, and T is 400. There are no back orders, but one scheduled receipt of 200 units. Now is the time to review. How much should be reordered?

$$\text{IP} \quad =$$

$$T - \text{IP} \ =$$

DECISION:

Chapter 13: Inventory Management

Application 13.7: Periodic Review System: Putting It All Together

Return to Discount Appliance Store (Application 13.8), but now use P system for the item.

    a.   Previous information

          Demand = 10 units/wk (assume 52 weeks per year)

          EOQ = 62 units (with reorder point system)

          Lead time (L) = 3 weeks

          Standard deviation in weekly demand = 8 units

          $z =$ 0.525 (for cycle-service level of 70%)

    b.   Reorder interval P, if you make the average lot size using the Periodic Review System <u>approximate</u> the EOQ.

       • $P = ($_____ / _____ $)($____$) =$ _____ , or ____ weeks

    c.   Safety stock

       • Safety stock = (   )(   )$\sqrt{\underline{\ }+\underline{\ }}$ = __ units

    d.   Target inventory T

       • $T =$ Average   +   Safety stock for
               demand during   protection interval
               protection interval

          $T = ($_____ + _____ $)($_____$) + ($_____$) =$ _____ units

Supplement G: Special Inventory Models

Application G.1: Noninstantaneous Replenishment

A domestic automobile manufacturer schedules 12 two-person teams to assemble 4.6 liter DOHC V-8 engines per work day. Each team can assemble 5 engines per day. The automobile final assembly line creates an annual demand for the DOHC engine at 10,080 units per year. The engine and automobile assembly plants operate 6 days per week, 48 weeks per year. The engine assembly line also produces SOHC V-8 engines. The cost to switch the production line from one type of engine to the other is $100,000. It costs $2000 to store one DOHC V-8 for one year.

a. What is the economic lot size?

$$ELS = \sqrt{\frac{2DS}{H}} \sqrt{\frac{p}{p-d}} = \sqrt{\frac{2(\quad)(\quad)}{\quad}} \sqrt{\frac{\quad}{\quad - \quad}}$$

$$= 1004\sqrt{2.4} = 1555.38, \quad \text{or } 1555 \text{ engines}$$

b. How long is the production run?

$$\frac{Q}{p} = \frac{\quad}{\quad} = 25.91, \quad \text{or } 26 \text{ production days}$$

c. What is the average quantity in inventory?

$$\frac{I_{max}}{2} = \frac{Q}{2}\left(\frac{p-d}{p}\right) = \frac{(\quad - \quad)}{2} = 324 \text{ engines}$$

d. What are the total annual costs?

$$C = \frac{Q}{2}\left(\frac{p-d}{p}\right)(H) + \frac{D}{Q}(S)$$

$$= \frac{\quad}{2}\left(\frac{\quad - \quad}{\quad}\right)\$2,000 + \frac{\quad}{\quad}(\$100,000)$$

$$= \$647,917 + \$648,231$$

$$= \$1,296,148$$

Supplement G: Special Inventory Models

Application G.2: Quantity Discounts

A supplier's price schedule is:

Order Quantity	Price per Unit
0–99	$50
100 or more	45

If ordering cost is $16 per order, annual holding cost is 20 percent of the per purchase price, and annual demand is 1800 items, what is the best order quantity?

Step 1.

$EOQ_{45.00} =$

$EOQ_{50.00} =$

Step 2.

$C_{76} =$

$C_{100} =$

The best order quantity is _____ units.

Supplement G: Special Inventory Models

Application G.3: One-Period Decisions

For one item, p = \$10 and l= \$5. The probability distribution for the season's demand is:

Demand (*D*)	**Demand Probability**
10	0.2
20	0.3
30	0.3
40	0.1
50	0.1

Complete the following payoff matrix, as well as the column on the right showing expected payoff. What is the best choice for Q?

			D			
Q	**10**	**20**	**30**	**40**	**50**	**Expected Payoff**
10	\$100	\$100	\$100	\$100	\$100	\$100
20	50	200	200	200	200	170
30	0	___	300	___	300	___
40	–50	100	250	400	400	175
50	–100	50	200	350	500	140

Payoff if Q = 30 and D = 20:

Payoff if Q = 30 and D = 40:

Expected payoff if Q = 30:

Application 14.1: Level Strategy with Overtime and Undertime

The Barberton Municipal Division of Road Maintenance is charged with road repair in the city of Barberton and surrounding area. Cindy Kramer, road maintenance director, must submit a staffing plan for the next year based on a set schedule for repairs and on the city budget. Kramer estimates that the labor hours required for the next four quarters are 6,000, 12,000, 19,000, and 9,000, respectively. Each of the 11 workers on the work force can contribute 520 hours per quarter. Overtime is limited to 20 percent of the regular-time capacity in any quarter. Subcontracting is not permitted.

a. Find a **level work-force plan** that allows no delay in road repair and minimizes undertime. Overtime can be used to its limits in any quarter.

Finding staff level (w):
$1.20w =$ _____
$w =$ _____

	Quarter				
	1	2	3	4	Total
Requirement (hrs)	6,000	12,000	19,000	9,000	46000
Workforce level (workers)					124
Undertime (hours)	10120				21360
Overtime (hours)	0				2880
Productive time (hours)	6000				43120
Hires (workers)	20				20
Layoffs (workers)	0				0

b. Payroll costs are $6,240 in wages per worker for regular time worked up to 520 hours, with an overtime pay rate of $18 for each overtime hour. Although unused overtime capacity has no cost, unused regular time is paid at $12 per hour. The cost of hiring a worker is $3,000, and the cost of laying off a worker is $2,000. What is the cost of your level work-force plan?

Costs					
Productive time	$72,000				$517,440
Undertime	121,440				256,320
Overtime	0				51,840
Hires	60,000				60,000
Layoffs	0				0

Total Cost $885,600

Chapter 14: Aggregate Planning

Application 14.2: Chase Strategy with Hiring and Layoffs

a. Now use a chase strategy for the Barberton Municipal Division that varies the work-force level without using overtime. Undertime should be minimized, except for the minimal amount mandated because the quarterly requirements are not integer multiples of 520 hours.

	Quarter				
	1	2	3	4	Total
Requirement (hrs)	6,000	12,000	19,000	9,000	46000
Workforce level (workers)	12				91
Undertime (hours)	240				1320
Overtime (hours)	0				0
Productive time (hours)	6000				46000
Hires (workers)	1				26
Layoffs (workers)	0				19

b. What is the total cost of this plan?

Costs					
Productive time	$72,000				$552,000
Undertime	2,880				15,840
Overtime	0				0
Hires	3,000				78,000
Layoffs	0				38,000

Total Cost $683,840

Chapter 14: Aggregate Planning

Application 14.3: Mixed Strategy

a. Now propose a plan of your own for the Barberton Municipal Division. Use the Chase Strategy as a base, but find a way to decrease the cost of hiring and layoffs by selectively using some overtime.

	Quarter				
	1	2	3	4	Total
Requirement (hrs)	6,000	12,000	19,000	9,000	46,000
Workforce level (workers)					
Undertime (hours)					
Overtime (hours)					
Productive time (hours)					
Hires (workers)					
Layoffs (workers)					

b. What is the cost of your mixed strategy plan?

Costs					
Productive time	$72,000	$144,000	$193,440	$108,000	$517,440
Undertime					
Overtime					
Hires					
Layoffs					

Total Cost

Chapter 14: Aggregate Planning

Application 14.4: Transportation Method of Production Planning

The Bull Grin Company makes an animal-feed supplement. Sales are seasonal, but Bull Grin's customers refuse to stockpile the supplement during slack sales periods; they insist on shipments according to their schedules to stockpile the supplement during slack sales periods and won't accept backorders. The reactive alternatives that they use, in addition to work-force variation, are regular time, overtime, subcontracting, and anticipation inventory. Backorders are not allowed.

a. Complete the tableau given below by entering the cost per pound produced with each production alternative to meet demand in each period. Bull Grin employs workers who produce 1,000 pounds of supplement for $830 on regular time and $910 on over-time. Holding 1000 pounds of feed supplement in inventory per quarter costs $100. There is no cost for unused regular-time, overtime or subcontracting capacity.

	Alternatives	Quarter 1	Quarter 2	Quarter 3	Quarter 4	Unused Capacity	Total Capacity
	Beginning Inventory	$0 / 40	$100	$200	$300	0	
1	Regular Time	$830 / 90	$930 / 220	$1,030 / -	$1,130 / 80	-	
1	Overtime	$910 / -	$1,010 / -	$1,110 / 20	$1,210 / -	-	
1	Subcontract	$1,000 / -	$1,100 / -	$1,200 / -	$1,300 / -	30	
2	Regular Time	$99,999	180	220	-	-	
2	Overtime	$99,999	-	20	-	-	
2	Subcontract	$99,999	-	30	-	-	
3	Regular Time	$99,999		460	-	-	
3	Overtime	$99,999		20	-	-	
3	Subcontract	$99,999		30	-	-	
4	Regular Time	$99,999			380	-	380
4	Overtime	$99,999			20	-	20
4	Subcontract	$99,999			30	-	30
	Requirements	130				30	1870

b. Now enter data for the capacity column of the tableau (final column to right). For simplicity, enter the data as thousands of pounds. The work-force plan being investigating now would provide regular-time capacities (in 000's pounds) of 390 in quarter 1, 400 in quarter 2, 460 in quarter 3, and 380 in quarter 4. Overtime is limited to production of a total of 20,000 pounds per quarter, and subcontractor capacity to only 30,000 pounds per quarter. The current inventory level is 40,000 pounds.

c. Next enter the data for the demand requirements row (last row in the tableau). The demand forecasts (in 000's pounds) are 130 in quarter 1, 400 in quarter 2, 800 in quarter 3, and 470 in quarter 4. Management wants 40,000 pounds available at the end the year. NOTE: Fourth-quarter demand should be increased in the requirements row to allow for the desired ending inventory.

d. What production levels, shipments, and anticipation inventories are called for by the optimal solution shown (bold numbers) in the tableau?

	Quarter 1	Quarter 2	Quarter 3	Quarter 4	Totals
Production					
Regular					1630
Overtime					80
Subcontract					90
Total Production					1800
Shipments					1800
Ending Inventory					810

e. What is the total cost of the optimal solution, except for the cost of hiring and layoffs?

Quarter 1:		= $ 74,700
Quarter 2:		= $ 354,000
Quarter 3:		= $ 710,000
Quarter 4:		= $ 454,000

Total   = $1,592,700

Supplement H: Linear Programming

Application H.1: Problem Formulation for Crandon Manufacturing

The Crandon Manufacturing Company produces two principal product lines. One is a portable circular saw, and the other is a precision table saw. Two basic operations are crucial to the output of these saws: fabrication and assembly. The maximum fabrication capacity is 4000 hours per month; each circular saw requires 2 hours, and each table saw requires 1 hour. The maximum assembly capacity is 5000 hours per month; each circular saw requires 1 hour, and each table saw requires 2 hours. The marketing department estimates that the maximum market demand next year is 3500 saws per month for both products. The average contribution to profits and overhead is $900 for each circular saw and $600 for each table saw.

Management wants to determine the best product mix for the next year so as to maximize contribution to profits and overhead. Also, it is interested in the payoff of expanding capacity or increasing market share.

a.   Definition of Decision Variables

$x_1 =$

$x_2 =$

b.   Formulation

Maximize:

Subject to:

Supplement H: Linear Programming

Application H.2: Graphical Solution for Crandon Manufacturing

a. Plot constraint equations

$2x_1 + x_2 \leq 4000$ (Fabrication)

$x_1 + 2x_2 \leq 5000$ (Assembly)

$x_1 + x_2 \leq 3500$ (Demand)

$x_1 \geq 0$ and $x_2 \geq 0$

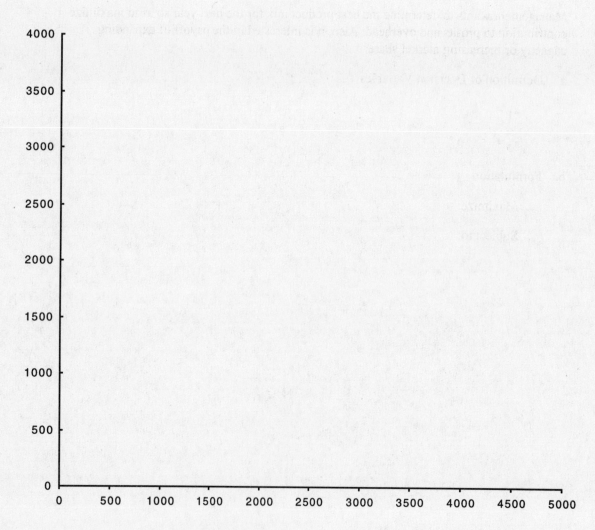

	Point 1			Point 2	
Constraint	x_1	x_2		x_1	x_2
1					
2					
3					

b. Shade feasible region

c. Plot isoprofit lines

    c. Let Z = $2,000,000 (arbitrary choice)

    d. Plot $900x_1 + $600x_2 = $2,000,000

	Point 1			Point 2	
Profit	x_1	x_2		x_1	x_2
$2,000,000	_____	_____		_____	_____

d. Identify optimal corner point

e. Solve algebraically, with two equations and two unknowns

      $2x_1 + 1x_2 \leq 4000$ (fabrication)
      $1x_1 + 2x_2 \leq 5000$ (assembly)

    Optimal Z: $900(_____) + $600(_____) = $2,100,000

f.   Find the slack at the optimal solution

   e. Slack in fabrication at (1000, 2000)

   f. Slack in assembly at (1000, 2000)

   g. Slack in demand at (1000, 2000)

Supplement H: Linear Programming

Application H.3: Range of Optimality for Crandon Manufacturing

What is the range of optimality for c_1 in Crandon Manufacturing? The two constraints defining the optimal solution are $2x_1 + 1x_2 \leq 4000$ and $1x_1 + 2x_2 \leq 5000$.

$$m_1 \quad \leq c_1/\underline{\hspace{1cm}} \quad \leq m_2$$

$$\underline{\hspace{1cm}} \leq c_1/\underline{\hspace{1cm}} \quad \leq \underline{\hspace{1cm}}$$

$$\underline{\hspace{1cm}} \leq \quad c_1 \quad \leq \underline{\hspace{1cm}}$$

Application H.4: Shadow Prices for Crandon Manufacturing

What is the shadow price of one hour of fabrication time at Crandon Manufacturing?

Original constraints

$2x_1 + 1x_2 = 4000$

$1x_1 + 2x_2 = 5000$

$x_1 = 1000$

$x_2 = 2000$

$Z = \$900(\underline{\hspace{1cm}}) + \$600(\underline{\hspace{1cm}})$

$ = \$2,100,000$

Relaxed constraints

$2x_1 + 1x_2 = 4001$

$1x_1 + 2x_2 = 5000$

$x_1 = 1000.67$

$x_2 = 1999.67$

$Z = \$900(1000.67) + \$600(1999.67)$

$ = \$2,100,400$

Shadow price = \underline{\hspace{1cm}} − \underline{\hspace{1cm}} = \underline{\hspace{1cm}}

Supplement H: Linear Programming

Application H.5: Product Mix Problem

The Trim-Look Company makes several lines of skirts, dresses, and sport coats for women. Recently it was suggested that the company reevaluate its South Islander line and allocate its resources to those products that would maximize contribution to profits and overhead. Each product must pass through the cutting and sewing departments. In addition, each product in the South Islander line requires the same polyester fabric. The following data were collected for the study.

Product	Processing Time (hr)		Material (yd)
	Cutting	Sewing	
Skirt	1	1	1
Dress	3	4	1
Sport coat	4	6	4

The cutting department has 100 hours of capacity, sewing has 180 hours, and 60 yards of material are available. Each skirt contributes $5 to profits and overhead; each dress, $17; and each sport coat, $30.

VARIABLE DEFINITIONS

FORMULATION

Supplement H: Linear Programming

Application H.6: Process Design

The plant manager of a plastic pipe manufacturer has the opportunity to use two different routings for a particular type of plastic pipe: Routing 1 uses extruder A, and routing 2 uses extruder B. Both routings require the same melting process. The following table shows the time requirements and capacities of these processes.

	Hours per 100 ft		
Process	Routing 1	Routing 2	Capacity (hr)
Melting	1	1	45
Extruder A	3	0	90
Extruder B	0	4	160

In addition, each 100 feet of pipe processed on routing 1 uses 5 pounds of raw material, whereas each 100 feet of pipe processed on routing 2 uses only 4 pounds. This difference results from differing scrap rates of the extruding machines. Consequently, the profit per 100 feet of pipe processed on routing 1 is $60 and on routing 2, $80. A total of 200 pounds of raw material is available.

VARIABLE DEFINITIONS

FORMULATION

Supplement H: Linear Programming

Application H.7: Blending Problem

A problem often of concern to managers in the process industry is blending. Consider the task facing the procurement manager of a company that manufactures special additives. She must determine the proper amounts of each raw material to purchase for the production of a certain product. Three raw materials are available. Each gallon of the finished product must have a combustion point of at least $220°$F. In addition, the gamma content (which causes hydrocarbon pollution) cannot exceed 6 percent of the volume. The zeta content (which cleans the internal moving parts of engines) must be at least 12 percent by volume. Each raw material has varying degrees of these characteristics.

Raw material Characteristic	A	B	C
Combustion point ($°$F)	200	180	280
Gamma content (%)	4	3	10
Zeta content (%)	20	10	8

Raw material A costs $0.60 per gallon; raw material B, $0.40; and raw material C, $0.50. The procurement manager wishes to minimize the cost of raw materials per gallon of product. What are the optimal proportions of each raw material to use in a gallon of finished product? *Hint:* Express your decision variables in terms of fractions of a gallon. The sum of the fractions must equal 1.00.

VARIABLE DEFINITIONS

FORMULATION

Application H.8: Portfolio Selection

Inside Traders, Inc. invests in various types of securities. The firm has $5 million for immediate investment and wishes to maximize the interest earned over the next year. Risk is not a factor. There are four investment possibilities, as outlined below. To further structure the portfolio, the board of directors has specified that at least 40 percent of the investment must be placed in corporate bonds and common stock. Furthermore, no more than 20 percent of the investment can be in real estate.

Investment	Earned (%)
Corporate bonds	8.5
Common stock	9.0
Gold certificates	10.0
Real estate	13.0

VARIABLE DEFINITIONS

FORMULATION

Supplement H: Linear Programming

Application H.9: Shift Scheduling

NYNEX has a scheduling problem. Operators work eight-hour shifts and can begin work at either midnight, 4 A.M., 8 A.M., noon, 4 P.M., or 8 P.M. Operators are needed according to the following demand pattern.

Time Period	Operators Needed
Midnight to 4 A.M.	4
4 A.M. to 8 A.M.	6
8 A.M. to noon	90
Noon to 4 P.M.	85
4 P.M. to 8 P.M.	55
8 P.M. to 12 midnight	20

Hint: Let x_j equal the number of operators beginning work (an eight-hour shift) in time period j, where $j = 1, 2, \ldots, 6$. Formulate the model to cover the demand requirements with the minimum number of operators.

VARIABLE DEFINITIONS

FORMULATION

Supplement H: Linear Programming

Application H.10: Production Planning

The Bull Grin Company produces a feed supplement for animal foods produced by a number of companies. Sales are seasonal, but Bull Grin's customers refuse to stockpile the supplement during slack sales periods. In other words, the customers want to minimize their inventory investments, insist on shipments according to their schedules, and won't accept back orders.

Bull Grin employs manual, unskilled labor, who require little or no training. Producing 1000 pounds of supplement costs $810 on regular time and $900 on overtime. These figures include materials, which account for over 80 percent of the cost. Overtime is limited to production of 30,000 pounds per quarter. In addition, subcontractors can be hired at $1100 per thousand pounds, but only 10,000 pounds per quarter can be produced this way.

The current level of inventory is 40,000 pounds, and management wants to end the year at that level. Holding 1000 pounds of feed supplement in inventory per quarter costs $110. The latest annual forecast follows.

Quarter	Demand (lb)
1	100,000
2	410,000
3	770,000
4	440,000
Total	1,720,000

The firm currently has 180 workers, a figure that management wants to keep in quarter 4. Each worker can produce 2000 pounds per quarter, so that regular-time production costs $1620 per worker. Idle workers must be paid at that same rate. Hiring one worker costs $1000, and laying off a worker costs $600.

VARIABLE DEFINITIONS

FORMULATION

Chapter 15: Material Requirements Planning

Application 15.1: Calculating an MRP Record

Item H10-A is a produced item (not purchased) with an order quantity of 80 units.
Complete the rest of its MRP record using the fixed order quatity (FOQ) rule.

Item: H10-A **Lot Size:** POQ=80 units

Description: Chair seat assembly **Lead Time:** 4 weeks

		Week									
		31	32	33	34	35	36	37	38	39	40
Gross requirements			60				35		45		60
Scheduled receipts			80								
Projected on-hand inventory	20										
Planned receipts											
Planned order releases											

Application 15.2: MRP Record with POQ Rule

Now complete the H10-A record using a POQ rule. The *P* should give an average lot size of 80 units. Assume the average weekly requirements are 20 units

P = _____ = _____ weeks.

Item: H10-A   **Lot Size:** POQ= 4

Description: Chair seat assembly   **Lead Time:** 4 weeks

		Week								
	31	32	33	34	35	36	37	38	39	40
Gross requirements		60				35		45		60
Scheduled receipts		80								
Projected on-hand inventory 20										
Planned receipts										
Planned order releases										

Chapter 15: Material Requirements Planning

Application 15.3: MRP Record using the lot-for-lot (L4L) Rule

Revise the H10-A record using the lot-for-lot (L4L) Rule.

Item: H10-A							Lot Size: L4L			
Description: Chair seat assembly							Lead Time: 4 weeks			
	Week									
	31	32	33	34	35	36	37	38	39	40
Gross requirements		60				35		45		60
Scheduled receipts		80								
Projected on-hand inventory 20										
Planned receipts										
Planned order releases										

Chapter 15: Material Requirements Planning

Application 15.4: Material Requirements Plan for Single Product Case.

A firm makes a product (Item A) from three components (Items B, C, and D). The latest MPS for product A calls for completeion of a 250-unit order in week 8, and its lead time is 2 weeks. The master schedule and bill of material for Product A are given below.

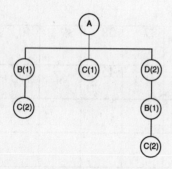

Item: End Item A							Lead Time: 2 wks.	
	Week							
	1	2	3	4	5	6	7	8
MPS Quantity								250
MPS Start						250		

A. Develop a material requirements plan for items B, C, and D, given the following inventory data. Blank MRP records are also provided.

ITEM

Data Category	B	C	D
Lot-sizing rule	L4tL	FOQ=1000	L4L
Lead time	2 weeks	1 week	3 weeks
Scheduled receipts	None	1000(week 1)	None
Beginning inventory	0	200	0

B.

Item: Description:						Lot Size: units Lead Time: weeks			
	Week								
	1	2	3	4	5	6	7	8
Gross requirements									
Scheduled receipts									
Projected on-hand inventory									
Planned receipts									
Planned order releases									

C.

Item: Description:					Lot Size: Lead Time:		units weeks
	Week						
	1	2	3	4	5	6	7	8
Gross requirements								
Scheduled receipts								
Projected on-hand inventory								
Planned receipts								
Planned order releases								

D.

Item: Description:					Lot Size: Lead Time:		units weeks
	Week						
	1	2	3	4	5	6	7	8
Gross requirements								
Scheduled receipts								
Projected on-hand inventory								
Planned receipts								
Planned order releases								

b. Why will there be no action notices for items B, D, and E?

AP 15.4 cont.

Chapter 15: Material Requirements Planning

Application 15.5: Material Requirements Plan for Multiple Product Case

A firm makes two products (Items A and B) from four components (Items C,D,E, and F). The master schedule and bills of material for the products are given below.

Master Schedule

Item: End item A										Lead Time: 2 weeks	
	Week										
	1	2	3	4	5	6	7	8	9	10
MPS quantity				50				60		
MPS start		50				60				

Master Schedule

Item: End item B										Lead Time: 1 week	
	Week										
	1	2	3	4	5	6	7	8	9	10
MPS quantity					200					
MPS start				200						

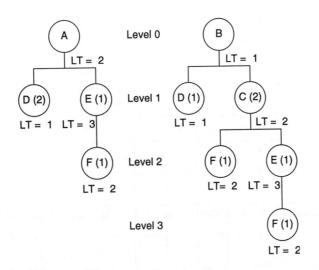

a. Develop a material requirements plan for items B,C,D, and E, given the following inventory data. Blamk MRP records are also provided.

ITEM

Data Category	C	D	E	F
Lot-sizing rule	FOQ=400	POQ(P=3)	L4L	L4L
Lead time	2 weeks	1 week	3 weeks	2 weeks
Scheduled receipts	None	None	450(week1)	None
Beginning inventory	100	70	0	425

B.

Item: Description:						Lot Size: units Lead Time: weeks			
	Week								
	1	2	3	4	5	6	7	8
Gross requirements									
Scheduled receipts									
Projected on-hand inventory									
Planned receipts									
Planned order releases									

C.

Item: Description:						Lot Size: units Lead Time: weeks			
	Week								
	1	2	3	4	5	6	7	8
Gross requirements									
Scheduled receipts									
Projected on-hand inventory									
Planned receipts									
Planned order releases									

AP 15.5 cont.

D.

Item: Description:							Lot Size:	units
							Lead Time:	weeks
					Week			
	1	2	3	4	5	6	7	8
Gross requirements								
Scheduled receipts								
Projected on-hand inventory								
Planned receipts								
Planned order releases								

E.

Item: Description:							Lot Size:	units
							Lead Time:	weeks
					Week			
	1	2	3	4	5	6	7	8
Gross requirements								
Scheduled receipts								
Projected on-hand inventory								
Planned receipts								
Planned order releases								

b.   What action notices will be given for items B,C,D, and E?

Supplement I: Master Production Scheduling

Application I.1: Developing a Master Production Schedule

Determine the MPS for an item with a 50-unit policy and 5 units on hand. The demand forecass and booked orders are shown in the partially complated plan given below. The lead time is one week.

Lot Size	50										
Lead Time	1										
Quantity on Hand	5	1	2	3	4	5	6	7	8	9	10
Forecast		20	10	40	10	0	0	30	20	40	20
Customer Orders (Booked)		30	20	5	8	0	2	0	0	0	0
Projected On-Hand Inventory											
MPS Quantity											
MPS start											
Available-to-Promise Inv (ATP)											

Chapter 16: Just-in-Time Systems

Application 16.1: Determining the Number of Containers

Item B52R has an average daily demand of 1000 units. The average waiting time per container of parts (which holds 100 units) is 0.5 day. The processing time per container is 0.1 day. If the policy variable is set at 10 percent, how many containers are required?

Application 17.1: Scheduling at One Operation Using SPT

Given the following information, devise an SPT schedule for the automatic routing machine.

Order	Standard time, Including Setup (hr)	Due Date (hrs from now)
AZ135	14	14
DM246	8	20
SX435	10	6
PC088	3	18

Order Sequence	Begin Work	End Work	Flow Time (hr)	Scheduled Customer Pickup Time	Actual Customer Pickup Time	Hours Early	Hours Past Due
1.							
2.							
3.							
4.							
Total			____		____	____	____
Average			____		____	____	____

Average work-in-process = _____   Average total Inventory   = _____

Application 17.2: Scheduling at One Operation Using CR and S/RO

The following four jobs must be scheduled on a drill press.

Job	Operation Time at Drill Press (wk)	Time Remaining to Due Date (wks)	Number of Operations Remaining*	Shop Time Remaining* (wks)
AA	4	5	3	4
BB	8	11	4	6
CC	13	16	10	9
DD	6	18	3	12
EE	2	7	5	3

* Including drill press

Create the sequences for two schedules, one using the Critical Ratio rule and one using the S/RO rule.

	Critical Ratio			Slack/Remaining Operation	
Job	Priority Index	Sequence on Drill Press	Job	Priority Index	Sequence on Drill Press
AA			AA		
BB			BB		
CC			CC		
DD			DD		
EE			EE		

Application 17.3: Sequencing Jobs at a Two-Station Flow Shop Using Johnson's Rule

Use the following data to schedule two machines arranged as a flow shop

| Job | Time (hr) | |
	Machine 1	Machine 2
A	4	3
B	10	20
C	2	15
D	8	7
E	14	13

Job Sequence

Chapter 17: Scheduling

Application 17.4: Developing a Work-Force Schedule

Given the following daily requirements (in employees required per day), show in the rows of space below a work-force schedule that involves the least number of employees and provides each employee two consecutive days off.

M 6	T 3	W 5	Th 3	F 7	S 2	Su 3	EMPLOYEE

Chapter 18: Managing Projects

Application 18.1: Diagramming the Network

Draw the network for a hospital project, given the following activities and immediate predecessors. Your instructor will indicate whether you should use the AOA or AON approach.

Activity	Description	Immediate Predecessor(s)
A	Select administrative and medical staff.	—
B	Select site and do site survey.	—
C	Select equipment.	A
D	Prepare final construction plans and layout.	B
E	Bring utilities to the site.	B
F	Interview applicants and fill positions in nursing, support staff, maintenance, and security.	A
G	Purchase and take delivery of equipment.	C
H	Construct the hospital.	D
I	Develop an information system.	A
J	Install the equipment.	E, G, H
K	Train nurses and support staff.	F, I, J

Start

Finish

AP 18.1

Chapter 18: Managing Projects

Application 18.2: Estimating Time of Completion

Given the data below, find the critical path for the hospital project.

Activity	Time
A	12
B	9
C	10
D	10
E	24
F	10
G	35
H	40
I	15
J	4
K	6

Path	Length
1. _____	____
2. _____	____
3. _____	____
4. _____	____
5. _____	____

Application 18.3: Earliest Start and Earliest Finish Times

Find the earliest start and earliest finish times for the hospital project. Let EF for the start node be 0. What is the project's "earliest expected completion time"?

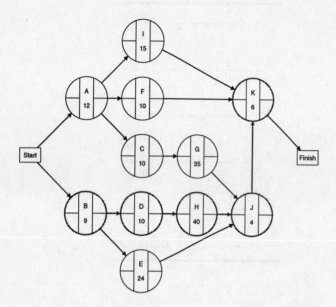

Activity	ES	EF
A		
B		
C		
D		
E		
F		
G		
H		
I		
J		
K		

Chapter 18: Managing Projects

Application 18.4: Latest Start and Latest Finish Times

Find the latest start and latest finish times for the hospital project. Let the ES of the finish mode be the project's earliest expected completion time.

Activity	LS	LF
A		
B		
C		
D		
E		
F		
G		
H		
I		
J		
K		

Chapter 18: Managing Projects

Application 18.5: Activity Slacks

Calculate each activity slack for the hospital project. What is the critical path?

Activity	LS	LF	Slack	Critical Path?
A				
B				
C				
D				
E				
F				
G				
H				
I				
J				
K				

Chapter 18: Managing Projects

Application 18.6: Calculating Time Statistics

Finish the table below for activities A and B.

| Activity | Time Estimates (wk) | | | Activity Statistics | |
	Most Optimistic (*a*)	Most Likely (*m*)	Most Pessimistic (*b*)	Expected Time (t_e)	Variance (σ^2)
A	11	12	13		
B	7	8	15		
C	5	10	15	10	2.78
D	8	9	16	10	1.78
E	14	25	30	24	7.11
F	6	9	18	10	4.00
G	25	36	41	35	7.11
H	35	40	45	40	2.78
I	10	13	28	15	9.00
J	1	2	15	4	5.44
K	5	6	7	6	0.11

A: t_e = _____

σ^2 = _____

B: t_e = _____

σ^2 = _____

Application 18.7: Analyzing Probabilities

How likely is it that the hospital project will be completed in 75 weeks? Use the normal table in Appendix 2.

σ^2 =   _____

z =   _____

Probability   =   _____

TRANSPARENCY MASTERS

Labor Productivity Calculations

	This Yr.	Last Yr.	Yr. Before Last
Factory Unit Sales	2,762,103	2,475,738	2,175,447
Employment	112,000	113,000	115,000

Calculate the year-to-year percentage in labor productivity:

Output/Employee

Productivity Improvement Calculation

To accompany *Operations Management Strategy and Analysis, 5/e,* by Krajewski and Ritzman. Copyright © 1999 by Addison Wesley Longman, Inc. All rights reserved. **TM 1.1a**

Multifactor Productivity Calculations

	This Yr.	Last Yr.
Sales of Mfd. Products (MM)	$49,363	$40,831
Total Mfg. Cost of Sales (MM)	$39,000	$33,000

Calculate the multifactor productivity:

Value of Output/Value of Input

Productivity Improvement Calculations

Supplement A: Decision Making

Denver Zoo Graphical Solution Axes

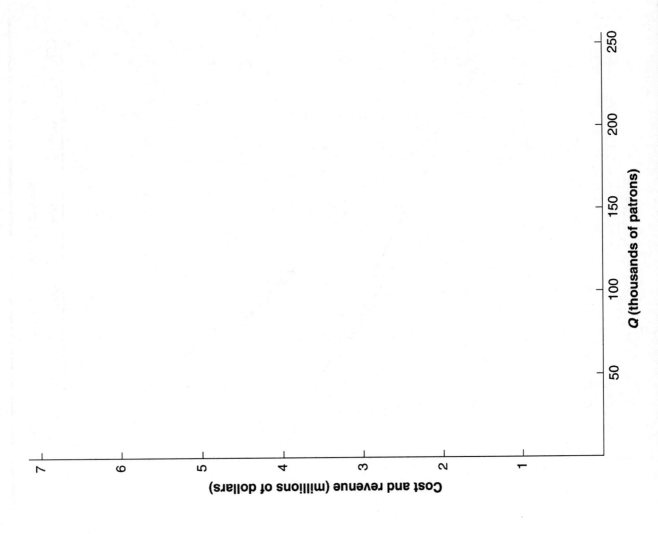

Q (thousands of patrons)

Cost and revenue (millions of dollars)

TM A.1a

Denver Zoo
Graphical Solution

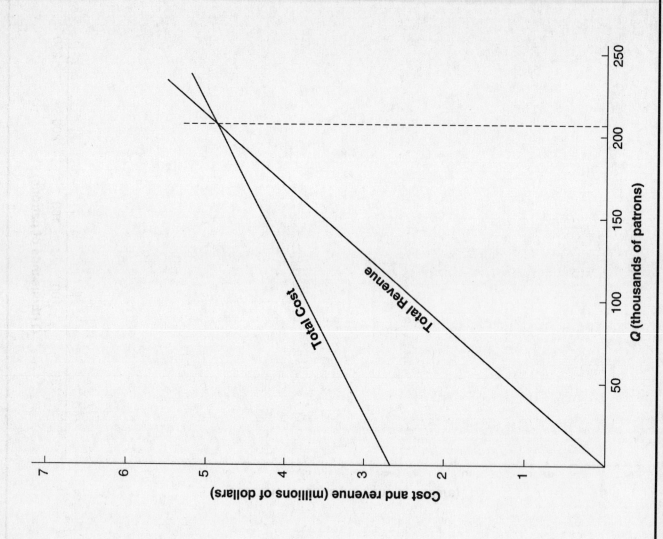

Denver Zoo Algebraic Solution

$$pQ = F + cQ$$

$$(4 + 5 + 15)Q = (2,400,000 + 220,000 + 30,000) + (2 + 9)Q$$

$$24Q = 2,650,000 + 11Q$$

$$13Q = 2,650,000$$

$$Q = 203,846 \text{ patrons}$$

Supplement A: Decision Making

Sensitivity Analysis

Variable Costs

Given $Q = 200,000$, find c

$$Q = F/(p - c)$$

$$p - c = F/Q$$

$$c = p - F/Q$$

$$= \$24 - \$2,650,000/200,000$$

$$= \$10.75$$

Supplement A: Decision Making

Sensitivity Analysis

Fixed Costs

Given $Q = 200{,}000$, $p = \$24$, and $c = \$11$, find F

$$Q = F/(p - c)$$

$$F = Q(p - c)$$

$$= 200{,}000(24 - 11)$$

$$= \$2{,}600{,}000$$

TM A.1e

Supplement A: Decision Making

Sensitivity Analysis

Price

Given $Q = 200,000$, $c = \$11$, $F = \$2,650,000$, concessions = $\$5$, and apparel = $\$15$, find the gate price

$$Q = F/(p - c)$$

$$p = F/Q + c$$

$$= \$2,650,000/200,000 + \$11$$

$$= \$24.25$$

and apparel = $\$20.00$

Gate price = $\$4.25$

Supplement A: Decision Making

Make-or-Buy Decision

Buy	Make
$F_b + c_b Q$	$F_m + c_m Q$

$$= $$

$$Q = \frac{F_b - F_m}{(c_b - c_m)}$$

Break-even quantity

Buy

Make

F_m

F_b

Dollars

Quantity (Q)

Supplement A: Decision Making

Make-or-Buy Decision

	Buy	Make
Fixed costs	$0	$300,000
Variable costs	$9	$7

$$Q = \frac{(\$300,000 - \$0)}{(\$9 - \$7)} = 150,000 \text{ patrons}$$

Preference Matrix

Initial

Performance Criterion	Weight	Score	Weighted Score
Market potential	10	5	
Unit profit margin	30	8	
Operations compatibility	20	10	
Competitive advantage	25	7	
Investment requirement	10	3	
Project risk	5	4	
		Weighted Score =	

Supplement A: Decision Making

Preference Matrix

Final

Performance Criterion	Weight	Score	Weighted Score
Market potential	10	5	50
Unit profit margin	30	8	240
Operations compatibility	20	10	200
Competitive advantage	25	7	175
Investment requirement	10	3	30
Project risk	5	4	20
Weighted Score =			715

Decision Analysis

CF&W Company

Payoffs (Profits)

Product	Land Route No Treaty	Land Route Treaty	Sea Route (	Maximin
Arrows	$840,000	$440,000	$190,000	
Barrels	$370,000	$220,000	$670,000	
Wagons	$25,000	$1,150,000	($25,000)	

Conclusion:

TM A.4a

Supplement A: Decision Making

Decision Analysis

CF&W Company

Payoffs (Profits)

Product	Land Route No Treaty	Land Route Treaty	Sea Route Only	Maximax
Arrows	$840,000	$440,000	$190,000	
Barrels	$370,000	$220,000	$670,000	
Wagons	$25,000	$1,150,000	($25,000)	

Conclusion:

Decision Analysis

CF&W Company

Payoffs (Profits)

Product	Land Route No Treaty	Land Route Treaty	Sea Route Only	Laplace
Arrows	$840,000	$440,000	$190,000	
Barrels	$370,000	$220,000	$670,000	
Wagons	$25,000	$1,150,000	($25,000)	

Conclusion:

Supplement A: Decision Making

Decision Analysis

CF&W Company

Payoffs (Profits)

Product	Land Route No Treaty	Land Route Treaty	Sea Route Only
Arrows	$840,000	$440,000	$190,000
Barrels	$370,000	$220,000	$670,000
Wagons	$25,000	$1,150,000	($25,000)

Regret Matrix

Product	Land Route No Treaty	Land Route Treaty	Sea Route Only	Minimax Regret
Arrows				
Barrels				
Wagons				

Conclusion:

Decision Making Under Risk

CF&W Company

Payoffs (Profits)

Product	Land Route No Treaty	Land Route Treaty	Sea Route Only
Arrows	$840,000	$440,000	$190,000
Barrels	$370,000	$220,000	$670,000
Wagons	$25,000	$1,150,000	($25,000)

Expected-Value Calculation

Product

Arrows (0.5)(   ) + (0.3)(   ) + (0.2)(   ) =

Barrels (0.5)(   ) + (0.3)(   ) + (0.2)(   ) =

Wagons (0.5)(   ) + (0.3)(   ) + (0.2)(   ) =

Conclusion:

Supplement A: Decision Making

Decision Tree
CF&W Company

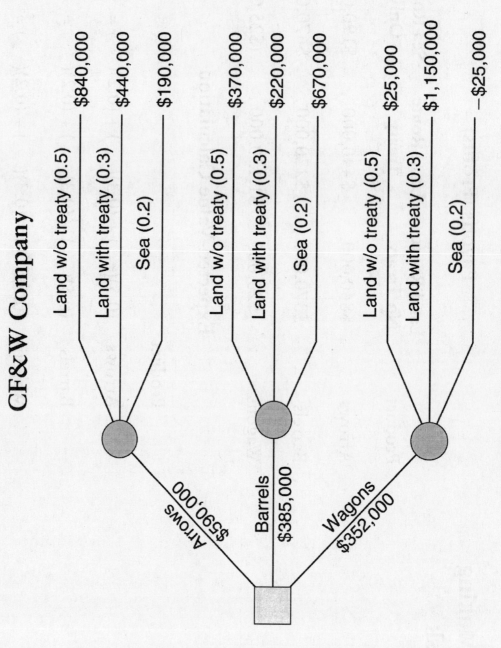

Land w/o treaty (0.5)		$840,000
Land with treaty (0.3)		$440,000
Sea (0.2)		$190,000
Land w/o treaty (0.5)		$370,000
Land with treaty (0.3)		$220,000
Sea (0.2)		$670,000
Land w/o treaty (0.5)		$25,000
Land with treaty (0.3)		$1,150,000
Sea (0.2)		−$25,000

Arrows $590,000

Barrels $385,000

Wagons $352,000

Conclusion: Choose Arrows

Decision Tree
(Figure A.6)

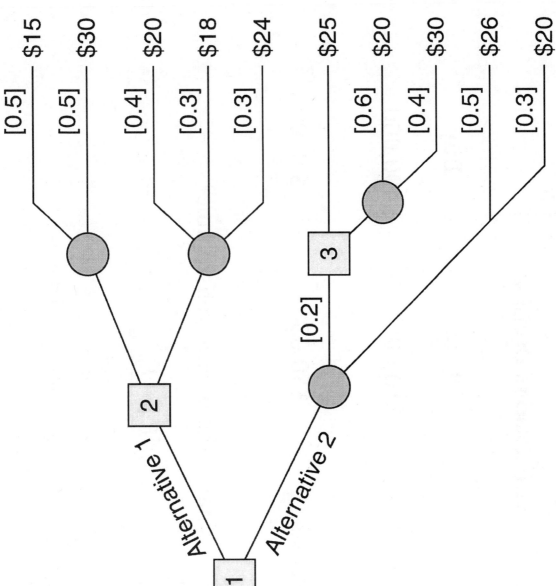

BBC Process Decision

	Make	Buy
Fixed costs	$10,000	$400,000
Variable costs	$50.00	$20.00

What is the break-even volume?

$$Q = \frac{F_m - F_b}{c_b - c_m} =$$

$$Q = \underline{\hspace{3cm}} \text{ frames}$$

Time Study Application

Element	Initial Observation Cycle, minutes									Select Time, $\bar{t}$	Standard Dev, σ
	1	2	3	4	5	6	7	8	9		
Wrap #1:	.10	.08	.08	.12	.10	.10	.12	.09	.11	0.1	0.015
Pack #2:	.10	.08	.08	.11	.06	.98*	.17	.11	.09	0.1	0.03295
Close #3:	.27	...	...	...	.34	...	...	...	.29	0.3	0.03606

To determine sample size, use the largest value of $\dfrac{\sigma}{\bar{t}}$

$$n = \left[\left(\frac{z}{p} \right) \left(\frac{\sigma}{\bar{t}} \right) \right]^2 = \left[\left(\frac{1.96}{0.06} \right) \left(\frac{0.03295}{0.01} \right) \right] = 116$$

Determining the Standard Time

Element	Select Time, t	Freq.	Rating Factor	Normal Time
Wrap #1:	0.10	1.00	1.2	0.12
Pack #2:	0.10	1.00	0.9	0.09
Close #3:	0.30	0.25	0.8	0.06

$$NTC = 0.12 + 0.09 + 0.06 = 0.27 \text{ min.}$$

$$ST = 0.27(1 + 0.185) = 0.32 \text{ min.}$$

Observation Form for Work Sampling

	Play or Acceptable Delay	Unacceptable Delay	Total
Pitchers			
Batters			

TM 5.2a

Recorded Data
for Work Sampling

	Play or Acceptable Delay	Unacceptable Delay	Total	p
Pitchers	289	96	385	0.25
Batters	339	46	385	0.18

Do we need a larger sample?

Pitchers : $n = \left(\dfrac{1.96}{0.04}\right)^2 (0.25)(1 - 0.25) = 450$

Batters : $n = \left(\dfrac{1.96}{0.04}\right)^2 (0.18)(1 - 0.18) = 254$

Conclusion?

Results of the Initial Study
(Figure 5.2)

	Accessing records	Attending to patients	Other support activities	Idle or break	Total observations
			Activity		
RN	124	258	223	83	688
LVN	28	251	46	19	344

Supplement C: Learning Curves

Calculations on Learning Curve

Given

$$k_1 = 1000$$

$$n = 50$$

$$r = 0.80$$

Calculations

$$k_n = k_1 n^b$$

$$k_{50} = 1000 \, (50)^{(\log 0.8)/(\log 2)}$$

$$= 1000 \, (50)^{-0.32192}$$

$$= 1000 \, (0.283827)$$

$$k_{50} = 283.8 \text{ hrs.}$$

Conversion Factors for the Cumulative Average Number of Direct Labor Hours per Unit (Table C.1)

80% Learning Rate (n = cumulative production)

n		n		n	
1	1.00000	19	0.53178	37	0.43976
2	0.90000	20	0.52425	38	0.43634
3	0.83403	21	0.51715	39	0.43304
4	0.78553	22	0.51045	40	0.42984
5	0.74755	23	0.50410	64	0.37382
6	0.71657	24	0.49808	128	0.30269
7	0.69056	25	0.49234	256	0.24405
8	0.66824	26	0.48688	512	0.19622
9	0.64876	27	0.48167	600	0.18661
10	0.63154	28	0.47668	700	0.17771
11	0.61613	29	0.47191	800	0.17034
12	0.60224	30	0.46733	900	0.16408
13	0.58960	31	0.46293	1000	0.15867
14	0.57802	32	0.45871	1200	0.14972
15	0.56737	33	0.45464	1400	0.14254
16	0.55751	34	0.45072	1600	0.13660
17	0.54834	35	0.44694	1800	0.13155
18	0.53979	36	0.44329	2000	0.12720

90% Learning Rate (n = cumulative production)

n		n		n	
1	1.00000	19	0.73545	37	0.67091
2	0.95000	20	0.73039	38	0.66839
3	0.91540	21	0.72559	39	0.66595
4	0.88905	22	0.72102	40	0.66357
5	0.86784	23	0.71666	64	0.62043
6	0.85013	24	0.71251	128	0.56069
7	0.83496	25	0.70853	256	0.50586
8	0.82172	26	0.70472	512	0.45594
9	0.80998	27	0.70106	600	0.44519
10	0.79945	28	0.69754	700	0.43496
11	0.78991	29	0.69416	800	0.42629
12	0.78120	30	0.69090	900	0.41878
13	0.77320	31	0.68775	1000	0.41217
14	0.76580	32	0.68471	1200	0.40097
15	0.75891	33	0.68177	1400	0.39173
16	0.75249	34	0.67893	1600	0.38390
17	0.74646	35	0.67617	1800	0.37711
18	0.74080	36	0.67350	2000	0.37114

TM C.2a

Learning Curve Calculations

First Job

$$\text{Average}_{38} = 1000(0.43634) = 436.34$$

$$\text{Total}_{38} = 436.34(38) = 16,581 \text{ hr}$$

Conclusion: Trouble

Second Job

$$\text{Average}_{64} = 1000(0.37382) = 373.82$$

$$\text{Total}_{64} = 373.82(64) = 23,924 \text{ hr}$$

$$\text{Total}_{64} - \text{Total}_{38} = 23,924 - 16,581$$
$$= 7,343 \text{ hr}$$

TM C.2b

Chapter 6: Total Quality Management

Reliability

	Old Car	New Car
Available keys	0.95	0.95
Fuel in tank	0.80	0.80
Charged battery	0.98	0.98
Functional computer	—	0.92

Old car reliability:　　$r_s =$

New car reliability:　　$r_s =$

Factors for Calculating Three-Sigma Limits
For $\bar{x}$-Chart and $\bar{R}$-Chart
(Table 7.1)

Size of Sample (n)	Factor for UCL and LCL for $\bar{x}$-Charts (A_2)	Factor for LCL for R-Charts (D_3)	Factor for UCL for R-Charts (D_4)
2	1.880	0	3.267
3	1.023	0	2.575
4	0.729	0	2.282
5	0.577	0	2.115
6	0.483	0	2.004
7	0.419	0.076	1.924
8	0.373	0.136	1.864
9	0.337	0.184	1.816
10	0.308	0.223	1.777

Source: 1950 ASTM *Manual on Quality Control of Materials*, copyright © American Society for Testing Materials. Reprinted with permission.

TM 7.1a

Webster Chemical Filling Process

Sample	Tube Number								Range
	1	2	3	4	5	6	7	8	
1	7.98	8.34	8.02	7.94	8.44	7.68	7.81	8.11	0.76
2	8.23	8.12	7.98	8.41	8.31	8.18	7.99	8.06	0.43
3	7.89	7.77	7.91	8.04	8.00	7.89	7.93	8.09	0.32
4	8.24	8.18	7.83	8.05	7.90	8.16	7.97	8.07	0.41
5	7.87	8.13	7.92	7.99	8.10	7.81	8.14	7.88	0.33
6	8.13	8.14	8.11	8.13	8.14	8.12	8.13	8.14	0.03
					Average				0.38

$$UCL_R = 1.864(0.38) = 0.708 \quad LCL_R = 0.136(0.38) = 0.052$$

What is the conclusion on process variability?

Webster Chemical Filling Process
Sample 6 Data Deleted

Sample	Tube Number								Avg	Range
	1	2	3	4	5	6	7	8		
1	7.98	8.34	8.02	7.94	8.44	7.68	7.81	8.11	8.040	0.76
2	8.23	8.12	7.98	8.41	8.31	8.18	7.99	8.06	8.160	0.43
3	7.89	7.77	7.91	8.04	8.00	7.89	7.93	8.09	7.940	0.32
4	8.24	8.18	7.83	8.05	7.90	8.16	7.97	8.07	8.050	0.41
5	7.87	8.13	7.92	7.99	8.10	7.81	8.14	7.88	7.980	0.33
Averages									8.034	0.45

$UCL_R = 1.864(0.45) = 0.839$ $UCL_{\bar{x}} = 8.0 + 0.373(0.45) = 8.168$

$LCL_R = 0.136(0.45) = 0.061$ $LCL_{\bar{x}} = 8.0 - 0.373(0.45) = 7.832$

Conclusions?

TM 7.1c

Webster Chemical Capping Process
Number of defective tubes in a box of 144)

Sample	Tubes	Sample	Tubes	Sample	Tubes
1	3	8	6	15	5
2	5	9	4	16	0
3	3	10	9	17	2
4	4	11	2	18	6
5	2	12	6	19	2
6	4	13	5	20	1
7	2	14	1	Total	72

TM 7.2a

p-Chart for Mastics and Caulking

$$\bar{p} = \frac{\text{Total number of leaky tubes}}{\text{Total number of tubes}} = \underline{\hspace{2cm}}$$

$$\bar{p} = \sqrt{\frac{\bar{p}(1-\bar{p})}{n}} = \sqrt{\phantom{\frac{a}{b}}} = \sqrt{144} = $$

$$UCL = $$

$$LCL = $$

TM 7.2b

Webster Chemical Caulking Defects

Tube #	Lumps	Tube #	Lumps	Tube #	Lumps
1	6	5	6	9	5
2	5	6	4	10	0
3	0	7	1	11	9
4	4	8	6	12	2

$$\bar{c} = \frac{6 + 5 + \cdots + 2}{12} = 4$$

$$\sigma_c = \sqrt{4} = 2$$

$$UCL_c = 4 + (2)(2) = 8$$

$$LCL_c = 4 - (2)(2) = 0$$

Conclusion?

Webster Chemical Process Capability

Nominal Weight: 8.00 ounces ± 0.60 ounce

$$\bar{\bar{x}} = 8.054 \text{ ounces} \qquad \sigma = 0.192 \text{ ounce}$$

Process Capability Ratio:

$$C_p = \frac{8.60 - 7.40}{6(0.192)} = 1.0417$$

Process Capability Index:

$$C_{pk} = \text{Min} \left[\frac{8.054 - 7.400}{3(0.192)} = 1.135, \ \frac{8.600 - 8.054}{3(0.192)} = 0.948 \right]$$

$$C_{pk} = 0.948$$

Conclusion?

TM 7.4

Supplement D: Acceptance Sampling

Application

A sampling plan is being evaluated where $c = 10$ and $n = 193$. If AQL $= 0.03$ and LTPD $= 0.08$, what are the producer's risk and consumer's risk for the plan?

- Finding α (probability of rejecting AQL quality)

$p =$

$np =$

$P_a =$

$\alpha = 1 - P_a =$

- Finding β (probability of accepting LTPD quality)

$p =$

$np =$

$P_a =$

$\beta = P_a =$

Supplement D: Acceptance Sampling

Drawing the OC Curve

For $n = 193$, $c = 10$, compute P_a for various values of proportion defective (p).

Proportion defective	np	P_a
1%	1.93	1.00
2%	3.86	1.00
3%	5.79	0.96
4%	7.72	0.85
5%	9.65	0.65
6%	11.58	0.40
7%	13.51	0.25
8%	15.44	0.10
9%	17.37	0.05
10%	19.30	0.01

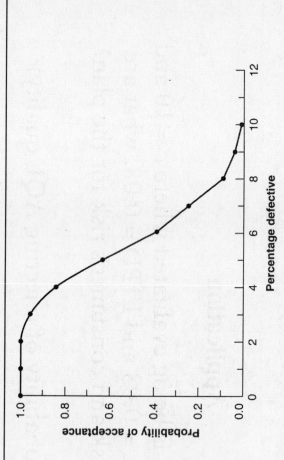

Supplement D: Acceptance Sampling

Cumulative Poisson Probabilities

x

np	0	1	2	3	4	5	6	7	8	9	10	11	12	13
4.2	.015	.078	.210	.395	.590	.753	.867	.936	.972	.989	.996	.999	1.000	
4.4	.012	.066	.185	.359	.551	.720	.844	.921	.964	.985	.994	.998	.999	1.000
4.6	.010	.056	.163	.326	.513	.686	.818	.905	.955	.980	.992	.997	.999	1.000
4.8	.008	.048	.143	.294	.476	.651	.791	.887	.944	.975	.990	.996	.999	1.000
5.0	.007	.040	.125	.265	.440	.616	.762	.867	.932	.968	.986	.995	.998	.999
5.2	.006	.034	.109	.238	.406	.581	.732	.845	.918	.960	.982	.993	.997	.999
5.4	.005	.029	.095	.213	.373	.546	.702	.822	.903	.951	.977	.990	.996	.999
5.6	.004	.024	.082	.191	.342	.512	.670	.797	.886	.941	.972	.988	.995	.998
5.8	.003	.021	.072	.170	.313	.478	.638	.771	.867	.929	.965	.984	.993	.997
6.0	.002	.017	.062	.151	.285	.446	.606	.744	.847	.916	.957	.980	.991	.996
6.2	.002	.015	.054	.134	.259	.414	.574	.716	.826	.902	.949	.975	.989	.995
6.4	.002	.012	.046	.119	.235	.384	.542	.687	.803	.886	.939	.969	.986	.994
6.6	.001	.010	.040	.105	.213	.355	.511	.658	.780	.869	.927	.963	.982	.992
6.8	.001	.009	.034	.093	.192	.327	.480	.628	.755	.850	.915	.955	.978	.990
7.0	.001	.007	.030	.082	.173	.301	.450	.599	.729	.830	.901	.947	.973	.987
7.2	.001	.006	.025	.072	.156	.276	.420	.569	.703	.810	.887	.937	.967	.984
7.4	.001	.005	.022	.063	.140	.253	.392	.539	.676	.788	.871	.926	.961	.980
7.6	.001	.004	.019	.055	.125	.231	.365	.510	.648	.765	.854	.915	.954	.976
7.8	.000	.004	.016	.048	.112	.210	.338	.481	.620	.741	.835	.902	.945	.971
8.0	.000	.003	.014	.042	.100	.191	.313	.453	.593	.717	.816	.888	.936	.966
8.2	.000	.003	.012	.037	.089	.174	.290	.425	.565	.692	.796	.873	.926	.960
8.4	.000	.002	.010	.032	.079	.157	.267	.399	.537	.666	.774	.857	.915	.952
8.6	.000	.002	.009	.028	.070	.142	.246	.373	.509	.640	.752	.840	.903	.945
8.8	.000	.001	.007	.024	.062	.128	.226	.348	.482	.614	.729	.822	.890	.936
9.0	.000	.001	.006	.021	.055	.116	.207	.324	.456	.587	.706	.803	.876	.926
9.2	.000	.001	.005	.018	.049	.104	.189	.301	.430	.561	.682	.783	.861	.916
9.4	.000	.001	.005	.016	.043	.093	.173	.279	.404	.535	.658	.763	.845	.904
9.6	.000	.001	.004	.014	.038	.084	.157	.258	.380	.509	.633	.741	.828	.892
9.8	.000	.001	.003	.012	.033	.075	.143	.239	.356	.483	.608	.719	.810	.879
10.0	0	.000	.003	.010	.029	.067	.130	.220	.333	.458	.583	.697	.792	.864
10.2	0	.000	.002	.009	.026	.060	.118	.203	.311	.433	.558	.674	.772	.849
10.4	0	.000	.002	.008	.023	.053	.107	.186	.290	.409	.533	.650	.752	.834
10.6	0	.000	.002	.007	.020	.048	.097	.171	.269	.385	.508	.627	.732	.817
10.8	0	.000	.001	.006	.017	.042	.087	.157	.250	.363	.484	.603	.710	.799
11.0	0	.000	.001	.005	.015	.038	.079	.143	.232	.341	.460	.579	.689	.781
11.2	0	.000	.001	.004	.013	.033	.071	.131	.215	.319	.436	.555	.667	.762
11.4	0	.000	.001	.004	.012	.029	.064	.119	.198	.299	.413	.532	.644	.743
11.6	0	.000	.001	.003	.010	.026	.057	.108	.183	.279	.391	.508	.622	.723
11.8	0	.000	.001	.003	.009	.023	.051	.099	.169	.260	.369	.485	.599	.702
12.0	0	.000	.001	.002	.008	.020	.046	.090	.155	.242	.347	.462	.576	.682

Cumulative Poisson Probabilities

np	\(x\) 0	1	2	3	4	5	6	7	8	9	10	11	12	13
12.2	0	0	0.000	0.002	0.007	0.018	0.041	0.081	0.142	0.225	0.327	0.439	0.553	0.660
12.4	0	0	0.000	0.002	0.006	0.016	0.037	0.073	0.131	0.209	0.307	0.417	0.530	0.639
12.6	0	0	0.000	0.001	0.005	0.014	0.033	0.066	0.120	0.194	0.288	0.395	0.508	0.617
12.8	0	0	0.000	0.001	0.004	0.012	0.029	0.060	0.109	0.179	0.269	0.374	0.485	0.595
13.0	0	0	0.000	0.001	0.004	0.011	0.026	0.054	0.100	0.166	0.252	0.353	0.463	0.573
13.2	0	0	.000	.001	.003	.009	.023	.049	.091	.153	.235	.333	.441	.551
13.4	0	0	.000	.001	.003	.008	.020	.044	.083	.141	.219	.314	.420	.529
13.6	0	0	.000	.001	.002	.007	.018	.039	.075	.130	.204	.295	.399	.507
13.8	0	0	.000	.001	.002	.006	.016	.035	.068	.119	.189	.277	.378	.486
14.0	0	0	.000	.000	.002	.006	.014	.032	.062	.109	.176	.260	.358	.464
14.2	0	0	0	.000	.002	.005	.013	.028	.056	.100	.163	.244	.339	.443
14.4	0	0	0	.000	.001	.004	.011	.025	.051	.092	.151	.228	.320	.423
14.6	0	0	0	.000	.001	.004	.010	.023	.046	.084	.139	.213	.302	.402
14.8	0	0	0	.000	.001	.003	.009	.020	.042	.077	.129	.198	.285	.383
15.0	0	0	0	.000	.001	.003	.008	.018	.037	.070	.118	.185	.268	.363
15.2	0	0	0	.000	.001	.002	.007	.016	.034	.064	.109	.172	.251	.344
15.4	0	0	0	.000	.001	.002	.006	.014	.030	.058	.100	.160	.236	.326
15.6	0	0	0	.000	.001	.002	.005	.013	.027	.053	.092	.148	.221	.308
15.8	0	0	0	.000	.000	.002	.005	.011	.025	.048	.084	.137	.207	.291
16.0	0	0	0	0	.000	.001	.004	.010	.022	.043	.077	.127	.193	.275
16.2	0	0	0	0	.000	.001	.004	.009	.020	.039	.071	.117	.180	.259
16.4	0	0	0	0	.000	.001	.003	.008	.018	.035	.065	.108	.168	.243
16.6	0	0	0	0	.000	.001	.003	.007	.016	.032	.059	.100	.156	.228
16.8	0	0	0	0	.000	.001	.002	.006	.014	.029	.054	.092	.145	.214
17.0	0	0	0	0	.000	.001	.002	.005	.013	.026	.049	.085	.135	.201
17.2	0	0	0	0	.000	.001	.002	.005	.011	.024	.045	.078	.125	.188
17.4	0	0	0	0	.000	.001	.002	.004	.010	.021	.041	.071	.116	.176
17.6	0	0	0	0	0	.000	.001	.004	.009	.019	.037	.065	.107	.164
17.8	0	0	0	0	0	.000	.001	.003	.008	.017	.033	.060	.099	.153
18.0	0	0	0	0	0	.000	.001	.003	.007	.015	.030	.055	.092	.143
18.2	0	0	0	0	0	.000	.001	.003	.006	.014	.027	.050	.085	.133
18.4	0	0	0	0	0	.000	.001	.002	.006	.012	.025	.046	.078	.123
18.6	0	0	0	0	0	.000	.001	.002	.005	.011	.022	.042	.072	.115
18.8	0	0	0	0	0	.000	.001	.002	.004	.010	.020	.038	.066	.106
19.0	0	0	0	0	0	.000	.001	.002	.004	.009	.018	.035	.061	.098
19.2	0	0	0	0	0	0	.000	.001	.003	.008	.017	.032	.056	.091
19.4	0	0	0	0	0	0	.000	.001	.003	.007	.015	.029	.051	.084
19.6	0	0	0	0	0	0	.000	.001	.003	.006	.013	.026	.047	.078
19.8	0	0	0	0	0	0	.000	.001	.002	.006	.012	.024	.043	.072
20.0	0	0	0	0	0	0	.000	.001	.002	.005	.011	.021	.039	.066

Supplement D: Acceptance Sampling

Average Outgoing Quality

AQL = 0.01 $\alpha = 0.05$

LTPD = 0.06 $\beta = 0.10$

$n = 100$ $c = 3$

What is the AOQ if $p = 0.05$ and $N = 3000$?

Use Appendix 3:

$np = 100(0.05) = 5$

$P_a = 0.265$

$$AOQ = \frac{(0.05)(0.265)(2900)}{3000} = 0.0128$$

Calculating Requirements

$$M = \frac{(80{,}000 \times 0.05) + (60{,}000 \times 0.10) + (120{,}000 \times 0.02) +}{(250 \text{ days/yr} \times 16 \text{ hr/day}) [1 - 0.05]}$$

$$\frac{(80{,}000/240)(0.5) + (60{,}000/180)(2.2) + (120{,}000/360)(3.8)}{}$$

$$M = 14{,}567/3{,}800 = 3.83 \text{ or } 4 \text{ machines}$$

Grandmother's Chicken Restaurant

Year	Demand (meals)	Gaps (meals) Kitchen	Dining
1	90,000	10,000	—
2	100,000	20,000	—
3	110,000	30,000	5,000
4	120,000	40,000	15,000
5	130,000	50,000	25,000

Current capacities: 80,000 meals in kitchen
105,000 in dining room

Cash Flows for Two-Stage Expansion at Grandmother's Chicken Restaurant
(Table 8.1)

Year	Projected demand (meals/yr)	Projected capacity (meals/yr)	Calculation of incremental cash flow compared to base case (80,000 meals/yr)	Cash inflow (outflow)
0	80,000	80,000	Increase kitchen capacity to 105,000 meals =	($80,000)
1	90,000	105,000	90,000 − 80,000 = (10,000 meals)($2/meal) =	$20,000
2	100,000	105,000	100,000 − 80,000 = (20,000 meals)($2/meal) =	$40,000
3	110,000	105,000	105,000 − 80,000 = (25,000 meals)($2/meal) =	$50,000
			Increase total capacity to 130,000 meals =	($170,000)
				($120,000)
4	120,000	130,000	120,000 − 80,000 = (40,000 meals)($2/meal) =	$80,000
5	130,000	130,000	130,000 − 80,000 = (50,000 meals)($2/meal) =	$100,000

Single-Server Model

Assumptions

Number of servers : 1

Number of phases : 1

Input source : infinite; no balking or reneging

Arrival distribution : Poisson; mean arrival rate – λ

Service distribution : exponential; mean service time = $1/\mu$

Waiting line : single line; unlimited length

Priority discipline : FCFS

Operating characteristics

$$W = \frac{1}{\mu - \lambda}$$

$$W_q = \rho W$$

$$\rho = \frac{\lambda}{\mu}$$

$$P_n = (1 - \rho)\rho^n$$

$$L = \frac{\lambda}{\mu - \lambda}$$

$$L_q = \rho L$$

TM E.1a

Supplement E: Waiting Line Models

Single-Server Application

$\lambda = 20$ customers per hour

$\mu = 25$ customers per hour

1. Average utilization

$$p = \frac{\lambda}{\mu} = \quad =$$

2. Average number of customers in the system

$$L = \frac{\lambda}{\mu - \lambda} =$$

3. Average number of customers in line

$$L_q = pL =$$

4. Average time spent in the system

$$W = \frac{1}{\mu - \lambda} =$$

5. Average time spent in line

$$W_q = pW =$$

Analyzing Service Rate

$\lambda = 20$ customers per hour

What service rate is required to achieve an average waiting time of 10 minutes in the system?

$$W = \frac{1}{\mu - \lambda}$$

Supplement E: Waiting Line Models

Multiple-Server Model

Assumptions

Input source : infinite; no balking or reneging

Arrival distribution : Poisson; mean arrival rate = λ

Service distribution : exponential; mean service time = $1/\mu$

Waiting line : single line; unlimited length

Priority discipline : FCFS

Number of servers : s

Number of phases : 1

Operating characteristics

$$\rho = \frac{\lambda}{s\mu}$$

$$P_0 = \left[\sum_{n=0}^{s-1} \frac{(\lambda/\mu)^n}{n!} + \frac{(\lambda/\mu)^s}{s!} \left(\frac{1}{1-\rho} \right) \right]^{-1}$$

$$P_n = \begin{cases} \dfrac{(\lambda/\mu)^n}{n!} P_0 & 0 < n < s \\ \dfrac{(\lambda/\mu)^n}{s!\, s^{n-s}} P_0 & n \geq s \end{cases}$$

$$L_q = \frac{P_0(\lambda/\mu)^s \rho}{s!(1-\rho)^2}$$

$$W_q = \frac{L_q}{\lambda}$$

$$W = W_q + \frac{1}{\mu}$$

$$L = \lambda W$$

Supplement E: Waiting Line Models

Multiple-Server Application

$s = 2$

$\mu = 12.5$ customers per hour

$\lambda = 20$ customers per hour

$$\rho = \frac{\lambda}{\mu s} =$$

$$P_0 = \frac{1}{\left[1 + \left(\dfrac{\lambda}{\mu} \right) + \dfrac{\left(\lambda/\mu \right)^2}{2} \left(\dfrac{1}{1 - \rho} \right) \right]} =$$

$$L_q = \frac{P_0 \left(\lambda/\mu \right)^2 \rho}{2! \left(1 - \rho \right)^2} =$$

$$W_q = \frac{L_q}{\lambda}$$

Supplement E: Waiting Line Models

Single-Server Model

Assumptions

Number of servers : 1

Number of phases : 1

Input source : finite; equals N customers

Arrival distribution : exponential interarrival times; mean $= 1/\lambda$

Service distribution : exponential; mean service time $= 1/\mu$

Waiting line : single line; no more than $N - 1$

Priority discipline : FCFS

Operating characteristics

$$W = L[(N - L)\lambda]^{-1}$$

$$P_0 = \left[\sum_{n=0}^{N} \frac{N!}{(N - n)!} \left(\frac{\lambda}{\mu} \right)^n \right]^{-1}$$

$$\rho = 1 - P_0$$

$$L_q = N - \frac{\lambda + \mu}{\lambda_0} (1 - P_0)$$

$$L = N - \frac{\mu}{\lambda}(1 - P_0)$$

$$W_q = L_q[(N - L)\lambda]^{-1}$$

Finite Source Application

$$\lambda_0 = 1/50 = 0.02 \text{ copiers per hour}$$

$$\mu = 1/4 = 0.25 \text{ copiers per hour}$$

$$P_0 = \left[\frac{8!}{8!}(0.08)^0 + \frac{8!}{7!}(0.08)^1 + \cdots + \frac{8!}{0}(0.08)^8 \right]^{-1} = 0.44$$

$$\rho = 1 - P_0 = 0.56$$

$$L = 8 - \left(\left(\frac{0.25}{0.02}(1 - 0.44) \right) \right) = 1$$

Supplement E: Waiting Line Models

Hilltop Produce

a. $\rho = \dfrac{20}{30} = 66.7\%$

b. $P_0 = (0.333)(0.667)^0 = 0.333$

$P_1 = (0.333)(0.667)^1 = 0.222$

$P_2 = (0.333)(0.667)^2 = 0.111$

c. $L_q = (0.667)\left(\dfrac{20}{30 - 20}\right) = 1.333$

d. $W = \dfrac{1}{30 - 20} = 0.1\ \text{hr} \times \dfrac{60\ \text{min}}{\text{hr}} = 6\ \text{min}$

Random Numbers
Famous Chamois

Minutes	Random Numbers
1	00–00
2	01–03
3	04–09
4	10–18
5	19–30
6	31–44
7	45–58
8	59–70
9	71–80
10	81–87
11	88–92
12	93–96
13	97–99

Supplement F: Simulation Analysis

Simulation
Famous Chamois

Random Number	Time to Arrival	Arrival Time	Max No. In Drive	Service Begins	Departure Time	Minutes in System
50	7	0:07	0	0:07	0:13	6
63	8	0:15	0	0:15	0:21	6
95	12	0:27	0	0:27	0:33	6
49	7	0:34	0	0:34	0:40	6
68	8	0:42	0	0:42	0:48	6
11	4	0:46	1	0:48	0:54	8
40	6	0:52	1	0:54	1:00	8
93	12	1:04	0	1:04	1:10	6
61	8	1:12	0	1:12	1:18	6
48	7	1:19	0	1:19	1:25	6
82	10	1:29	0	1:29	1:35	6
09	3	1:32	1	1:35	1:41	9
08	3	1:35	1	1:41	1:47	12
72	9	1:44	1	1:47	1:53	9
98	13	1:57	0	1:57	2:03	6
41	6	2:03	0	2:03	2:09	6
39	6	2:09	0	2:09	2:15	6
67	8	2:17	0	2:17	2:23	6
11	4	2:21	1	2:23	2:29	8
11	4	2:25	1	2:29	2:35	10
00	1	2:26	2	2:35	2:41	15
07	3	2:29	2	2:41	2:47	18
66	8	2:37	2	2:47	2:53	16
00	1	2:38	3	2:53	2:59	21
29	5	2:43	3	2:59	3:05	22

TM F.1b

Location Decision
Preference Matrix

Location Factor	Weight	The Neighborhood		Sesame Street		Peewee's Playhouse	
Material Supply	0.1	5	0.5	9	0.9	8	0.8
Quality of Life	0.2	9	1.8	8	1.6	4	0.8
Mild Climate	0.3	10*	3.0	6	1.8	8	2.4
Labor Skills	0.4	3	1.2	4	1.6	7	2.8
			6.5		5.9		6.8

Distance Measures

Euclidean Distance

$$d_{AB} = \sqrt{\left(x_A - x_B\right)^2 + \left(y_A - y_B\right)^2}$$

$$d_{AB} = \sqrt{\left(20 - 80\right)^2 + \left(10 - 60\right)^2} = \underline{\underline{78.1}}$$

Rectilinear Distance

$$d_{AB} = \left|x_A - x_B\right| + \left|y_A - y_B\right|$$

$$d_{AB} = \left|20 - 80\right| + \left|10 - 60\right| = \underline{\underline{110}}$$

TM 9.2

Load-Distance Method
(Using Rectilinear Distance)

Cincinatti $= 15(0) + 20(9) + 30(9) + 25(8) + 40(4) = 810$

Dayton $= 15(9) + 20(0) + 30(10) + 25(5) + 40(9) = 920$

Cleveland $= 15(9) + 20(10) + 30(0) + 25(5) + 40(5) = 660$

Toledo $= 15(8) + 20(5) + 30(5) + 25(0) + 40(8) = 690$

Lima $= 15(4) + 20(9) + 30(5) + 25(8) + 40(0) = \boxed{590}$

Chapter 9: Location

Center of Gravity

$$x^* = \frac{\sum\limits_i l_i x_i}{\sum\limits_i l_i} \quad \text{and} \quad y^* = \frac{\sum\limits_i l_i y_i}{\sum\limits_i l_i}$$

$$x^* = \frac{[(20 \times 11) + (15 \times 12) + (30 \times 4)]}{(20 + 15 + 30)} = 8.0$$

$$y^* = \frac{[(20 \times 8.5) + (15 \times 9.5) + (30 \times 1.5)]}{(20 + 15 + 30)} = 5.5$$

Atlantic City
Community Chest
The Situation

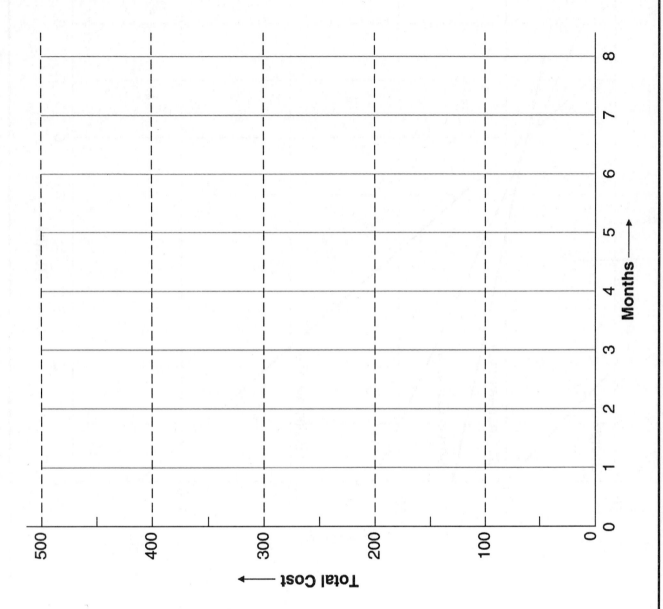

TM 9.5a

Chapter 9: Location

Atlantic City
Community Chest
The Solution

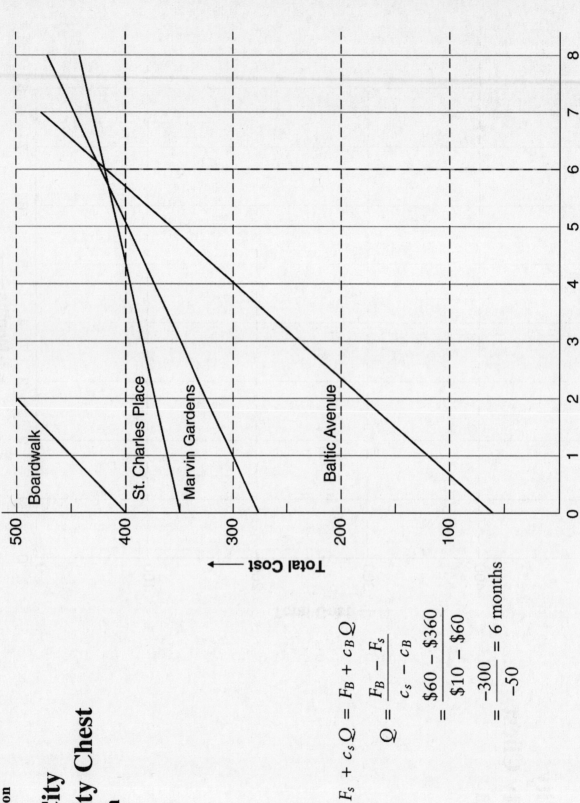

$$F_s + c_s Q = F_B + c_B Q$$

$$Q = \frac{F_B - F_s}{c_s - c_B}$$

$$= \frac{\$60 - \$360}{\$10 - \$60}$$

$$= \frac{-300}{-50} = 6 \text{ months}$$

Transportation Method

Sources	Destinations				Capacity
	Atlanta	Omaha	Seattle	Dummy Unused	
San Antonio	$4	$5	$6	$0	12,000
New York City	$3	$7	$9	$0	10,000
Demand	8,000	6,000	5,000	3,000	22,000

Blank
Tableaus

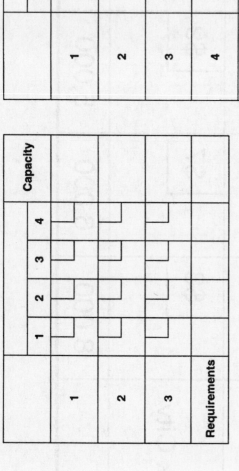

	1	2	3	4	5	6	Capacity
1							
2							
3							
4							
Requirements							

	1	2	3	4	5	Capacity
1						
2						
3						
4						
Requirements						

	1	2	3	4	Capacity
1					
2					
3					
Requirements					

	1	2	3	4	5	Capacity
1						
2						
3						
Requirements						

TM 9.6b

Finding Good Block Plans

Trips Between Departments

Department	1	2	3	4	5	6
1	—	25	90			165
2		—			105	
3			—		125	125
4				—	25	
5					—	105
6						—

Original Plan

3	6	1
2	5	4

Proposed Plan

Original Plan

3	6	1
2	5	4

Department Pair	Closeness Factor	Distance	Score
1, 6	165	1	165
3, 5	125	2	250
3, 6	125	1	125
2, 5	105	1	105
5, 6	105	1	105
1, 3	90	2	180
1, 2	25	3	75
4, 5	25	1	25
Total			1030

TM 10.1b

Proposed Plan

4	6	1
2	5	3

Department Pair	Closeness Factor	Distance	Score
1, 6	165	1	165
3, 5	125	1	125
3, 6	125	2	250
2, 5	105	1	105
5, 6	105	1	105
1, 3	90	1	90
1, 2	25	3	75
4, 5	25	2	50
Total			965

Warehouse Layout

Section Data

Section	Distance
1	50
2	60
3	200
4	210
5	220
6	230
7	920
8	930
9	940
10	1680
11	1690
12	1700

Parts Data

Part	Trips per Day	No. of Sections
A	50	3
B	75	1
C	120	2
D	150	1
E	80	2
F	140	2
G	25	1

TM 10.2a

Warehouse Layout Solution

Part	Ratio of Trips to Area	Priority	Sections Assigned
A	50	5	7, 8, 9
B	75	2	2
C	60	4	5, 6
D	150	1	1
E	40	6	10, 11
F	70	3	3, 4
G	25	7	12

Information on Work Elements

Element	Time (sec)	Predecessor
A	12	–
B	60	1
C	36	–
D	24	–
E	38	3, 4
F	72	2, 5
G	14	–
H	72	–
I	35	7, 8
J	60	9
K	12	6, 10
Total =	435	

Chapter 10: Layout

Precedence Diagram

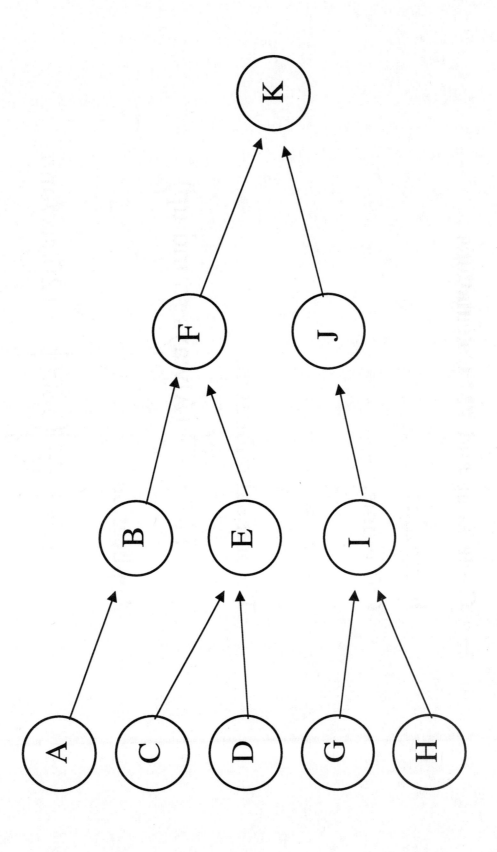

Cycle Time and TM Calculations

Formulas

Cycle time:

$$c = \frac{1}{r}$$

Theoretical minimum:

$$TM = \frac{\Sigma t}{c} \quad \text{(Always round up)}$$

Application

$$c = \left(\frac{1}{30}\right)(3600) = 120 \text{ sec/unit}$$

$$TM = \frac{435}{120} = 3.6 \text{ or 4 stations}$$

Performance Measures

Formulas

Idle time $= nc - \Sigma t$

Efficiency (%) $= \left(\dfrac{\Sigma t}{nc}\right)(100)$

Balance delay (%) $= 100 - \text{Efficiency}$

Application

Idle time $= 4(120) - 435 = 45 \text{ sec}$

Efficiency $= (435/480)(100) = 90.6\%$

Balance delay $= 100 - 90.6 = 9.4\%$

TM 10.3d

Finding a Solution

Station (Step 1)	Candidate (Step 2)	Choice (Step 3)	Cumulative Time (Step 4)	Idle Time ($c = 120$) (Step 4)
1	A,C,D,G,H	H	72	48
2				
3	E,I	E	38	82
4	F,I	F	110	10
	I	I	35	85
	J	J	95	25
	K	K	107	13

Line Balancing Solution

Station (Step 1)	Candidate (Step 2)	Choice (Step 3)	Cumulative Time (Step 4)	Idle Time ($c = 120$) (Step 4)
1	A,C,D,G,H	H	72	48
	A,C,D,G	**C**	**108**	**12**
	A	**A**	**120**	**0**
2	**B,D,G**	**B**	**60**	**60**
	D,G	**D**	**84**	**36**
	G	**G**	**98**	**22**
3	E,J	E	38	82
	F,I	F	110	10
4	I	I	35	85
	J	J	95	25
	K	K	107	13

Inventory Measures

A recent accounting statement showed total inventories (raw materials + WIP + finished goods) to be $6,821,000. This year's "cost of goods sold" is $19.2 million. The company operates 52 weeks per year. How many weeks of supply are being held? What is the inventory turnover?

$$\text{Weeks of supply} = \frac{\$6,821,000}{(\$19,200,000)/(52 \text{ weeks})} = 18.5 \text{ weeks}$$

$$\text{Inventory turnover} = \frac{\$19,200,000}{\$6,821,000} = 2.8 \text{ turns}$$

Moving Average Method

$$F_{t-1} = \frac{D_t + D_{t-1} + \cdots + D_{t-n+1}}{n}$$

where: F_{t-1} = Forecast for period $t + 1$

- Use a 3-month moving average to forecast customer arrivals for month 5.

$$F_5 = \frac{}{3} =$$

Forecast for   =
    month 5

- If the actual demand of month 5 is 805 customers, what is the forecast for month 6?

$$F_6 = \frac{}{3} =$$

Forecast for   =
    month 6

  TM 12.1a

Chapter 12: Forecasting

Weighted Moving Average

$$F_{t+1} = W_1 D_t + W_2 D_{t-1} + \ldots + W_n D_{t-n+1}$$

where: F_{t+1} = Forecast for period $t + 1$

- Let $W_1 = 0.50$, $W_2 = 0.30$, and $W_3 = 0.20$.
  Calculate the forecast for month 5.

  F_5 =

  Forecast for =
  month 5

- If the actual demand of month 5 is 805 patients, what is the forecast for month 6?

  F_6 =

  Forecast for =
  month 6

Exponential Smoothing

$$F_{t+1} = \alpha D_t + (1 - \alpha)F_t$$

where: F_{t+1} = Forecast for period $t + 1$

- Suppose $A_3 = 783$ customers and $\alpha = 0.20$. What is forecast for month 5?

$$F_5 \quad =$$

Forecast for   =
month 5

- If $D_5 = 805$, what is the forecast for month 6?

$$F_6 \quad =$$

Forecast for   =
month 6

Trend-Adjusted Exponential Smoothing Method

Average: $$A_t = \alpha D_t + (1 - \alpha)(A_{t-1} + T_{t-1})$$

Average trend: $$T_t = \beta(A_t - A_{t-1}) + (1 - \beta)T_{t-1}$$

Forecast for p periods ahead: $$A_t + pT_t$$

Trend Adjusted Exponential Smoothing

$A_{\text{Mar}} = 300{,}000 \text{ cases};$ $\qquad T_{\text{Mar}} = +8{,}000 \text{ cases}$

$D_{\text{Apr}} = 330{,}000 \text{ cases};$ $\qquad \alpha = 0.20; \beta = 0.10$

What are the forecasts for May and July?

$A_{\text{Apr}} = 0.2(330) + 0.8(300 + 8) = 312.4$

$T_{\text{Apr}} = 0.1(312.4 - 300.0) + 0.9(8) = 8.44$

$$\begin{aligned}
\text{Forecast for May} \;&=\; 312.4 + (1)(8.44) \\
&=\; 320.84, \text{ or } 320{,}840 \text{ cases}
\end{aligned}$$

$$\begin{aligned}
\text{Forecast for July} \;&=\; 312.4 + (3)(8.44) \\
&=\; 337.72, \text{ or } 337{,}720 \text{ cases}
\end{aligned}$$

Multiplicative Seasonal Method

Step 1: Calculate the average demand per period for each year of past data.

Step 2: Divide the actual demand for each period by the average demand per period to get a *seasonal factor*. Repeat for each year of data.

Step 3: Calculate the average seasonal factor for each period.

Step 4: To get a forecast for a given period in a future year, multiply the seasonal factor by the estimated average demand per period in that year.

Multiplicative Seasonal Method Application

| Qtr | Year 1 | | Year 2 | | Average |
	Demand	Index	Demand	Index	Index
1	100	0.40	192	0.64	0.52
2	400	1.60	408	1.36	1.48
3	300	1.20	384	1.28	1.24
4	200	0.80	216	0.72	0.76
Avg.	250		300		

Suppose the projected demand for Year 3 is 1320 units.

Forecast for Quarter 1 = 0.52(330)
$\approx$ 172

Forecast for Quarter 2 = 1.48(330)
$\approx$ 488

Forecast for Quarter 3 = 1.24(330)
$\approx$ 409

Forecast for Quarter 4 = 0.76(330)
$\approx$ 251

Forecast Error Measures

1. Cumulative sum
   of forecast errors

   $$CFE = \sum_{t=1}^{n} E_t$$

2. Average forecast error

   $$\bar{E} = \frac{CFE}{n}$$

3. Main squared error

   $$MSE = \frac{\sum_{t=1}^{n} E_t^2}{n}$$

4. Standard deviation

   $$\sigma = \sqrt{\frac{\sum_{t=1}^{n} (E_t - \bar{E})^2}{n-1}}$$

5. Mean absolute error

   $$MAD = \frac{\sum_{t=1}^{n} |E_t|}{n}$$

6. Mean percent absolute error

   $$MAPE = \frac{\sum_{t=1}^{n} \frac{|E_t|(100)}{D_t}}{n}$$

Calculations for Forecast Error Measures

Month (t)	Demand (D_t)	Forecast (F_t)	Error (E_t)	Error Squared (E_t^2)	Absolute Error ($\lvert E_t \rvert$)	Absolute Percent Error ($\lvert E_t \rvert / D_t)100$
1	200	225	–25	625	25	12.5%
2	240	220	20	400	20	8.3
3	300	285	15	225	15	5.0
4	270	290	–20	400	20	7.4
5	230	250	–20	400	20	8.7
6	260	240	20	400	20	7.7
7	210	250	–40	1,600	40	19.0
8	275	240	35	1,225	35	12.7
Total			**–15**	**5275**	**195**	**81.3%**

$$\text{CFE} \quad = \quad -15$$

$$E_t \quad = \quad \frac{-15}{8} = -1.875$$

$$\text{MSE} \quad = \quad \frac{5275}{8} = 659.4$$

$$s \quad = \quad \sqrt{\frac{\Sigma E_t - (-1.875)^2}{7}} = 27.4$$

$$\text{MAD} \quad = \quad \frac{195}{8} = 24.4$$

$$\text{MAPE} \quad = \quad \frac{81.3\%}{8} = 10.2\%$$

Estimating
Inventory Levels

- **Cycle inventory at each DC?**

$$\left(\frac{350}{2}\right)(650) = \$113,750$$

- **Safety stock at each DC?**

$$(1)(50)(650) = \$32,500$$

- **Pipeline inventory in transit to each DC?**

$$(2)(50)(650) = \$65,000$$

- **Total inventory at each DC?**

$$\$113,750 + \$32,500 + \$65,000 = \$211,250$$

- **First candidate for reduction?**

Cycle inventory (\$113,750 is biggest)

Finding the EOQ, Total Cost, and TBO

A. EOQ

$$EOQ = \sqrt{\frac{2(3120)(30)}{20}} = 97 \text{ units}$$

B. Total Cost

Current policy

$Q = 360$ units

$C = (360/2) + (3120/360)(30)$

$C = 3600 + 260$

$C = \$3860$

EOQ policy

$Q = 97$ units

$C = (97/2)(20) + (3120/97)(30)$

$C = 970 + 965$

$C = \$1935$

C. TBO's of EOQ and Current Policy

$$TBO_{360} = \frac{360}{3120} \quad (52 \text{ weeks per year}) = 6 \text{ weeks}$$

$$TBO_{EOQ} = \frac{97}{3120} \quad (52 \text{ weeks per year}) = 1.6 \text{ weeks}$$

Placing Orders with a Continuous Review System

Whenever a withdrawal brings IP down to the reorder point (R), place an order for Q (fixed) units.

Example

$IP = 10 + 200 - 0 = 210$

$R = 100$

Decision: Place no new order.

Finding Safety Stock and *R*

95% Cycle-Service Level

Safety stock = $z\sigma_L$ = 1.645(40) = 65.8 or 66 units

R = Average demand during lead time + Safety stock

R = 85 + 66

R = 151 units

85% Cycle-Service Level

Safety stock = $z\sigma_L$ = 1.04(40) = 41.6 or 42 units

R = 85 + 42

R = 127 units

Continuous Review System: Putting It All Together

a. EOQ

$$D = 10/\text{wk} \times 52 \text{ wk/yr} = 520$$

$$EOQ = \sqrt{\frac{2(520)(45)}{12}} = 62$$

b. Safety Stock B

$$\sigma_L = 8\sqrt{3} = 14$$

$$\text{Safety stock} = z\sigma_L = 0.525(14) = 8$$

c. Reorder Point R

R = Average demand during lead time + safety stock

$$= 3(10) + 8 = 38$$

d. Inventory Reductions

- Reducing Q from 80 to 62:
- Safety stock reduction = 120 − 8 = 112 units
- Cycle inventory reduction = 40 − 31 = 9 units
- Reducing R from 150 to 38

Placing Orders with a Periodic Review System

$$IP = 10 + 200 - 0 = 210$$

$$T - IP = 400 - 210 = 190$$

Decision: Order 190 units

To accompany *Operations Management Strategy and Analysis*, 5/e, by Krajewski and Ritzman. Copyright © 1999 by Addison Wesley Longman, Inc. All rights reserved. TM 13.6

Chapter 13: Inventory Management

Application
P System

a. Previous Information

- D = 520
- EOQ = 62
- z = 0.525
- σ_t = 8
- t = 1
- L = 3

b. Reorder Interval P

- P = (EOQ/D)(52)

    = (62/520)(52) = 6.2 or 6 wk

c. Safety Stock

- Safety stock = $z\sigma_t\sqrt{P + L}$

    = $(0.525)(8)\sqrt{6 + 3}$

d. Target Inventory T

- T = Average demand during protection interval + Safety stock during protection interval

    = $(6 + 3)(10) + 13 = 103$ units

TM 13.7

Noninstantaneous Replenishment

a. What is the economic lot size?

$$ELS = \sqrt{\frac{2DS}{H}}\sqrt{\frac{p}{p-d}} = \sqrt{\frac{2(10,080)(100,000)}{2,000}}\sqrt{\frac{60}{60-35}}$$

b. How long is the production run?

$$\frac{Q}{p} = \frac{1,555}{60} = 25.91, \text{ or } 26 \text{ production days}$$

c. What is the average quantity in inventory?

$$I_{max} = \frac{Q}{2}\left(\frac{p-d}{p}\right) = \frac{1,555}{2}\left(\frac{60-35}{60}\right) = 324 \text{ engines}$$

d. What is the total of the annual relevant costs?

$$C = \frac{Q}{2}\left(\frac{p-d}{p}\right)(H) + \frac{D}{Q}(s)$$

$$= \frac{1,555}{2}\left(\frac{60-35}{60}\right)\$2,000 + \frac{10,080}{1,555}(\$100,000)$$

$$= \$647,917 + \$648,231$$

$$= \$1,296,148$$

Supplement G: Special Inventory Models

Quantity Discounts

Step 1.

$$EOQ_{45.00} = \sqrt{\frac{2(1,800)(16)}{(0.2)(45)}}$$

$$= 80 \text{ units (infeasible)}$$

$$EOQ_{50.00} = \sqrt{\frac{2(1,800)(16)}{(0.2)(50)}}$$

$$= 76 \text{ units (feasible)}$$

Step 2.

$$C_{76} = \frac{76}{2}(0.20 \times 50.00) + \frac{1,800}{76}(16) + 50(1,800)$$

$$= \$90,759$$

$$C_{100} = \frac{100}{2}(0.20 \times 45.00) + \frac{1,800}{100}(16) + 45(1,800)$$

$$= \$81,738$$

The best order quantity is 100 units.

To accompany *Operations Management Strategy and Analysis, 5/e*, by Krajewski and Ritzman. Copyright © 1999 by Addison Wesley Longman, Inc. All rights reserved.

Supplement G: Special Inventory Models

One-Price Decisions

Q	D					Expected Payoff
	10	20	30	40	50	
10	$100	$100	$100	$100	$100	$100
20	50	200	200	200	200	170
30	0	150	300	300	300	**195**
40	–50	100	250	400	400	175
50	–100	50	200	350	500	140

- Payoff if $Q = 30$ and $D = 20$:
  $pD - I(Q - D) = 10(20) - 5(30) - 20) = \$150$

- Payoff if $Q = 30$ and $D = 40$:
  $pQ = 10(30) = \$300$

- Expected payoff if $Q = 30$:
  $0(0.2) + 150(0.3) + 300(0.3 + 0.1 + 0.1) = \$195$

Level Strategy
with Overtime
and Undertime

The Plan

Finding staff level (w):

$1.20w =$ _____

$w =$ _____

	Quarter				Total
	1	2	3	4	
Requirement (hrs)	6,000	12,000	19,000	9,000	46000
Workforce level (workers)	31	31	31	31	124
Undertime (hours)	10120	4120	0	7120	21360
Overtime (hours)	0	0	2880	0	2880
Productive time (hours)	6000	12000	16120	9000	43120
Hires (workers)	20	0	0	0	20
Layoffs (workers)	0	0	0	0	0

Cost of Plan

Costs					
Productive time	$72,000	$144,000	$193,440	$108,000	$517,440
Undertime	121,440	49,440	0	85,440	256,320
Overtime	0	0	51,840	0	51,840
Hires	60,000	0	0	0	60,000
Layoffs	0	0	0	0	0

Total Cost $885,600

All Alternatives and 13 Periods

	1	2	3	4	5	6	7	8	9	10	11	12	13	Total
Requirement														
Work-force level														
Undertime														
Overtime														
Vacation time														
Subcontracting time														
Backorders														
Productive time														
Inventory														
Hires														
Layoffs														
Costs														
Productive time														
Undertime														
Overtime														
Vacation time														
Inventory														
Backorders														
Hires														
Layoffs														
Subcontracting														
Totals														

TM **14.1b**

Selected Alternatives and 13 Periods

	1	2	3	4	5	6	7	8	9	10	11	12	13	Total
Requirement														
Work-force level														
Undertime														
Overtime														
Productive time														
Hires														
Layoffs														
Costs														
Productive time														
Undertime														
Overtime														
Hires														
Layoffs														
Totals														

Chapter 14: Aggregate Planning

All Alternatives and 6 Periods

	1	2	3	4	5	6	Total
Requirement							
Work-force level							
Undertime							
Overtime							
Vacation time							
Subcontracting time							
Backorders							
Productive time							
Inventory							
Hires							
Layoffs							
Costs							
Productive time							
Undertime							
Overtime							
Vacation time							
Inventory							
Backorders							
Hires							
Layoffs							
Subcontracting							
Totals							

Selected Alternatives and 6 Periods

	1	2	3	4	5	6	Total
Requirement							
Work-force level							
Undertime							
Overtime							
Productive time							
Hires							
Layoffs							
Costs							
Productive time							
Undertime							
Overtime							
Hires							
Layoffs							
Totals							

TM 14.1e

Chase Strategy with Hiring and Layoffs

The Plan

	Quarter				
	1	2	3	4	Total
Requirement (hrs)	6,000	12,000	19,000	9,000	46000
Workforce level (workers)	12	24	37	18	91
Undertime (hours)	240	480	240	360	1320
Overtime (hours)	0	0	0	0	0
Productive time (hours)	6000	12000	19000	9000	46000
Hires (workers)	1	12	13	0	26
Layoffs (workers)	0	0	0	19	19

Cost of Plan

Costs					
Productive time	$72,000	$144,000	$228,000	$108,000	$552,000
Undertime	2,880	5,760	2,880	4,320	15,840
Overtime	0	0	0	0	0
Hires	3,000	36,000	39,000	0	78,000
Layoffs	0	0	0	38,000	38,000

Total Cost $683,840

Mixed Strategy

The Plan

		Quarter			
	1	2	3	4	Total
Requirement (hrs)	6,000	12,000	19,000	9,000	46,000
Workforce level (workers)	12	24	31	18	85
Undertime (hours)	240	480	0	360	1,080
Overtime (hours)	0	0	2,880	0	2,880
Productive time (hours)	6,000	12,000	16,120	9,000	43,120
Hires (workers)	1	12	7	0	20
Layoffs (workers)	0	0	0	13	13

Cost of Plan

Costs					
Productive time	$72,000	$144,000	$193,440	$108,000	$517,440
Undertime	2,880	5,760	0	4,320	12,960
Overtime	0	0	51,840	0	51,840
Hires	3,000	36,000	21,000	0	60,000
Layoffs	0	0	0	26,000	26,000

Total Cost $668,240

Transportation Method of Production Planning

Alternatives		Quarter 1	Quarter 2	Quarter 3	Quarter 4	Unused Capacity	Total Capacity
	Beginning Inventory	$0 **40**	$100	$200	$300	0	
1	Regular Time	$830 **90**	$930 **220**	$1,030	$1,130 **80**		
	Overtime	$910	$1,010	$1,110 **20**	$1,210		
	Subcontract	$1,000	$1,100	$1,200	$1,300		
2	Regular Time	$99,999	$830 **180**	$930 **220**	$1,030		
	Overtime	$99,999	$910	$1,010 **20**	$1,110		
	Subcontract	$99,999	$1,000	$1,100 **30**	$1,200	30	
3	Regular Time	$99,999	$99,999	$830 **460**	$930		
	Overtime	$99,999	$99,999	$910 **20**	$1,010		
	Subcontract	$99,999	$99,999	$1,000 **30**	$1,100		
4	Regular Time	$99,999	$99,999	$99,999	$830 **380**		380
	Overtime	$99,999	$99,999	$99,999	$910 **20**		20
	Subcontract	$99,999	$99,999	$99,999	$1,000 **30**		30
	Requirements	130				30	1870

Chapter 14: Aggregate Planning

Transportation Method of Production Planning

Alternatives		Quarter 1	Quarter 2	Quarter 3	Quarter 4	Unused Capacity	Total Capacity
	Beginning Inventory	0 · **40**	100	200	300	0	40
1	Regular Time	$830 · **90**	$930 · **220**	$1,030	$1,130 · **80**		390
1	Overtime	$910	$1,010	$1,110 · **20**	$1,210		20
1	Subcontract	$1,000	$1,100	$1,200	$1,300	30	30
2	Regular Time	$99,999	$830 · **180**	$930 · **220**	$1,030		400
2	Overtime	$99,999	$910	$1,010 · **20**	$1,110		20
2	Subcontract	$99,999	$1,000	$1,100 · **30**	$1,200		30
3	Regular Time	$99,999	$99,999	$830 · **460**	$930		460
3	Overtime	$99,999	$99,999	$910 · **20**	$1,010		20
3	Subcontract	$99,999	$99,999	$1,000 · **30**	$1,100		30
4	Regular Time	$99,999	$99,999	$99,999	$830 · **380**		380
4	Overtime	$99,999	$99,999	$99,999	$910 · **20**		20
4	Subcontract	$99,999	$99,999	$99,999	$1,000 · **30**		30
	Requirements	130	400	800	510	30	1870

Production, Shipments, and Inventories

	Quarter 1	Quarter 2	Quarter 3	Quarter 4	Totals
Production					
Regular					1630
Overtime					80
Subcontract					90
Total Production					1800
Shipments					1800
Ending Inventory					810

Production, Shipments, and Inventories

	Quarter 1	Quarter 2	Quarter 3	Quarter 4	Totals
Production					
Regular	390	400	460	380	1630
Overtime	20	20	20	20	80
Subcontract	0	30	30	30	90
Total Production	410	450	570	430	1800
Shipments	130	400	800	470	1800
Ending Inventory	320	370	80	40	810

Total Cost of Plan

Quarter 1:	= $ 74,700
Quarter 2:	= $ 354,000
Quarter 3:	= $ 710,000
Quarter 4:	= $ 454,000

Total = $1,592,700

Total Cost of Plan

Quarter 1:	40($0) + 90($830) = $ 74,700
Quarter 2:	220($930) + 180($830) = $ 354,000
Quarter 3:	20($1110) + 220($930) + 20($1010) + 30($1100) + 460($830) + 20($910) + 30($1000) = $ 710,000
Quarter 4:	80($1130) + 380($830) + 20($910) + 30($1000) = $ 454,000

Total = $1,592,700

Chapter 14: Aggregate Planning

Six-Period Tableau

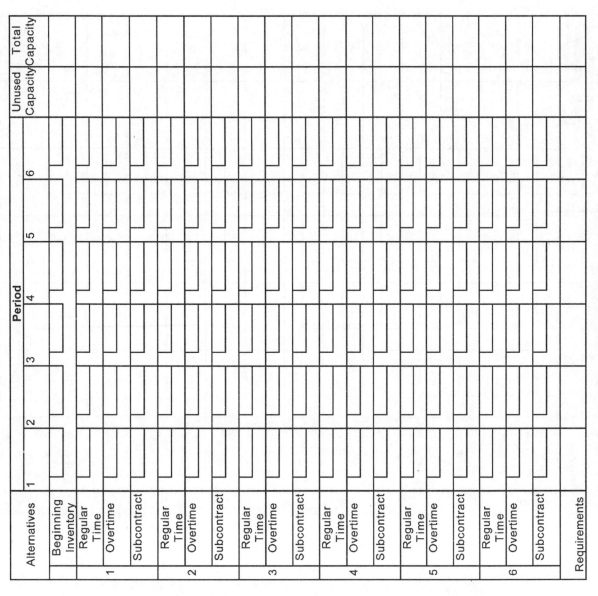

NOTE: Remember to include the desired ending inventory in the final period's requirement.

TM 14.4g

Four-Period Tableau

Quarter	Alternatives	Period 1	Period 2	Period 3	Period 4	Unused Capacity	Total Capacity
	Beginning inventory						
1	Regular time						
	Overtime						
	Subcontract						
2	Regular time						
	Overtime						
	Subcontract						
3	Regular time						
	Overtime						
	Subcontract						
4	Regular time						
	Overtime						
	Subcontract						
Requirements							

Crandon Manufacturing Formulation

Maximize: $900x_1 + 600x_2 = Z$

Subject to:

$$2x_1 + 1x_2 \leq 4{,}000 \text{ (Fabrication)}$$

$$1x_1 + 2x_2 \leq 5{,}000 \text{ (Assembly)}$$

$$1x_1 + 1x_2 \leq 3{,}500 \text{ (Demand)}$$

$$x_1, x_2 \geq 0 \text{ (Nonnegativity)}$$

Supplement H: Linear Programming

Plotting Constraints for Crandon

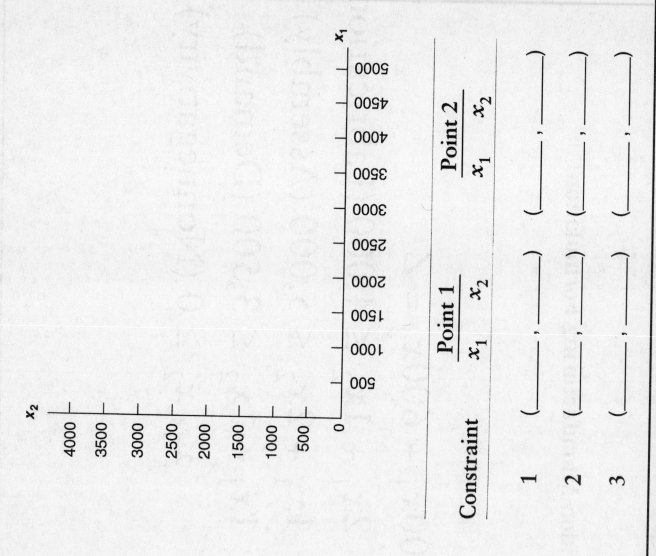

Constraint	Point 1		Point 2	
	x_1	x_2	x_1	x_2
1	(	,)	(	,)
2	(	,)	(	,)
3	(	,)	(	,)

Supplement H: Linear Programming

Constraints and Feasible Region for Crandon

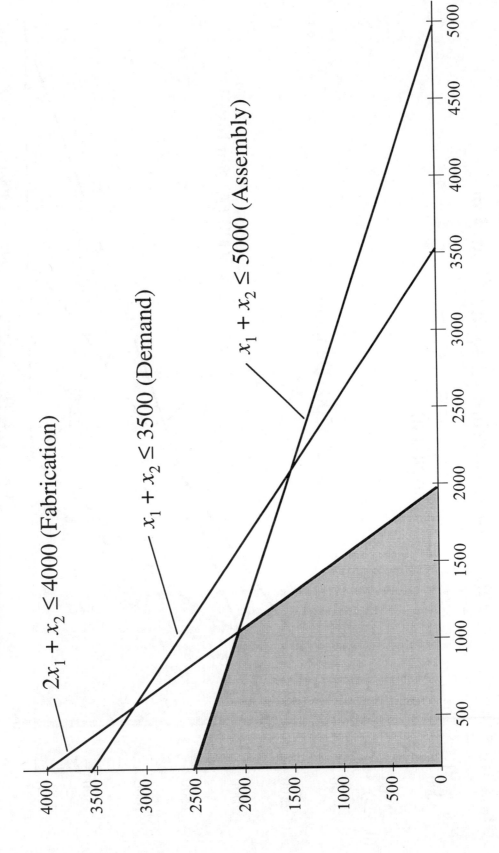

$2x_1 + x_2 \leq 4000$ (Fabrication)

$x_1 + x_2 \leq 3500$ (Demand)

$x_1 + x_2 \leq 5000$ (Assembly)

Supplement H: Linear Programming

Objective Function Line for Crandon

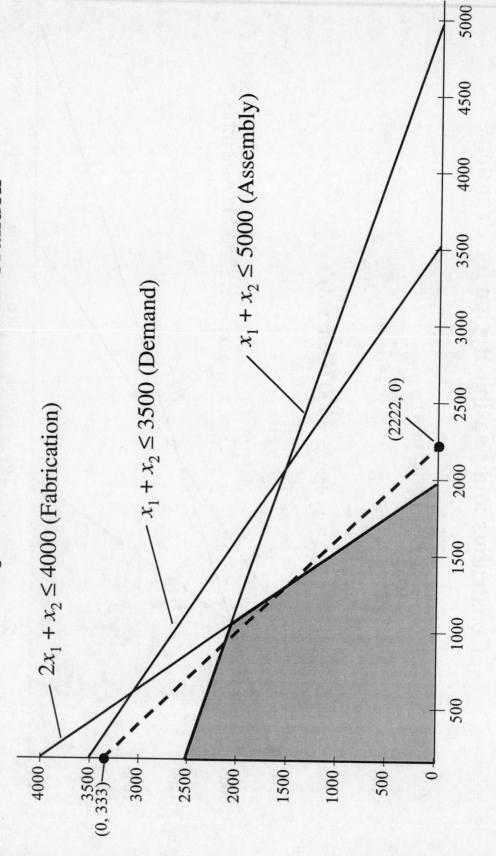

TM H.2c

Algebraic Solution
for Crandon

$$2x_1 + 1x_2 \leq 4,000 \quad \text{(fabrication)}$$
$$1x_1 + 2x_2 \leq 5,000 \quad \text{(assembly)}$$

$$2x_1 + 1x_2 = 4,000$$
$$-(2x_1 + 4x_2 = 10,000)$$
$$\overline{\quad -3x_2 = -6,000}$$
$$x_2 = 2,000$$

$$2x_1 + 1(2,000) = 4,000$$
$$2x_1 = 2,000$$
$$x_1 = 1,000$$

The optimal point is (1,000, 2,000). The Crandon Manufacturing Company should produce 1,000 circular saws and 2,000 table saws per month. This solution gives a total profit of $900(1,000) + $600(2,000) = $2,100,000.

To accompany *Operations Management Strategy and Analysis, 5/e,* by Krajewski and Ritzman. Copyright © 1999 by Addison Wesley Longman, Inc. All rights reserved. **TM H.2d**

Slack/Surplus
Variables for Crandon

- **Slack in fabrication at (1,000, 2,000)**

$$2x_1 + x_2 \leq 4,000$$

$$2x_1 + x_2 + s_1 = 4,000$$

$$2(1,000) + 2,000 + s_1 = 4,000$$

$$s_1 = 0$$

- **Slack in assembly at (1,000, 2,000)**

$$x_1 + 2x_2 \geq 5,000$$

$$x_1 + 2x_2 + s_2 = 5,000$$

$$1,000 + 2(2,000) + s_2 = 5,000$$

$$s_2 = 0$$

- **Slack in demand at (1,000, 2,000)**

$$x_1 + x_2 \leq 3,500$$

$$x_1 + x_2 + s_3 = 3,500$$

$$1,000 + 2,000 + s_3 = 3,500$$

$$s_3 = 500$$

Range of Optimality for Crandon

$$m_1 \leq \frac{c_1}{600} \leq m_2$$

$$-2 \leq \frac{c_1}{600} \leq -\frac{1}{2}$$

$$1200 \geq c_1 \geq 300$$

$$300 \leq c_1 \leq 1200$$

Shadow Price of Fabrication Time at Crandon Manufacturing

Original Constraints

$2x_1 + 1x_2 = 4,000$

$1x_1 + 2x_2 = 5,000$

Relaxed Constraints

$2x_1 + 1x_2 = 4,001$

$1x_1 + 2x_2 = 5,000$

Original Solution

$x_1 = 1,000$

$x_2 = 2,000$

$Z = \$900(1,000)$
$\quad + \$600(2,000)$
$\quad = \$2,100,000$

New Solution

$x_1 = 1,000.67$

$x_2 = 1,999.67$

$Z = \$900(1,000.67)$
$\quad + \$600(1,999.67)$
$\quad = \$2,100,400$

Shadow price = $\$2,100,400 - \$2,100,000 = \$400/\text{hour}$

OMS Software Output

Solution

Variable Label	Variable Value	Original Coefficient	Coefficient Sensitivity
Var1	1000	900.0000	0
Var2	2000	600.0000	0

Constraint Label	Original RHV	Slack or Surplus	Shadow Price
Const1	4000	0	400.0000
Const2	5000	0	100.0000
Const3	3500	500	0

Objective Function Value: 2100000

Sensitivity Analysis and Ranges

Objective Function Coefficients

Variable Label	Lower Limit	Original Coefficient	Upper Limit
Var1	300	900	1200
Var2	450	600	1800

Right-Hand-Side Values

Constraint Label	Lower Limit	Original Value	Upper Limit
Const1	2500	4000	5500
Const2	2000	5000	6500
Const3	3000	3500	No Limit

Product Mix Problem

Variable Definitions

x_1 = number of skirts produced and sold

x_2 = number of dresses produced and sold

x_3 = number of sports coats produced and sold

Formulation

Maximize:

$$5x_1 + 17x_2 + 30x_3 = Z$$

Subject to:

$$x_1 + 3x_2 + 4x_3 \leq 100 \quad \text{(Cutting)}$$

$$x_1 + 4x_2 + 6x_3 \leq 180 \quad \text{(Sewing)}$$

$$x_1 + x_2 + 4x_3 \leq 60 \quad \text{(Material)}$$

$$x_1, x_2, x_3 \geq 0 \quad \text{(Non-negativity)}$$

Process Design

Variable Definitions

x = Amount of pipe processed on routing 1, as 100 ft.
y = Amount of pipe processed on routing 2, as 100 ft.

Formulation

Maximize:

$$60x + 80y = Z$$

Subject to:

$$
\begin{aligned}
x \ + y &\leq \ 45 \quad \text{(Melting)} \\
3x \quad\ &\leq \ 90 \quad \text{(A)} \\
4y &\leq 160 \quad \text{(B)} \\
5x + 4y &\leq 200 \quad \text{(Material)} \\
x, y &\geq \quad 0 \quad \text{(Non-negativity)}
\end{aligned}
$$

Blending Problem

Variable Definitions

A = fraction of material A in finished product
B = fraction of material B in finished product
C = fraction of material C in finished product

Formulation

Minimize:

$$0.6A + 0.4B + 0.5C = Z$$

Subject to:

$$200A + 180B + 280C \geq 220 \quad \text{(Combustion Point)}$$
$$4A + 3B + 10C \leq 6 \quad \text{(Gamma)}$$
$$20A + 10B + 8C \geq 12 \quad \text{(Zeta)}$$
$$A + B + C = 1.0 \quad \text{(Fractions)}$$

$$A, B, C \geq 0 \quad \text{(Non-negativity)}$$

Portfolio Selection

Variable Definitions

x_{CB} = Millions of dollars invested in corporate bonds

x_{CS} = Millions of dollars invested in common stock

x_{GC} = Millions of dollars invested in gold certificates

x_{RE} = Millions of dollars invested in real estate

Formulation

Maximize:

$$8.5x_{CB} + 9x_{CS} + 10x_{GC} + 13x_{RE} = Z$$

Subject to:

$$x_{CB} + x_{CS} + x_{GC} + x_{RE} \leq 5 \quad \text{(Total)}$$

$$x_{CB} + x_{CS} \geq 2 \quad (40\%)$$

$$x_{RE} \leq 1 \quad (20\%)$$

$$x_{CB}, x_{CS}, x_{GC}, x_{RE} \geq 0 \quad \text{(Non-negativity)}$$

Shift Scheduling

Variable Definitions

x_j = Number of operators beginning work in time period j

Formulation

Minimize:

$$x_1 + x_2 + x_3 + x_4 + x_5 + x_6 = Z$$

Subject to:

$$x_1 + \qquad\qquad\qquad x_6 \geq 4$$
$$x_1 + x_2 \qquad\qquad\qquad \geq 6$$
$$x_2 + x_3 \qquad\qquad \geq 90$$
$$x_3 + x_4 \qquad \geq 85$$
$$x_4 + x_5 \qquad \geq 55$$
$$x_5 + x_6 \geq 20$$

$$x_1, x_2, x_3, x_4, x_5, x_6 \geq 0$$

Production Planning

Variable Definitions

I_t = Thousands of pounds of supplement in inventory in quarter t

W_t = Number of workers in quarter t

O_t = Thousands of pounds of supplement produced on overtime in quarter t

H_t = Number of workers hired in quarter t

F_t = Number of workers fired in quarter t

S_t = Thousands of pounds of supplements produced by subcontracting in quarter t

D_t = Thousands of pounds of supplement forecasted as demand for quarter t

Formulation

Minimize:

$$\sum_{t=1}^{4} 110I_t + 1,620W_t + 1,800O_t + 1,000H_t + 600F_t + 1,100S_t = Z$$

Subject to:

$$2W_t + O_t + S_t + I_{t-1} - I_t = D_t \qquad (t = 1, 2, 3, 4)$$
$$W_t - W_{t-1} - H_t + F_t = 0 \qquad (t = 1, 2, 3, 4)$$
$$O_t \leq 30 \qquad (t = 1, 2, 3, 4)$$
$$S_t \leq 10 \qquad (t = 1, 2, 3, 4)$$
$$I_4 = 40$$
$$W_4 = 180$$
$$I_o = 40$$
$$W_o = 180$$
$$I_t, O_t, S_t, W_t \geq 0 \qquad (t = 1, 2, 3, 4)$$

Chapter 15: Material Requirements Planning

Partially Completed MRP Inventory Record: FOQ

Item: H10—A
Description: Chair seat assembly

Lot Size: 80 units
Lead Time: 4 weeks

	Week									
	31	32	33	34	35	36	37	38	39	40
Gross requirements		60				35		45		60
Scheduled receipts		80								
Projected on-hand inventory	20									
Planned receipts										
Planned order releases										

Completed MRP Record: FOQ

Item: H10—A
Description: Chair seat assembly

Lot Size: 80 units
Lead Time: 4 weeks

						Week				
	31	32	33	34	35	36	37	38	39	40
Gross requirements		60				35		45		60
Scheduled receipts		80								
Projected on-hand inventory 20	20	40	40	40	40	5	5	40	40	60
Planned receipts								80		80
Planned order releases				80		80				

Chapter 15: Material Requirements Planning

Partially Completed MRP Inventory Record: POQ

Item: H10—A
Description: Chair seat assembly

Lot Size: POQ = 4
Lead Time: 4 weeks

		Week							
	31	32	33	34	35	36	37	38	39	40
Gross requirements		60				35		45		60
Scheduled receipts		80								
Projected on-hand inventory	20									
Planned receipts										
Planned order releases										

Completed MRP Inventory Record: POQ

Item: H10—A
Description: Chair seat assembly

Lot Size: POQ = 4
Lead Time: 4 weeks

	Week									
	31	32	33	34	35	36	37	38	39	40
Gross requirements		60				35		45		60
Scheduled receipts		80								
Projected on-hand inventory	20	40	40	40	40	5	5	60	60	0
Planned receipts								100		
Planned order releases				100						

Chapter 15: Material Requirements Planning

Partially Completed MRP Inventory Record: L4L

Item: H10—A
Description: Chair seat assembly

Lot Size: L4L
Lead Time: 4 weeks

		Week								
		31	32	33	34	35	36	37	38	39	40
Gross requirements			60				35		45		60
Scheduled receipts			80								
Projected on-hand inventory	20										
Planned receipts											
Planned order releases											

Completed MRP Inventory Record: L4L

Item: H10—A
Description: Chair seat assembly

Lot Size: L4L
Lead Time: 4 weeks

		Week								
		31	32	33	34	35	36	37	38	39	40
Gross requirements			60				35		45		60
Scheduled receipts			80								
Projected on-hand inventory	20	20	40	40	40	40	5	5	0	0	0
Planned receipts							60		40		60
Planned order releases					40						

　TM 15.3b

Chapter 15: Material Requirements Planning

Master Schedule and BOM for Item A

Item: End item A								Lead Time: 2 wk
	Week							
	1	2	3	4	5	6	7	8
MPS quantity								250
MPS start						250		

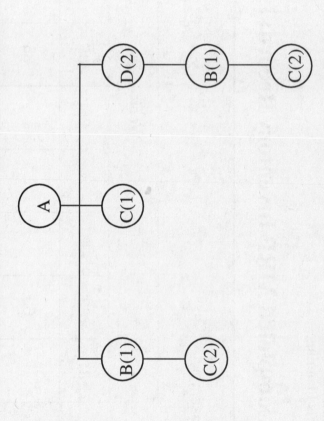

Inventory Data for Items B, C, and D

Data Category	Item		
	B	C	D
Lot sizing rule	L4L	FOQ = 1000	L4L
Lead time	2 weeks	1 week	3 weeks
Scheduled receipts	none	1000 (week 1)	None
Beginning inventory	0	200	0

MRP Record for Item B

Item: B
Description:

Lot Size: L4L
Lead Time: 2 weeks

	Week							
	1	2	3	4	5	6	7	8
Gross requirements			500			250		
Scheduled receipts								
Projected on-hand inventory	0	0	0	0	0	0		
Planned receipts			500			250		
Planned order releases	500			250				

TM 15.4c

MRP Record for Item C

Item: C
Description:

Lot Size: 1000 units
Lead Time: 1 week

		Week							
		1	2	3	4	5	6	7	8
Gross requirements		1000			500		250		
Scheduled receipts		1000							
Projected on-hand inventory	200	200	200	200	700	700	450		
Planned receipts						1000			
Planned order releases					1000				

Chapter 15: Material Requirements Planning

MRP Record for Item D

Item: D
Description:

Lot Size: L4L
Lead Time: 3 weeks

		Week							
		1	2	3	4	5	6	7	8
Gross requirements							500		
Scheduled receipts									
Projected on-hand inventory	0	0	0	0	0	0	0		
Planned receipts							500		
Planned order releases				500					

Master Schedules and BOMs for Items A and B

Master Schedule

Item: End item A

Lead Time: 2 weeks

	Week									
	1	2	3	4	5	6	7	8	9	10
MPS quantity				50				60		
MPS start		50				60				

Master Schedule

Item: End item B

Lead Time: 1 week

	Week									
	1	2	3	4	5	6	7	8	9	10
MPS quantity					200					
MPS start				200						

Master Schedules and BOMs for Items A and B (Cont.)

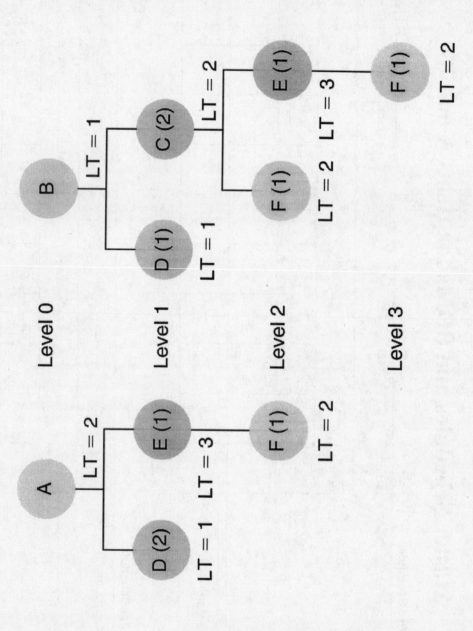

Inventory Record Data

Data Category	Item			
	C	D	E	F
Lot-sizing rule	FOQ = 400	POQ (P = 3)	L4L	L4L
Lead time	2 weeks	1 week	3 weeks	2 weeks
Scheduled receipts	None	None	450 (week 1)	None
Beginning (on-hand) inventory	100	70	0	425

TM 15.5c

Chapter 15: Material Requirements Planning

Solution for Item C

Item: C
Description:

Lot Size: FOQ = 400 units
Lead Time: 2 weeks

		1	2	3	4	5	6	7	8	9	10
						Week					
Gross requirements					400						
Scheduled receipts											
Projected on-hand inventory	100	100	100	100	100	100	100	100	100	100	100
Planned receipts					400						
Planned order releases		400									

Chapter 15: Material Requirements Planning

Solution for Item D

Item: D
Description:

Lot Size: POQ ($P = 3$)
Lead Time: 1 week

		Week								
	1	2	3	4	5	6	7	8	9	10
Gross requirements		100		200		120				
Scheduled receipts										
Projected on-hand inventory 70	70	200	200	0	0	0	0	0	0	0
Planned receipts		230				120				
Planned order releases	230				120					

Chapter 15: Material Requirements Planning

Solutions for Item E

Item: E
Description:

Lot Size: L4L
Lead Time: 3 weeks

						Week					
		1	2	3	4	5	6	7	8	9	10
Gross requirements			450				60				
Scheduled receipts		450									
Projected on-hand inventory	0	450	0	0	0	0	0	0	0	0	0
Planned receipts							60				
Planned order releases				60							

Chapter 15: Material Requirements Planning

Solutions for Item F

Item: E
Description:

Lot Size: L4L
Lead Time: 2 weeks

					Week					
	1	2	3	4	5	6	7	8	9	10
Gross requirements		450	60							
Scheduled receipts										
Projected on-hand inventory [425]	425	25	0	0	0	0	0	0	0	0
Planned receipts			35							
Planned order releases	[35]									

Chapter 15: Material Requirements Planning

8-Period MRP Record

Item:								
Description:					**Lot Size:**	units		
					Lead Time:	weeks		

					Week			
	1	2	3	4	5	6	7	8
Gross requirements								
Scheduled receipts								
Projected on-hand inventory								
Planned receipts								
Planned order releases								

10-Period MRP Record

Item:								Lot Size:	units	
Description:								Lead Time:	weeks	

	Week									
	1	2	3	4	5	6	7	8	9	10
Gross requirements										
Scheduled receipts										
Projected on-hand inventory										
Planned receipts										
Planned order releases										

Chapter 15: Material Requirements Planning

12-Period MRP Record

Item: Description:												Lot Size: _____ units Lead Time: _____ weeks

						Date						
	1	2	3	4	5	6	7	8	9	10	11	12
Gross requirements												
Scheduled receipts												
Projected on-hand inventory ☐												
Planned receipts												
Planned order releases												

TM 15.5j

Supplement I: Master Production Scheduling

Lot Size 50
Lead Time 1

Quantity on Hand	5	1	2	3	4	5	6	7	8	9	10	11	12	13	14	15
Forecast		20	10	40	10	0	0	30	20	40	20					
Customer Orders (Booked)		30	20	5	8	0	2	0	0	0	0					
Projected On-Hand Inventory																
MPS Quantity																
MPS start																
Available-to-Promise Inv (ATP)																

Supplement I: Master Production Scheduling

Lot Size 50
Lead Time 1

Quantity on Hand 5

	1	2	3	4	5	6	7	8	9	10	11	12	13	14	15
Forecast	20	10	40	10	0	0	30	20	40	20					
Customer Orders (Booked)	30	20	5	8	0	2	0	0	0	0					
Projected On-Hand Inventory	25	5	15	5	5	3	23	3	13	43					
MPS Quantity	50	0	50	0	0	50	50	50	50	50					
MPS start	0	50	0	0	0	50	0	50	50	0					
Available-to-Promise Inv (ATP)	5	50	35	0	0	50	50	50	50	50					

TM I.1b

Supplement I: Master Production Scheduling

	Lot Size Lead Time	1	2	3	4	5	6	7	8	9	10	11	12	13	14	15
Quantity on Hand																
Forecast																
Customer Orders (Booked)																
Projected On-Hand Inventory																
MPS Quantity																
MPS start																
Available-to-Promise Inv (ATP)																

Item B52R

$$k = \frac{d(\overline{w} + \overline{p})(1 + \alpha)}{c}$$

$$= \frac{1{,}000(0.5 + 0.1)(1 + 0.1)}{100}$$

$$= 6.6 \text{ or } 7 \text{ containers}$$

Schedule at One Operation Using SPT Priority Rule

Order Sequence	Begin Work	End Work	Flow Time (hr)	Scheduled Customer Pickup Time	Actual Customer Pickup Time	Hours Early	Hours Past Due
1.							
2.							
3.							
4.							
Total			_____	_____	_____	_____	_____
Average			_____	_____	_____	_____	_____

Average work-in-process = _____   Average total inventory = _____

Schedule at One Operation Using SPT Priority Rule

Order Sequence	Begin Work	End Work	Flow Time (hr)	Scheduled Customer Pickup Time	Actual Customer Pickup Time	Hours Early	Hours Past Due
1. PC088	0	3	3	18	18	15	
2. DM246	3	11	11	20	20	9	
3. SX435	11	21	21	6	21		15
4. AZ135	21	35	35	14	35		25
Total			70		94	24	40
Average			17.5		23.5	6	10

Average work-in-process = $\dfrac{70}{35} = 2$ Average total inventory = $\dfrac{94}{35} = 2.68$

Drill Press
CR and S/RO Schedules

	Critical Ratio			Slack/Remaining Operation	
		Sequence on			Sequence on
Job	Priority Index	Drill Press	Job	Priority Index	Drill Press
AA			AA		
BB			BB		
CC			CC		
DD			DD		
EE			EE		

Schedule at One Operation Using CR and S/RO Priority Rules

Critical Ratio

Job	Priority Index	Sequence on Drill Press
AA	1.25	First
BB	1.83	Fourth
CC	1.44	Second
DD	1.50	Third
EE	2.33	Fifth

Slack/Remaining Operation

Job	Priority Index	Sequence on Drill Press
AA	0.33	First
BB	1.25	Fourth
CC	0.70	Second
DD	2.00	Fifth
EE	0.80	Third

Two-Machine Flow Shop Problem Using Johnson's Rule

| Job | Time (hr) | |
	Machine 1	Machine 2
A	4	3
B	10	20
C	2	15
D	8	7
E	14	13

Job Sequence

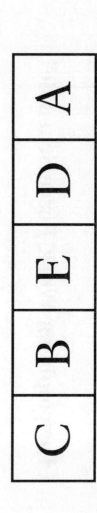

Developing a Work-Force Schedule

M	T	W	Th	F	S	Su	EMPLOYEE
6	3	5	3	7	2	3	

Developing a Work-Force Schedule

M	T	W	Th	F	S	Su	EMPLOYEE
6	3	5	3	7	2	3	1 : S/Su off
5	2	4	2	6	2	3	2 : S/Su off
4	1	3	1	5	2	3	3 : T/W off
3	1	3	0	4	1	2	4 : S/Su off
2	0	2	0	3	1	2	5 : M/T off
2	0	1	0	2	0	1	6 : S/Su off
1	0	0	0	1	0	1	7 : T/W off
0	0	0	0	0	0	0	

Diagramming the Network

Activity	Description	Immediate Predecessor(s)
A	Select administrative and medical staff.	—
B	Select site and do site survey.	—
C	Select equipment.	A
D	Prepare final construction plans and layout.	B
E	Bring utilities to the site.	B
F	Interview applicants and fill positions in nursing support staff, maintenance, and security.	A
G	Purchase and take delivery of equipment.	C
H	Construct the hospital.	D
I	Develop an information system.	A
J	Install the equipment.	E, G, H
K	Train nurses and support staff.	F, I, J

AON Network for the Hospital Project

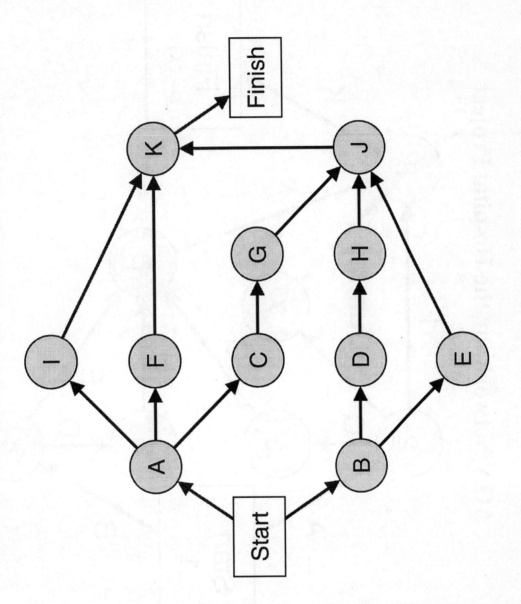

AOA Network for the Hospital Project

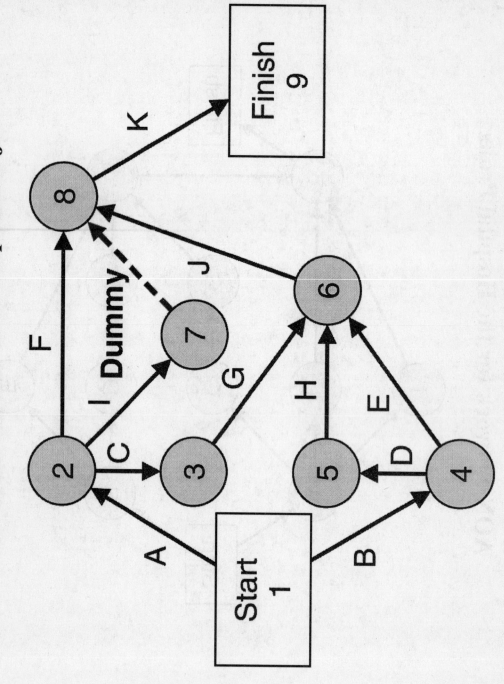

Activity Paths for the Hospital Project

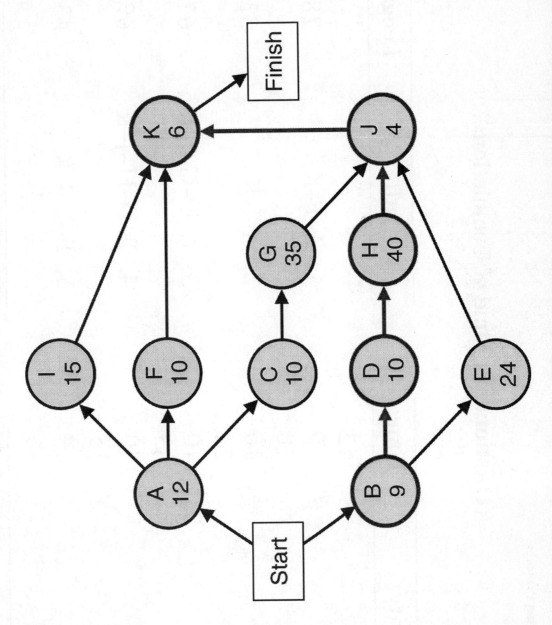

Estimating Time of Completion

Activity	Time
A	12
B	9
C	10
D	10
E	24
F	10
G	35
H	40
I	15
J	4
K	6

	Path	Length
1.	A–F–K	28
2.	A–I–K	33
3.	A–C–G–J–K	67
4.	B–D–H–J–K	69**
5.	B–E–J–K	43

Network for the Hospital Project, Showing Earliest Start and Earliest Finish Times

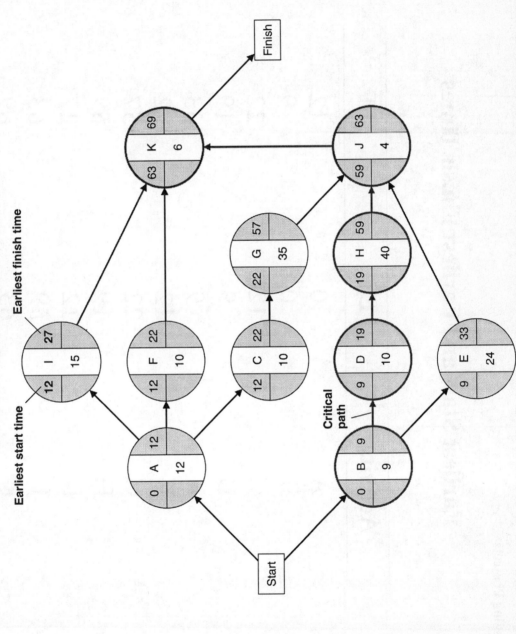

Earliest start time

Earliest finish time

Critical path

Earliest Start and Earliest Finish Times

Activity	ES	EF
A	0	12
B	0	9
C	12	22
D	9	19
E	9	33
F	12	22
G	22	57
H	19	59
I	12	27
J	59	63
K	63	69

Latest Start and Finish Times

Activity	LS	LF
A	2	14
B	0	9
C	14	24
D	9	19
E	35	59
F	53	63
G	24	59
H	19	59
I	48	63
J	59	63
K	63	69

Network for the Hospital Project, Showing Data Needed for Activity Slack Calculation

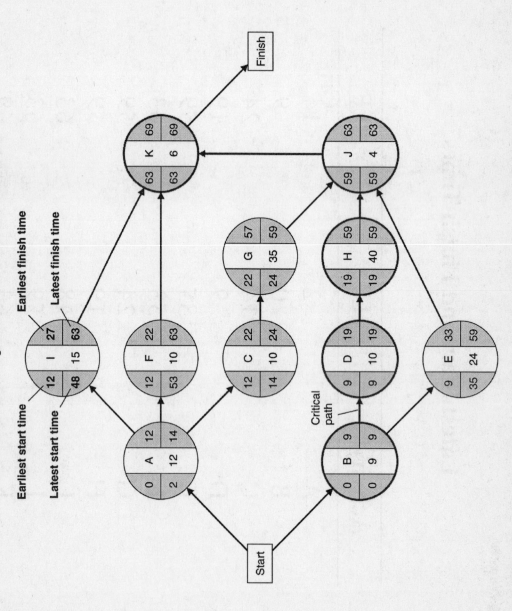

Calculating Activity Slacks
Activity slack: LS – ES or LF – EF

Activity	LF	EF	Slack	Critical Path?
A	14	12	2	
B	9	9	0	yes
C	24	22	2	
D	19	19	0	yes
E	59	33	26	
F	63	22	41	
G	59	57	2	
H	59	59	0	yes
I	63	27	36	
J	63	63	0	yes
K	69	69	0	yes

Chapter 18: Managing Projects

Calculating
Time Statistics

| | Time Estimates (weeks) | | | Activity Statistics | |
| | Optimistic | Most Likely | Pessimistic | Expected Time | Variance |
Activity	(a)	(m)	(b)	(t_e)	(σ^2)
A	11	12	13		
B	7	8	15		
C	5	10	15	10	2.78
D	8	9	16	10	1.78
E	14	25	30	24	7.11
F	6	9	18	10	4.00
G	25	36	41	35	7.11
H	36	40	45	40	2.78
I	10	13	28	15	9.00
J	1	2	15	4	5.44
K	5	6	7	6	0.11

Activity A

$$t_e = \frac{a + 4m + b}{6} = \frac{11 + 4 + (12) + 13}{6} = 12$$

$$\sigma^2 = \left(\frac{b - a}{6}\right)^2 = \left(\frac{13 - 11}{6}\right)^2 = 0.11$$

Activity B

$$t_e = \frac{7 + 4(8) + 15}{6} = 9$$

$$\sigma^2 = \left(\frac{15 - 7}{6}\right)^2 = 1.78$$

Probability of Completion in 75 Weeks

Critical path is B–D–H–J–K

$$\sigma^2 = 1.78 + 1.78 + 2.78 + 5.44 + 0.11$$

$$= 11.89$$

$$z = \frac{T - T_E}{\sqrt{\sigma^2}} = \frac{75 - 69}{\sqrt{11.89}} = \frac{6}{3.448}$$

$$= 1.74$$

The probability that the project time will not exceed 75 weeks is 0.9591.

Normal Distribution

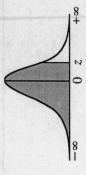

	.00	.01	.02	.03	.04	.05	.06	.07	.08	.09
.0	.5000	.5040	.5080	.5120	.5160	.5199	.5239	.5279	.5319	.5359
.1	.5398	.5438	.5478	.5517	.5557	.5596	.5636	.5675	.5714	.5753
.2	.5793	.5832	.5871	.5910	.5948	.5987	.6026	.6064	.6103	.6141
.3	.6179	.6217	.6255	.6293	.6331	.6368	.6406	.6443	.6480	.6517
.4	.6554	.6591	.6628	.6664	.6700	.6736	.6772	.6808	.6844	.6879
.5	.6915	.6950	.6985	.7019	.7054	.7088	.7123	.7157	.7190	.7224
.6	.7257	.7291	.7324	.7357	.7389	.7422	.7454	.7486	.7517	.7549
.7	.7580	.7611	.7642	.7673	.7704	.7734	.7764	.7794	.7828	.7852
.8	.7881	.7910	.7939	.7967	.7995	.8023	.8051	.8078	.8106	.8133
.9	.8159	.8186	.8212	.8238	.8264	.8289	.8315	.8340	.8365	.8389
1.0	.8413	.8438	.8461	.8485	.8508	.8531	.8554	.8577	.8599	.8621
1.1	.8643	.8665	.8686	.8708	.8729	.8749	.8770	.8790	.8810	.8830
1.2	.8849	.8869	.8888	.8907	.8925	.8944	.8962	.8980	.8997	.9015
1.3	.9032	.9049	.9066	.9082	.9099	.9115	.9131	.9147	.9162	.9177
1.4	.9192	.9207	.9222	.9236	.9251	.9265	.9279	.9292	.9306	.9319
1.5	.9332	.9345	.9357	.9370	.9382	.9394	.9406	.9418	.9429	.9441
1.6	.9452	.9463	.9474	.9484	.9495	.9505	.9515	.9525	.9535	.9545
1.7	.9554	.9564	.9573	.9582	.9591	.9599	.9608	.9616	.9625	.9633
1.8	.9641	.9649	.9656	.9664	.9671	.9678	.9686	.9693	.9699	.9706
1.9	.9713	.9719	.9726	.9732	.9738	.9744	.9750	.9756	.9761	.9767
2.0	.9772	.9778	.9783	.9788	.9793	.9798	.9803	.9808	.9812	.9817
2.1	.9821	.9826	.9830	.9834	.9838	.9842	.9846	.9850	.9854	.9857
2.2	.9861	.9864	.9868	.9871	.9875	.9878	.9881	.9884	.9887	.9890
2.3	.9893	.9896	.9898	.9901	.9904	.9906	.9909	.9911	.9913	.9916
2.4	.9918	.9920	.9922	.9925	.9927	.9929	.9931	.9932	.9934	.9936
2.5	.9938	.9940	.9941	.9943	.9945	.9946	.9948	.9949	.9951	.9952
2.6	.9953	.9955	.9956	.9957	.9959	.9960	.9961	.9962	.9963	.9964
2.7	.9965	.9966	.9967	.9968	.9969	.9970	.9971	.9972	.9973	.9974
2.8	.9974	.9975	.9976	.9977	.9977	.9978	.9979	.9979	.9980	.9981
2.9	.9981	.9982	.9982	.9983	.9984	.9984	.9985	.9985	.9986	.9986
3.0	.9987	.9987	.9987	.9988	.9988	.9989	.9989	.9989	.9990	.9990
3.1	.9990	.9991	.9991	.9991	.9992	.9992	.9992	.9992	.9993	.9993
3.2	.9993	.9993	.9994	.9994	.9994	.9994	.9994	.9995	.9995	.9995
3.3	.9995	.9995	.9995	.9996	.9996	.9996	.9996	.9996	.9996	.9997
3.4	.9997	.9997	.9997	.9997	.9997	.9997	.9997	.9997	.9997	.9998